ADOBE® ACROBAT® X

W9-DFL-828

CLASSROOM IN A BOOK®

The official training workbook from Adobe Systems

www.adobepress.com

Adobe

Adobe Press books are published by Peachpit, a division of Pearson Education located in Berkeley, California. For the latest on Adobe Press books, go to www.adobepress.com. To report errors, please send a note to errata@peachpit.com. For information on getting permission for reprints and excerpts, contact permissions@peachpit.com.

Printed and bound in the United States of America

ISBN-13:   978-0-321-75125-6

ISBN-10:   0-321-75125-6

9 8 7 6 5 4 3 2

WHAT'S ON THE DISC

Here is an overview of the contents of the Classroom in a Book disc

The *Adobe Acrobat X Classroom in a Book* disc includes the lesson files that you'll need to complete the exercises in this book, as well as other content to help you learn more about Adobe Acrobat X and use it with greater efficiency and ease. The diagram below represents the contents of the disc, which should help you locate the files you need.

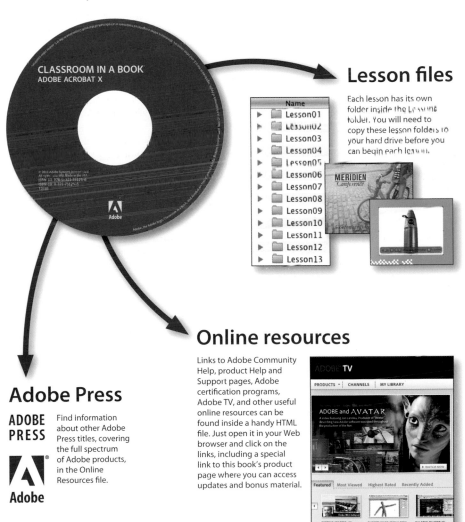

Lesson files

Each lesson has its own folder inside the Lessons folder. You will need to copy these lesson folders to your hard drive before you can begin each lesson.

Online resources

Links to Adobe Community Help, product Help and Support pages, Adobe certification programs, Adobe TV, and other useful online resources can be found inside a handy HTML file. Just open it in your Web browser and click on the links, including a special link to this book's product page where you can access updates and bonus material.

Adobe Press

ADOBE PRESS Find information about other Adobe Press titles, covering the full spectrum of Adobe products, in the Online Resources file.

CONTENTS

GETTING STARTED

Adobe® Acrobat® X is an essential tool in today's electronic workflow. As in earlier versions, you can use Acrobat Standard or Acrobat Pro to convert virtually any document to Adobe Portable Document Format (PDF), preserving the exact look and content of the original, complete with fonts and graphics. Additionally, Acrobat provides native support for Adobe Flash technology, so you can be sure that multimedia components in a PDF will play smoothly.

Adobe has completely redesigned the Acrobat user interface to make it more intuitive. If you're new to Acrobat, you'll be able to get up to speed quickly. If you've used earlier versions, the new user interface may take a little getting used to. However, you'll likely appreciate the uncluttered work area and streamlined design. You can customize the Quick Tools and Common Tools toolbars to give you quick access to the tools you use most frequently.

Whether you're using Acrobat Standard or Acrobat Pro, you can distribute PDF documents reliably and securely by email or store them on the web, an intranet, a file system, a CD, or a web service such as Acrobat.com. With shared reviews, you and your colleagues can collaborate easily as you perfect a document. Reviewers can view and comment on your work, regardless of the platform they work on. Acrobat makes it easy to collect and organize data from reviews or from forms. You can create interactive forms and enable users of the free downloadable Adobe Reader X software to save the completed form.

If you're using Acrobat Pro, you can automate processes and make them more consistent using the new Action Wizard. Acrobat includes several actions for common tasks, such as making documents accessible. And you can create your own actions, including instructional comments, for processes you perform.

Additionally, in Acrobat Pro, you can unify documents, spreadsheets, presentations, email, rich media, and more into a single, cohesive PDF Portfolio. You can also apply redaction to confidential information, compare versions of documents, and use advanced print production controls for a faster, more reliable print workflow.

About Classroom in a Book

Adobe Acrobat X Classroom in a Book® is part of the official training series for Adobe graphics and publishing software, developed with the support of Adobe product experts. The lessons are designed to let you learn at your own pace. If you're new to Adobe Acrobat, you'll learn the fundamental concepts and features you'll need to master the program. If you've been using Acrobat for a while, you'll find that Classroom in a Book teaches many advanced features, helps you become familiar with the new user interface, and includes lessons targeted specifically for legal professionals and for print professionals.

The lessons in this edition include information on a host of Adobe Acrobat features, including:

- Creating and using actions.
- Creating PDF Portfolios.
- Creating Adobe PDF files with a single click.
- Saving websites and other clipboard content as PDF files.
- Repurposing the content of Adobe PDF files for use in other applications (if permitted by the author).
- Editing PDF documents.
- Creating multimedia presentations.
- Reviewing and commenting on Adobe PDF documents, including the ability to share a document for live review.
- Creating, distributing, and gathering data from forms.
- Redacting information and using Bates numbering (for legal professionals).
- Securing PDF documents.

Although each lesson provides step-by-step instructions for specific projects, there's room for exploration and experimentation. You can follow the book from start to finish or do only the lessons that match your interests and needs.

Acrobat Pro and Acrobat Standard

This book covers features included in Acrobat Pro and Acrobat Standard. We've noted where a tool or feature described in this book is available only in Acrobat Pro. Features available only in Acrobat Pro include:

- Preflighting documents and other print production tasks.
- Creating PDF Portfolios.
- Modifying the reflow order of objects on a page to optimize accessibility.
- Applying Bates numbering and redaction.
- Comparing versions of a document.
- Using and creating actions.

Prerequisites

Before beginning to use *Adobe Acrobat X Classroom in a Book*, you should have a working knowledge of your computer and its operating system. Make sure you know how to use the mouse, standard menus and commands, and also how to open, save, and close files. If you need to review these techniques, see the printed or online documentation included with your system.

Installing Adobe Acrobat

Before beginning to use *Adobe Acrobat X Classroom in a Book*, make sure that your system is set up correctly and that you've installed the required software and hardware. You must purchase Adobe Acrobat X software separately. For system requirements, see the Adobe website at www.adobe.com/products/acrobat/main.html.

You must install the application from the Adobe Acrobat X CD onto your hard drive; you cannot run Acrobat X from the CD. Follow the onscreen installation instructions.

Starting Adobe Acrobat

You start Acrobat just as you would any other software application.

- **Windows:** Choose Start > Programs or All Programs > Adobe Acrobat X Standard or Adobe Acrobat X Pro.

- **Mac OS:** Open the Adobe Acrobat X Standard folder or the Adobe Acrobat X Pro folder, and double-click the program icon.

Copying the Classroom in a Book files

The *Adobe Acrobat X Classroom in a Book* CD includes folders that contain all the electronic files for the lessons. Each lesson has its own folder, and you must copy the folders to your hard drive to work through the lessons. To save room on your drive, you can install only the folder necessary for each lesson as you need it, and remove the folder when you're done.

To copy the Classroom in a Book files:

Note: If you overwrite the lesson files as you work through the lessons, you can restore the original files by recopying the corresponding lesson folder from the Classroom in a Book CD to the AcrobatX_CIB folder on your hard drive.

1 Insert the *Adobe Acrobat X Classroom in a Book* CD into your CD-ROM drive.

2 Create a folder named **AcrobatX_CIB** on your hard drive.

3 Copy all the lessons, or only those you want to work with now, to the hard drive:

- To copy all of the lessons, drag the Lessons folder from the CD into the AcrobatX_CIB folder.

- To copy a single lesson, drag the individual lesson folder from the CD into the AcrobatX_CIB folder.

Additional resources

Adobe Acrobat X Classroom in a Book is not meant to replace documentation provided with the Adobe Acrobat X program. Only the commands and options used in the lessons are explained in this book. For comprehensive information about program features, refer to these resources:

Acrobat Help and Support: www.adobe.com/support/acrobat, where you can find and browse Help and Support content on Adobe.com.

Adobe TV: http://tv.adobe.com is an online video resource for everything from getting started to expert instruction and inspiration about Adobe products.

AcrobatUsers.com: the official site for the Acrobat user community, where you'll find tutorials, videos, interviews, forum posts, and more.

Adobe Forums: http://forums.adobe.com lets you tap into peer-to-peer discussions, questions, and answers on Adobe products.

Resources for educators: www.adobe.com/education includes a wealth of resources for educators and students.

Adobe Acrobat X product home page: www.adobe.com/products/acrobat

Adobe Labs: http://labs.adobe.com gives you access to early builds of cutting-edge technology, as well as forums where you can interact with both the Adobe development teams building that technology and other like-minded members of the community.

Adobe certification

The Adobe training and certification programs are designed to help Adobe customers improve and promote their product-proficiency skills. There are four levels of certification:

- Adobe Certified Associate (ACA)
- Adobe Certified Expert (ACE)
- Adobe Certified Instructor (ACI)
- Adobe Authorized Training Center (AATC)

The Adobe Certified Associate (ACA) credential certifies that individuals have the entry-level skills to plan, design, build, and maintain effective communications using different forms of digital media.

The Adobe Certified Expert program is a way for expert users to upgrade their credentials. You can use Adobe certification as a catalyst for getting a raise, finding a job, or promoting your expertise.

If you are an ACE-level instructor, the Adobe Certified Instructor program takes your skills to the next level and gives you access to a wide range of Adobe resources.

Adobe Authorized Training Centers offer instructor-led courses and training on Adobe products, employing only Adobe Certified Instructors. A directory of AATCs is available at http://partners.adobe.com.

Accelerate your workflow with Adobe CS Live

Adobe CS Live is a set of online services that harness the connectivity of the web and integrate with Adobe Creative Suite 5 to simplify the creative review process, speed up website compatibility testing, deliver important web user intelligence, and more, allowing you to focus on creating your most impactful work. CS Live services are complimentary for a limited time* and can be accessed online or from within Creative Suite 5 applications.

Adobe BrowserLab is for web designers and developers who need to preview and test their web pages on multiple browsers and operating systems. Unlike other browser-compatibility solutions, BrowserLab renders screenshots virtually on demand with multiple viewing and diagnostic tools, and can be used with Dreamweaver CS5 to preview local content and different states of interactive pages. Being an online service, BrowserLab has fast development cycles, with greater flexibility for expanded browser support and updated functionality.

Adobe CS Review is for creative professionals who want a new level of efficiency in the creative review process. Unlike other services that offer online review of creative content, only CS Review lets you publish a review to the web directly from within InDesign, Photoshop, Photoshop Extended, and Illustrator and view reviewer comments back in the originating Creative Suite application.

Acrobat.com is for creative professionals who need to work with a cast of colleagues and clients in order to get a creative project from creative brief to final product. Acrobat.com is a set of online services that includes web conferencing, online file-sharing and workspaces. Unlike collaborating via email and attending time-consuming in-person meetings, Acrobat.com brings people to your work instead of sending files to people, so you can get the business side of the creative process done faster, together, from any location.

Adobe Story is for creative professionals, producers, and writers working on or with scripts. Story is a collaborative script-development tool that turns scripts into metadata that can be used with the Adobe CS5 Production Premium tools to streamline workflows and create video assets.

SiteCatalyst NetAverages is for web and mobile professionals who want to optimize their projects for wider audiences. NetAverages provides intelligence on how users are accessing the web, which helps reduce guesswork early in the creative process. You can access aggregate user data such as browser type, operating system, mobile device profile, screen resolution, and more, which can be shown over time. The data is derived from visitor activity to participating Omniture SiteCatalyst customer sites. Unlike other web intelligence solutions, NetAverages innovatively displays data using Flash, creating an engaging experience that is robust yet easy to follow.

You can access CS Live three different ways:

1   Set up access when you register your Creative Suite 5 products, and get complimentary access that includes all of the features and workflow benefits of using CS Live with Creative Suite 5.

2   Set up access by signing up online, and get complimentary access to CS Live services for a limited time. Note that this option does not give you access to the services from within your products.

3   Desktop product trials include a 30-day trial of CS Live services.

CS Live services are complimentary for a limited time. See www.adobe.com/go/cslive for details.

1 INTRODUCING ADOBE ACROBAT X

Lesson overview

In this lesson, you'll do the following:

- Get acquainted with the Adobe PDF document format, Acrobat X, and Adobe Reader.

- Take a first look at the Acrobat work area.

- Analyze examples of PDF documents designed for printing and for viewing online.

- Examine some formatting and design decisions you need to make when creating an electronic publication.

- View a PDF in Read mode.

- Learn to use Adobe Acrobat X Help.

 This lesson will take approximately 45 minutes to complete. Copy the Lesson01 folder onto your hard drive if you haven't already done so.

With Adobe Acrobat X, you can view, create, edit, and enhance Adobe PDF documents, which preserve all the formatting of the original file.

About Adobe PDF

Adobe Portable Document Format (PDF) is a universal file format that preserves all of the fonts, formatting, colors, and graphics of any source document, regardless of the application and platform used to create the original document. Adobe PDF files are compact and secure. Anyone using the free Adobe Reader can view, navigate, comment on, and print a PDF file. You can extend additional rights to Adobe Reader users, allowing them to fill in and save a PDF form, and to participate in PDF review processes. If you're using Acrobat Pro, you can also enable Reader users to digitally sign a PDF.

- Adobe PDF preserves the exact layout, fonts, and text formatting of electronic documents, regardless of the computer system or platform used to view these documents.

- PDF documents can contain multiple languages, such as Japanese and English, on the same page.

- PDF documents print predictably with proper margins and page breaks.

- You can secure PDF files to prevent unauthorized changes or printing, or to limit access to confidential documents.

- You can change the view magnification of a PDF page in Acrobat or Adobe Reader, which is especially useful for zooming in on graphics or diagrams containing intricate details.

About Adobe Acrobat

Acrobat lets you create, work with, read, and print PDF documents.

Creating Adobe PDF files

Almost any document—a text file, a file created in a page-layout application, a scanned document, a web page, or a digital photo—can be converted to Adobe PDF using Acrobat software or third-party authoring applications. Your workflow and document type determine the best way to create a PDF.

- Use the Create commands in the Acrobat File menu to quickly convert a variety of file formats to Adobe PDF and open them in Acrobat. You can also access these commands from the Create button in the Quick Tools toolbar. You can convert files one at a time, or convert multiple files at once. You can combine converted files into a single, compact PDF file, or, if you're using Acrobat Pro, you can assemble them in a PDF Portfolio with built-in navigation tools. You can also create a blank PDF page using the Insert Blank Page tool.

- Use the Print command to convert almost any file to Adobe PDF from within any application. In most applications, you can adjust settings for PDF creation from within the Print dialog box.

- Use Acrobat PDFMaker from Microsoft Office for Windows and other popular applications. When you install Acrobat, Acrobat PDFMaker is added automatically to supported applications that are installed on the computer. Simply click the Create PDF button (🖷) on the Acrobat ribbon (Office 2007 or 2010) or the Convert To Adobe PDF button (🅰) on the authoring application's toolbar. You can change settings to include bookmarks, hyperlinks, and accessibility features.

- Scan paper documents and convert them to searchable Adobe PDF documents.

- Use the Create PDF From Web Page command to download web pages and convert them to Adobe PDF, keeping links intact. Or, use Acrobat PDFMaker in Mozilla Firefox or Microsoft Internet Explorer to save web pages quickly.

- Convert email messages to Adobe PDF in Microsoft Outlook or Lotus Notes in Windows. You can convert an individual email to PDF, or convert an entire folder of messages into a merged PDF or a PDF Portfolio.

Lesson 3, "Creating Adobe PDF Files," Lesson 5 "Using Acrobat with Microsoft Office Files (Windows)" and Lesson 13, "Using Acrobat in Professional Printing," give step-by-step instructions for creating Adobe PDF files using several of these methods.

Working with PDF files

You can manage, edit, assemble, and search PDF files in Acrobat. Additionally, you can create forms, initiate review processes, and even apply legal features.

- Configure the Acrobat work area to suit your needs. The user interface in Acrobat X features customizable toolbars, task panes, and a navigation pane. (Lesson 2, "Exploring the Work Area")

- In Acrobat Pro, assemble multiple documents into a PDF Portfolio, in which the individual files are maintained as separate documents that can be read, edited, and printed independently. (Lesson 7, "Combining Files in PDF Portfolios")

- Run a simple search using the Find command or run a more complex search from the powerful Search pane in Acrobat. (Lesson 4, "Reading and Working with PDF Files")

- Rotate and crop PDF pages, insert PDF files and pages into a document, customize bookmarks, and renumber pages. (Lesson 6, "Enhancing and Editing PDF Documents")

- Make minor edits to PDF content including text, and, in Acrobat Pro, objects. Reuse the content of a PDF file in other applications (if allowed by the creator of the document) by saving the contents to other file formats, extracting images, and converting PDF pages to image formats. (Lesson 6, "Enhancing and Editing PDF Documents")

- Create sophisticated multimedia presentations. Embedded video, animation, or sound files require no additional software for viewing. The PDF file includes everything the recipient needs to view the file in Acrobat or the free, downloadable Adobe Reader. (Lesson 6, "Enhancing and Editing PDF Documents")

- Approve the contents or certify the validity of a document by adding your digital signature. You can also add sophisticated protection to a confidential PDF file, preventing users from copying text and graphics, printing the document, or even opening the file. (Lesson 8, "Adding Signatures and Security")

- Add comments and mark up text in an electronic document review cycle. In Acrobat, you can set up email, web, or shared reviews. You can collaborate live using the Acrobat.com online service. You can also invite Adobe Reader users to participate in reviews. (Lesson 9, "Using Acrobat in a Review Cycle")

- Create interactive PDF forms from any electronic document or a scanned paper form. You can enable forms so that Adobe Reader users can complete and save them, too. Tools in Acrobat also help you distribute forms, track responses, and analyze form data. (Lesson 10, "Working with Forms in Acrobat")

- In Acrobat Pro, automate workflows using customized actions that combine tasks according to your needs. (Lesson 11, "Using Actions")

- Process and deliver legal documents electronically. To serve the needs of courts and law offices, Acrobat Pro includes a redaction feature for removing privileged content from a PDF document and a Bates numbering feature for labeling documents. (Lesson 12, "Using the Legal Features.")

- Generate high-quality PDF files. Specialized prepress tools in Acrobat Pro enable you to preview color separations, adjust how transparent objects are imaged, and print color separations from PDF files. The Standards pane identifies PDF/X, PDF/A, and PDF/E files, and the Preflight feature makes it easy to verify that a PDF file meets your criteria before printing. (Lesson 13, "Using Acrobat in Professional Printing")

Reading PDF files

You can read PDF documents using Adobe Reader, Acrobat Standard, or Acrobat Pro. You can share your PDF files using network and web servers, CDs, DVDs, other removable media, and the Acrobat.com web service.

About Adobe Reader

Adobe Reader, available free online, is the global standard for viewing PDF files. It is the only PDF viewer that can open and interact with all PDF documents. Adobe Reader makes it possible to view, search, digitally sign, verify, print, and collaborate on PDF files without having Acrobat installed.

Adobe Reader can natively display rich media content, including video and audio files. You can also view PDF Portfolios in Reader. New in Adobe Reader X, anyone can comment on PDF files using the Sticky Note and Highlight tools that are built into the application. However, you can extend additional rights to Adobe Reader users if you want them to be able to complete a PDF form or participate fully in collaborative document reviews.

By default, Adobe Reader for Windows opens PDF files in Protected Mode (known as "sandboxing" to IT professionals). In Protected Mode, Reader confines any processes to the application itself, so that potentially malicious PDF files do not have access to your computer and its system files. To verify that Adobe Reader is in Protected Mode, choose File > Properties, select the Advanced tab, and view the Protected Mode status.

Adobe PDF on the web

The web has greatly expanded the possibilities for delivering electronic documents to a wide and varied audience. Because web browsers can be configured to run other applications inside the browser window, you can post PDF files as part of a website. Visitors to your site can download or view these PDF files inside the browser window using Adobe Reader.

When including a PDF file as part of your web page, consider directing users to the Adobe website so that the first time they encounter a PDF, they can download Adobe Reader, free of charge, if necessary.

PDFs can be viewed one page at a time and printed from the web. With page-at-a-time downloading, the web server sends only the requested page, decreasing downloading time. In addition, you can easily print selected pages or all pages from the document. PDF is a suitable format for publishing long electronic documents on the web, and PDF documents print predictably, with proper margins and page breaks.

You can also download and convert web pages to Adobe PDF, making it easy to save, distribute, and print them. (For more information, see Lesson 3, "Creating Adobe PDF Files.")

Note: Accessibility features, including the Read Out Loud feature, may not work in Adobe Reader in Windows XP when Protected Mode is enabled. In Windows Vista and Windows 7, accessibility features work as expected in Protected Mode.

Note: Adobe strongly recommends that you use Adobe Reader in Protected Mode. However, if you need to disable it, choose Edit > Preferences. Then, select General from the list of categories, and deselect Enable Protected Mode At Startup In the Application Startup panel. You'll need to restart Adobe Reader for the change to take effect.

Adding Adobe Reader installers

Adobe Reader is available free of charge, making it easier for users to view your PDF documents. You can point users to the Adobe Reader installers on the Adobe website at www.adobe.com. If you're distributing documents on a CD or DVD, you can include a copy of the Adobe Reader installers on the disc.

If you're including the Adobe Reader installers on a disc, you should include a ReadMe text file at the top level of the CD or DVD that describes how to install Adobe Reader and provides any last-minute information.

You may make and distribute unlimited copies of Adobe Reader, including copies for commercial distribution. For complete information on distributing and giving your users access to Adobe Reader, visit the Adobe website at http://www.adobe.com/products/acrobat.

A special logo is available from Adobe for use when distributing Adobe Reader.

A first look at the work area

First you'll take a look at some PDFs in Acrobat to get acquainted with the Acrobat X interface and to get a feel for electronic document design considerations.

1 Start Acrobat. In the Welcome screen, click Open.

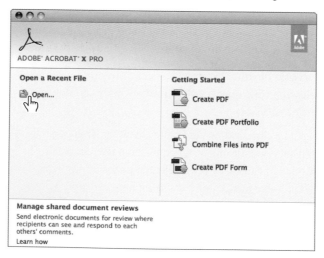

The Acrobat Welcome screen is a gateway to recent files and PDF creation tools.

2 Navigate to the Lesson01 folder on your hard drive, select the file named Hilaptorex.pdf, and click Open.

This document is a one-page article that has been converted to Adobe PDF for easy electronic distribution.

3 Take a look at the work area. It includes a menu bar at the top of the screen. Click any of the menu names to see a menu of commands. We clicked View.

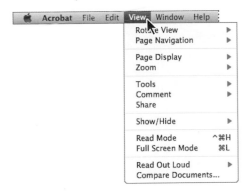

The menu bar is usually open when you're working in Acrobat. If you ever do close the menu bar by choosing View > Show/Hide > Menu Bar, you won't be able to access any menu commands to reopen it. To reopen the menu bar, press F9 (Windows) or Command+Shift+M (Mac OS) on your keyboard.

4 Notice the task pane buttons on the right side of the window: Tools, Comment, and Share. Click Tools.

The Tools pane organizes the Acrobat tools into task-related panels.

5 Notice the toolbars directly beneath the menu bar. The toolbars contain buttons to let you access certain features quickly.

You can customize the Quick Tools toolbar by adding buttons for any of the tools listed in the task panes. You'll learn about customizing the toolbar in Lesson 2, "Exploring the Work Area."

6 Click the Create button on the Quick Tools toolbar. Choosing one of the Create commands initiates a process for creating a PDF file. Click outside the menu to close it without selecting a command.

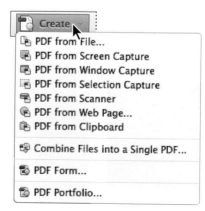

7 Move your pointer down to the lower-left corner of the document pane to reveal the size of this page. (The document pane is the part of the workspace that displays an open document.) The page size display disappears when you move the pointer away from the area.

Notice that the page size is a standard 8.5-by-11 inches. The designer chose this size so that the page could be printed on a desktop printer in addition to being read electronically.

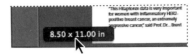

8 Choose File > Open, and open the Application.pdf file, located in the Lesson01 folder. Notice that the file opens in a separate workspace with its own set of toolbars. You can switch between viewing the two open documents, Hilaptorex.pdf and Application.pdf, by selecting the one you want to view from the Window menu.

9 From the Window menu, select the Application.pdf file (in the list of open files at the bottom of the menu). Later you'll learn how to tile windows so that you can view several files at once.

10 Click the Bookmarks button (▯) in the navigation pane on the left side of the work area. Click the Harry Tanaka CV bookmark in the Bookmarks panel to jump directly to that bookmark's destination page in the document.

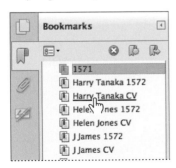 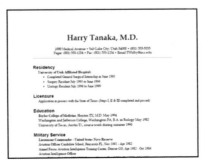

The navigation pane displays the default navigation panels, including the Bookmarks panel. To open additional navigation panels, choose View > Show/Hide > Navigation Panes > [panel name]. You'll learn more about the navigation pane and its panels in Lesson 2, "Exploring the Work Area."

11 With the Application.pdf file active, choose File > Close, and close that file without saving any changes. Close the Hilaptorex.pdf file in the same way.

You've had a brief look at the major components of the Acrobat X work area—the menu bar, toolbars, task panes, document pane, and navigation pane. You'll learn more about these elements as you work through this book.

Viewing PDF presentations in Full Screen mode

In Full Screen mode, the menu bar and toolbars are hidden.

1 Choose File > Open, and double-click the Aquo_Financial.pdf file, located in the Lesson01 folder.

2 Click Yes in the Full Screen message box to open this document in Full Screen mode.

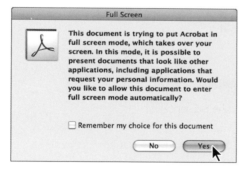 

Notice that in Full Screen mode the document occupies all available space on the monitor. All the Acrobat toolbars, menus, and panes have disappeared.

This document is an informational presentation, designed to be viewed exclusively onscreen. The graphics, large type size, and horizontal page layout have been designed for optimal display on a monitor.

To set a file to open in Full Screen mode, choose File > Properties, click the Initial View tab in the Document Properties dialog box, select Open In Full Screen Mode, and click OK. Then save the document. For more information, see Lesson 6, "Enhancing and Editing PDF Documents."

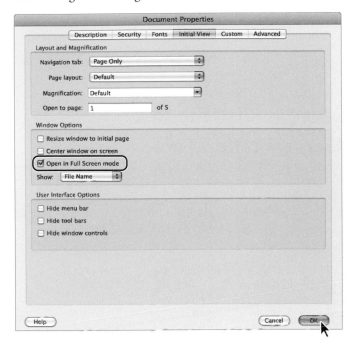

You can view any PDF file in Full Screen mode by opening the document in Acrobat and choosing View > Full Screen Mode.

3 Press Enter or Return to page through the presentation.

4 Press the Escape key to exit Full Screen mode.

5 To ensure that navigation controls are always accessible to you, even in Full Screen mode, choose Edit > Preferences (Windows) or Acrobat > Preferences (Mac OS), and select Full Screen from the list of categories in the Preferences dialog box. Select the Show Navigation Bar option, and click OK to apply your changes.

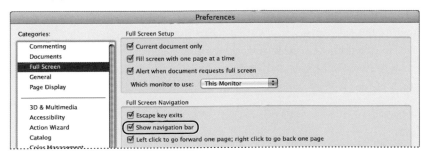

From this point on, whenever you open a document in Acrobat on your computer in Full Screen mode, Acrobat will display Next Page, Previous Page, and Exit Full Screen View buttons at the bottom left of the document pane. The buttons appear when you first view the document in Full Screen mode, and then disappear so that they don't obstruct the presentation. To access the buttons, move the pointer over the lower-left corner of the screen. Keep in mind that Full Screen viewing preferences are specific to the computer on which you run a PDF presentation, not to the document.

Viewing PDF files in Read mode

You can maximize the screen space available to your PDF document without entering Full Screen mode. Read mode hides all the elements of the work area except the document and the menu bar.

1 Choose View > Read Mode.

2 Move the pointer near the bottom of the window. A semi-transparent floating toolbar appears briefly when you move the pointer near the bottom of the page. This floating toolbar includes navigational tools that let you zoom in and out or move to different pages.

3 To restore the work area, click the Show Main Toolbar button in the floating toolbar, or choose View > Read Mode again.

4 Choose File > Close, and close the file without saving any changes.

Designing documents for online viewing

If you expect readers to view your document online, you need to make the design and production decisions that will help make the publication attractive and easy to use. If you're simply converting an existing paper document to electronic format, you'll need to weigh the benefits of reworking the design against the time and cost required to do so. If your publication will be viewed both onscreen and on paper, make sure that the design accommodates the requirements of both.

First, you'll take a look at a printed document that was converted unchanged to electronic format. Converting a document to Adobe PDF is a good way to distribute a document cheaply and easily. It also enables you to use features such as links and bookmarks to make navigation of a longer document, such as a company FAQ, both easy and intuitive. Using OCR (optical character recognition), you can also make text in the document searchable.

1 Choose File > Open, and open the Aquo_FAQs_Print.pdf file, located in the Lesson01 folder.

Notice that this long and narrow document is difficult to read onscreen. You must scroll down to read the entire page.

2 To view the entire page in the document pane, choose View > Zoom > Zoom To Page Level or click the Fit One Full Page button (⊞) in the Common Tools toolbar.

Even though the page fits onscreen, you can see that this document was designed for print. The long and narrow page is inconveniently shaped for the screen, and the small image and type sizes make reading a strain for the user.

Now you'll look at the same document redesigned and optimized for online reading.

3 Choose File > Open, and double-click the Aquo_FAQs_Web.pdf file, also in the Lesson01 folder.

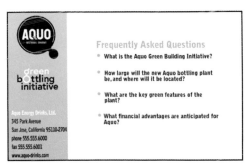

Notice that the horizontal page orientation makes this document better suited for display on a monitor than the vertical orientation of the previous document.

4 Click the Bookmarks button (📑) in the navigation pane to open the Bookmarks panel.

5 Click the bookmark labeled "Size and location of the plant."

The question and answer about the plant's size and location appear. Notice how the larger type and different page size make this document easier to view than the document designed for print.

6 Click the bookmark labeled "FAQs."

7 Click one of the questions to jump to its page.

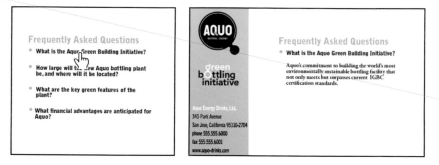

Each question on the first page of the document is a link that takes the viewer to the corresponding question. The original document has been redesigned to accommodate a navigational structure based on self-contained, screen-sized units.

The formatting considerations of onscreen publications—fonts, page size, layout, color, and resolution—are the same as those of other kinds of publications; however, each element must be re-evaluated in the context of onscreen viewing. Decisions about issues such as color and resolution, which in traditional publishing may require a trade-off between quality and cost, may require a parallel trade-off between quality and file size in electronic publishing. Once you have determined the page elements that are important to you, choose the publishing tools and format that will best maintain those elements.

8 Choose File > Close to close each open PDF file.

You have examined a variety of electronic documents designed in different file formats for different purposes, while getting acquainted with the Acrobat X work area. Later in this book, you'll get some hands-on practice in creating and tailoring electronic documents.

Getting help

Acrobat offers complete, accessible resources to help you learn and use the program:

- Adobe Acrobat X Help contains in-depth information about all the Acrobat commands and features.
- From Acrobat, you have a direct link to up-to-date support resources online at the Adobe website.

Using Adobe Acrobat X Help

The lessons in this book focus on commonly used tools and features of Acrobat X. However, you can get complete information on all the Acrobat tools, commands, and features for both Windows and Mac OS systems from Adobe Acrobat X Help. Adobe Acrobat X Help is easy to use because you can look for topics in several ways:

- Scan the table of contents.
- Search for keywords.
- Jump from topic to topic using related topics links.

You'll use Adobe Acrobat X Help to find information about the application.

1 Choose Help > Adobe Acrobat X Help to open Adobe Acrobat X Help in your default browser.

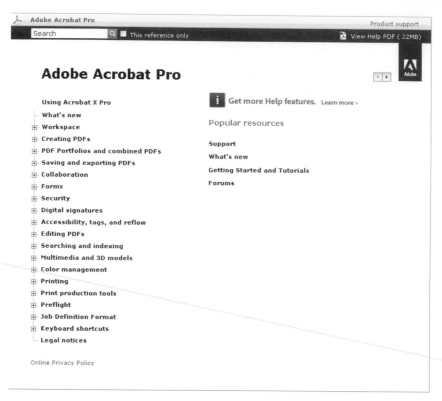

Adobe Acrobat X Help opens online. The table of contents appears, with links for each topic.

If you do not have an Internet connection, Acrobat displays a message suggesting you verify your Internet connection. If you plan to work in Acrobat without an Internet connection, you can download the Acrobat Help topics as a PDF document from the Adobe Acrobat X Help screen online, and then open and search the PDF file as you would any other.

2 Click the icon to the left of a heading to expand it.

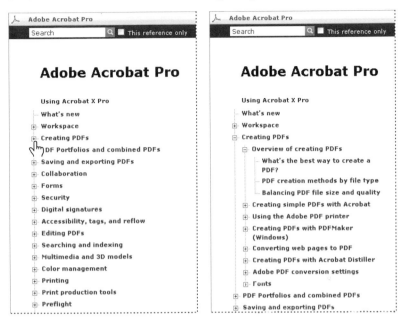

3 Click on any heading or subheading to view help content on that topic.

4 Use the links included in the topic to view related information. Or click the breadcrumbs at the top of the window to navigate back to the table of contents or to a higher-level heading.

5 In the Search box at the top of the window, type **PDF Portfolio**, and then press Enter or Return.

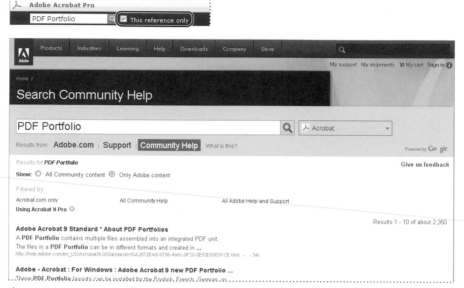

If you select This Reference Only when you search, only Acrobat Help topics are displayed.

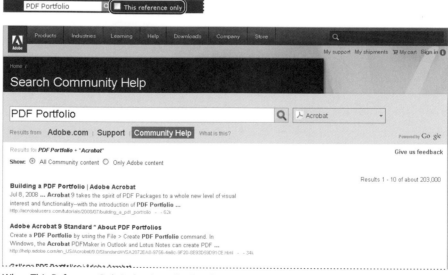

When This Reference Only is deselected, related community resources are displayed in addition to Acrobat Help topics.

The search results are listed in the window. You can view the Help topics onscreen, or you can print them.

6 To print a Help topic, choose File > Print, or click the Print button in the toolbar of your browser application.

7 Close the browser to close Adobe Acrobat X Help.

8 Quit Acrobat by choosing File > Exit (Windows) or Acrobat > Quit Acrobat (Mac OS).

Now that you've been introduced to Acrobat, you'll learn how to create and work with Adobe PDF files as you move through the lessons in this book.

Review questions

1 Name one way you can create a PDF document.

2 Name two advantages of PDF documents.

3 How can you return to your usual work area from Full Screen mode?

Review answers

1 To create a PDF document, you can use the Create command in Acrobat, use the Print command from any application, use Acrobat PDFMaker from Microsoft Office in Windows or another supported application, scan a document and convert it to PDF, or create a PDF file from a web page using the From Web Page command in Acrobat.

2 Adobe PDF provides several advantages, including the following:

- Adobe PDF preserves the exact layout, fonts, and text formatting of electronic documents, regardless of the computer system or platform used to view these documents.

- PDF documents can contain multiple languages, such as Japanese and English, on the same page.

- PDF documents print predictably with proper margins and page breaks.

- You can secure PDF files to prevent unauthorized changes or printing, or to limit access to confidential documents.

- You can change the view magnification of a PDF page in Acrobat or Adobe Reader, which is especially useful for zooming in on graphics or diagrams containing intricate details.

3 To exit Full Screen mode and return to your normal work area, press the Esc key on your keyboard.

2 EXPLORING THE WORK AREA

Lesson overview

In this lesson, you'll do the following:

- Select tools in the Quick Tools and Common Tools toolbars.

- Select tools in the Tools and Comment panes.

- Add tools to the Quick Tools toolbar.

- Navigate a PDF document using the Common Tools toolbar, menu commands, page thumbnails, and bookmarks.

- Change the view of a document in the document pane.

 This lesson will take approximately 45 minutes to complete. Copy the Lesson02 folder onto your hard drive if you haven't already done so.

The Acrobat X workspace puts the tools you need at your fingertips, without cluttering up the screen. You can customize the toolbars for quicker access to tools you use frequently.

Opening a PDF file

The default Acrobat X work area is streamlined to ensure easy access to the tools you'll use most often as you work with PDF files.

1 Start Acrobat.

2 Click Open in the Welcome screen.

3 Navigate to the Lesson02 folder on your hard drive, and select the Conference Guide.pdf file.

4 Click Open.

▶ **Tip:** In Windows, you can move between open PDF documents by clicking a file's icon in the Windows Taskbar.

The menu bar and two toolbars are visible at the top of the work area. In Acrobat X, each open document has its own work area and toolbars. You can access common commands in the menu bar.

Acrobat can open in two different ways—as a standalone application or in a web browser. The associated work areas differ in small but important ways. This book assumes that you are using Acrobat as a standalone application.

Working with the toolbars

The Acrobat toolbars, known as the Quick Tools toolbar and the Common Tools toolbar, contain commonly used tools and commands for working with PDF files. Most of the tools available in Acrobat are included in the Tools pane at the right side of the window. However, you can add tools to the Quick Tools toolbar so that you can access them more quickly.

Using the toolbars

By default, the Quick Tools toolbar includes the Create button that provides several commands for creating PDF files, output buttons, basic commenting tools, and common page-manipulation tools. It also includes a button for customizing the Quick Tools toolbar.

Quick Tools toolbar

The Common Tools toolbar includes page navigation buttons.

Common Tools toolbar

To see the name or description of a tool in either toolbar, hover the pointer over the tool.

Selecting tools

The default tool in Acrobat is the Selection tool (🔸). To select a tool from a toolbar, click its button in the toolbar. A selected tool usually remains active until you select another tool.

1 Click the Zoom In button (⊕) in the Common Tools toolbar three times.

Acrobat enlarges the view. Only part of the document appears in the application window.

2 Click the Hand tool (🖐) in the Common Tools toolbar.

The Hand tool lets you pan around the document.

3 With the Hand tool selected, drag the document across the application window to see a different portion of the image.

4 Click the Zoom Out button (⊖) once to see more of the page.

The Zoom tools do not change the actual size of a document. They change only its magnification on your screen.

▶ **Tip:** A black arrow to the right of a tool indicates that there is a menu associated with that tool. Click the arrow to reveal that menu.

5 Click the arrow to the right of the magnification text box, and choose 100% from the pop-up menu to display the document at 100%.

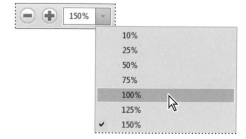

Same tools, different locations

If you've used Adobe Acrobat 9 or earlier, the Acrobat X work area can require a little adjustment. But don't worry. The tools you rely on are still there—they're just tucked into panels instead of taskbars.

If you looked for a tool in the taskbar in Acrobat 9, it's probably in the task panes in Acrobat X. Most of the taskbars map directly to panels in the Tools pane. The Comment taskbar, of course, maps to the Comment pane. And the Collaborate taskbar maps to the Share pane. Many of the menu commands have moved to the Tools pane, as well.

▶ **Tip:** If you use a tool frequently, add it to the Quick Tools toolbar to access it more quickly.

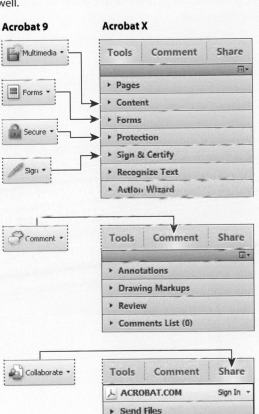

Working with task panes

The task panes on the right side of the application window contain many of the tools you'll need to perform a wide variety of tasks in Acrobat. The Tools pane displays panels with tools for tasks ranging from page manipulation to form creation and text recognition. The Comment pane gives you access to reviewing tools. The Share pane makes it easy to share files on Acrobat.com, an online file-sharing service, or to send them as attachments. To display the contents of a pane, click its name.

Selecting tools in the Tools pane

Tools are grouped by task in panels in the Tools pane. By default, Acrobat displays the most commonly used panels. See "Panels in the Tools pane" for a description of the available panels.

You'll use tools to rotate a page and edit some text.

1　Click Tools to open the Tools pane, if it's not already open.

2　Click Pages to display the Pages panel, if it's not already open.

3　In the Common Tools toolbar, type **9** in the page number box, and then press Enter or Return to go to page 9 in the document. The map of Meridien is oriented incorrectly.

4　In the Pages panel, click Rotate. The Rotate Pages dialog box opens.

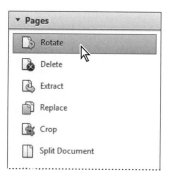

5　Choose Clockwise 90 Degrees from the Direction menu. Then select Pages in the Page Range area, and make sure you're rotating from page 9 to page 9 of 12.

6 Click OK to close the Rotate Pages dialog box and rotate the page.

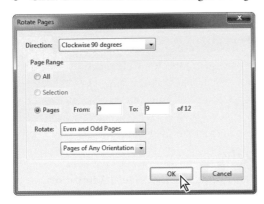

7 Go to page 12.

8 Click Content in the Tools pane.

The Content panel opens. By default, Acrobat displays only one panel at a time. When you open a panel, Acrobat closes the panel that was previously open.

9 Select the Edit Document Text tool in the Edit Text & Objects area of the Content panel.

● **Note:** If this is the first time you've used the Edit Document Text tool, there may be a delay while Acrobat loads system fonts.

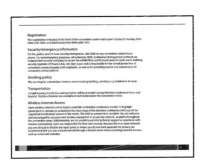

The pointer changes to an I-beam when you move it over text.

10 On page 12, select the word *and* in the second sentence of the Wireless Internet Access topic.

11 Type **but** to replace the word *and*.

Conference via 802.11 b/g high-Meridien Conference *and* may not be nnect to is meridien. You are welcome ess our network, available throughout de technical support or assistance with curity. Because this is an open network, hot want exposed. For privacy, we

Conference via 802.11 b/g high-Meridien Conference but may not be nnect to is meridien. You are welcome ess our network, available throughout de technical support or assistance with curity. Because this is an open network, hot want exposed. For privacy, we

12 Click OK if Acrobat informs you that it needs to substitute the font.

13 Choose File > Save As > PDF.

14 Name the file **Conference Guide_final.pdf**, and click Save. Leave the file open.

Panels in the Tools pane

By default, the Tools pane displays the most commonly used panels. To add or remove panels from the pane, select panels in the Tools pane menu. Acrobat uses the current Tools pane configuration in all PDF documents you open until you change the configuration again. (Some of the tools—and some entire panels—are available only in Acrobat Pro.)

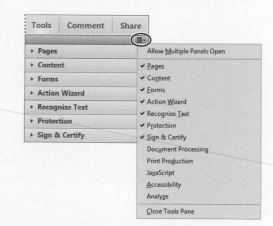

- The Pages panel contains tools for manipulating pages and page design.
- The Content panel contains tools for editing the content of the document, including text.
- The Forms panel contains tools for creating and editing PDF forms.
- The Protection panel contains tools for file encryption, redaction, and other security features.
- The Sign & Certify panel contains tools for working with digital signatures.
- The Recognize Text panel contains tools for converting scanned text to editable text.
- The Action Wizard panel contains existing actions and tools for creating new actions.
- The Document Processing panel contains tools for preparing a document for distribution.
- The Print Production panel contains tools for preparing a document for professional printing.
- The JavaScript panel contains tools for creating and editing scripts in Acrobat.
- The Accessibility panel contains tools for ensuring your PDF document is accessible to people with disabilities.
- The Analyze panel contains tools for working with data in your document.

Using the Comment pane

Acrobat provides many ways for you to add comments or otherwise mark up a document. The Comment pane gives you access to commenting tools and lists comments included in the document.

You'll view comments in a document, and add one of your own. You'll work extensively with the Comment pane in Lesson 9, "Using Acrobat in a Review Cycle."

1 Choose File > Open.

2 In the Open dialog box, navigate to the Lesson02 folder, select the Meridien Rev.pdf file, and click Open.

This document is a screen capture of a web page for the conference. The designer is soliciting review comments.

3 In the Common Tools toolbar, click the arrow next to the zoom percentage, and choose Zoom To Page Level so that you can see the entire page.

4 Click Comment in the upper-right corner of the application window to open the Comment pane.

 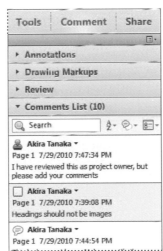

Comments in the document are displayed in the Comments List area of the pane.

5 Select a comment. Its markup is highlighted on the page, so that you can see the comment in context.

6 Click Annotations to open the Annotations panel if it's not already open.

7 Select the Sticky Note tool (💬).

8 Click anywhere on the page. A sticky note icon appears, and a message box opens. Type **This is much better than the last version!**

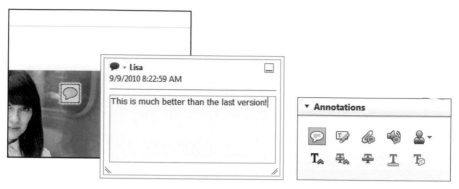

9 Click anywhere on the page to deselect your comment. Your comment appears in the Comments List.

10 Click Comment to close the Comment pane.

Customizing the Quick Tools toolbar

● **Note:** You can add and remove tools to the right of the Customize Quick Tools button in the Quick Tools toolbar, but you cannot move or remove anything to its left, such as the Save and Print buttons.

The task panes keep a wealth of tools readily available, but tucked out of sight. However, it's faster to access tools on the Quick Tools toolbar than it is to open a pane, select a panel, and select a tool. You can add tools you use frequently to the Quick Tools toolbar, remove tools you don't need, and arrange the order of tools in the toolbar. Changes you make to the Quick Tools toolbar are application-wide, so the toolbar appears the same, no matter which PDF file you have open.

1 In the Quick Tools toolbar, click the Customize Quick Tools button.

The Customize Quick Tools dialog box opens. The right side displays the tools currently in the toolbar. The left side lists the tools you can add.

2 From the list on the left, expand Content, and then select Edit Document Text.

3 Click the right arrow button to copy the tool to the list on the right.

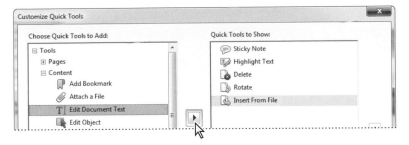

4 Click the up arrow button multiple times to move the Edit Document Text tool to the top of the list, so that it will appear first in the Quick Tools toolbar.

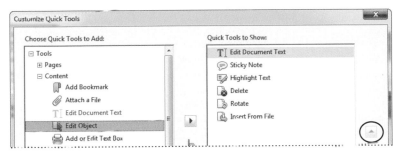

5 Click OK to save your changes.

The Edit Document Text tool has been added to the Quick Tools toolbar, and it appears immediately after the Customize Quick Tools button.

Using keyboard shortcuts to select tools

You can set your Acrobat preferences so that you can use keyboard shortcuts to select tools.

1 Choose Edit > Preferences (Windows) or Acrobat > Preferences (Mac OS), and select General from the categories on the left.

● **Note:** Not all tools have keyboard shortcuts associated with them.

2 Select the Use Single-Key Accelerators To Access Tools option. A check mark appears in the box when this option is selected.

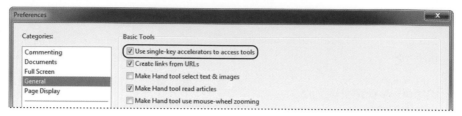

3 Click OK to apply the change.

Now when you position the pointer over some of the tools, you'll see a letter or a combination of keys in parentheses following the tool name. This is the keyboard shortcut for that tool.

4 Move your pointer over the Add Sticky Note tool in the Quick Tools toolbar, and notice that the tool tip now displays the keyboard shortcut for the tool.

5 Move the pointer into the document pane, and press Ctrl+6 or Command+6 on the keyboard. The pointer changes to the Sticky Note tool, and Acrobat adds a sticky note to the page.

6 Click anywhere on the page to deselect the note.

Navigating PDF documents

You can zoom in and out, move to different pages, show multiple pages at a time, view multiple documents at a time, and even split a document to view different areas of the same document at a time. Many navigation tools are available in more than one place; you can use the method that best suits your workflow.

Changing magnification

Earlier in this lesson, you used the Zoom In and Zoom Out tools, as well as the Preset Magnification menu, all in the Common Tools toolbar. You can also change the magnification using commands in the View menu.

1 If the Meridien Rev.pdf file isn't open, open it now.

2 Choose View > Zoom > Fit Width.

The PDF document fills the entire width of the application window.

3 Choose View > Zoom > Zoom To.

4 In the Zoom To dialog box, scroll down to choose 125% from the Magnification pop-up menu, and then click OK.

Accessing specific pages

You've used the page number text box in the Common Tools toolbar to go to a specific page. You can also use commands in the View menu or the Page Thumbnails panel in the navigation pane to quickly move to a different page in the document.

1 Choose Window > Conference Guide_final.pdf to display the file you worked with earlier. If the Conference Guide_final.pdf file isn't open, open it.

2 Choose View > Page Navigation > Page.

3 In the Go To Page dialog box, type **7**, and click OK.

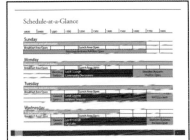

Acrobat displays page 7 of the document.

4 Choose View > Page Navigation > Previous Page.

Acrobat displays page 6 of the document. The Previous Page and Next Page commands serve the same purpose as the Previous Page and Next Page buttons in the Common Tools toolbar.

5 In the navigation pane on the left side of the application window, click the Page Thumbnails button ( ).

Acrobat displays thumbnails of all the pages in the document. Acrobat automatically creates thumbnails for the pages of a PDF document when you open it, if they do not already exist in the document.

6 Select the thumbnail for page 3.

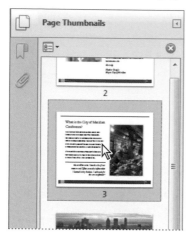 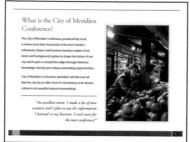

Acrobat displays page 3 of the document.

Note: The navigation pane also contains the Attachments and Digital Signatures panels. You'll work with these panels in later lessons.

7 Zoom in to 200%. Notice that the thumbnail highlights the area of the page that is visible at this magnification.

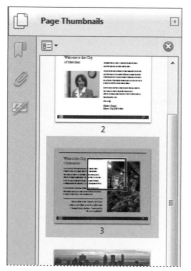 

8 Select the Hand tool in the Common Tools toolbar.

9 Drag in the document window to see a different area of the page. Notice that the highlighted area in the thumbnail moves accordingly.

Using bookmarks to navigate documents

You can create bookmarks to help viewers navigate PDF documents. Bookmarks act as an electronic table of contents page, providing links directly to the content they describe.

1 Click the Bookmarks button (📑) directly below the Page Thumbnails button in the navigation pane.

Acrobat displays the bookmarks that have been created for this PDF document.

2 Click the Meridien Wi-Fi bookmark.

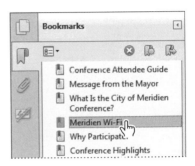 

Acrobat displays page 4, which contains information about Meridien wireless access.

3 Click the General Sessions bookmark.

Acrobat displays page 8, where the descriptions of the conference sessions begin. You do not need to create a bookmark for each page.

4 Click the General Information bookmark.

Acrobat displays page 10, where the general information begins. You'll create another bookmark to help conference attendees locate information about accessing first aid quickly.

5 Click the Next Page button (⬇) in the Common Tools toolbar to go to page 11.

6 Select the Selection tool (I⯅) in the Common Tools toolbar, and then select the First aid information heading on the page.

▶ **Tip:** You can create bookmarks for a PDF document in Acrobat, or you can generate them automatically using PDFMaker or by generating a table of contents in InDesign and specifying to include bookmarks when you create a PDF file.

7 Click the New Bookmark button (📑) at the top of the Bookmarks panel.

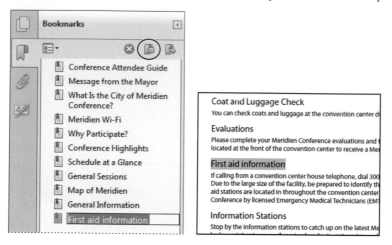

Acrobat adds a new bookmark with the text you selected beneath the General Information bookmark.

8 Drag the new bookmark over the General Information bookmark (directly over the words "General Information") until you see a small right triangle, and then release the mouse.

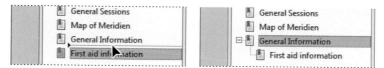

Acrobat indents the new bookmark, nesting it inside the General Information bookmark.

Viewing multiple documents

You can work with more than one PDF file at a time, displaying the documents vertically or horizontally.

1 Choose Window > Tile > Vertically.

Acrobat displays all the open PDF files side by side. Notice that each document has its own application window, complete with toolbars and panes.

2 Choose Window > Tile > Horizontally.

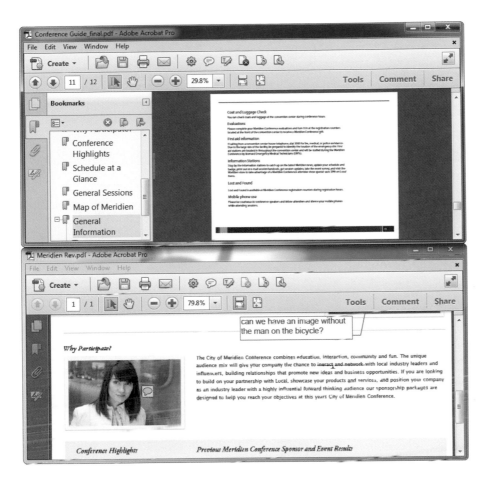

Acrobat displays the PDF documents in their own application windows once again, but this time they're displayed horizontally.

3 Choose Window > Cascade.

Acrobat displays the active document in front of the others, but you can see the title bar for each of the other open documents.

Splitting the view of a document

Sometimes you need to work with different portions of a single document simultaneously, whether it's to ensure you've used consistent wording or to examine differences in images. You can split a document into two views, with the ability to navigate each individually.

1 Choose Window > Split.

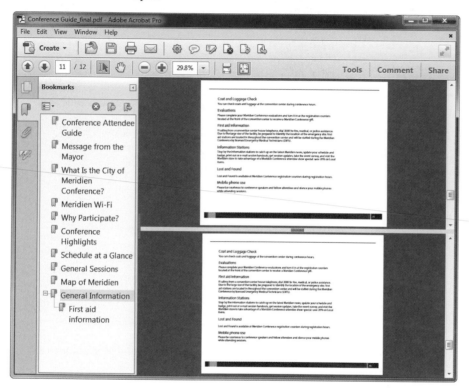

Acrobat displays the same document twice, each with its own scroll bar. Notice that both copies of the document share the same toolbars and panes.

2 Click anywhere in the top version of the document. It's now the active view.

3 Click the Previous Page button to go to the previous page in the top view. Only the top view changes.

4 Click anywhere in the bottom view to make it active.

5 Zoom in to 150%. Only the bottom view changes.

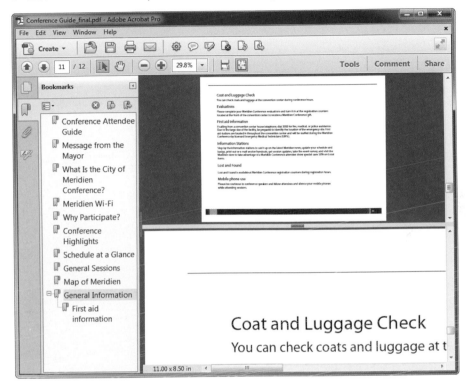

6 Choose Window > Remove Split.

Acrobat restores the document to a single view, displaying whichever view was active when you chose the Remove Split command.

7 Close all open documents without saving changes.

Review questions

1 How do you navigate to a different page?

2 How can you show additional panels in the Tools pane?

3 How can you add tools to the Quick Tools toolbar?

4 How can you access commenting tools?

Review answers

1 To navigate to a different page, you can do any of the following:

- Click the Next Page or Previous Page button in the Common Tools toolbar.

- Type a page number in the Common Tools toolbar.

- Choose a command from the View > Page Navigation menu.

- Select a thumbnail in the Page Thumbnails panel in the navigation pane.

- Select a bookmark in the Bookmarks panel in the navigation pane.

2 To display additional panels in the Tools pane, select them in the Tools pane menu.

3 To add tools to the Quick Tools toolbar, click the Customize Quick Tools button in the Quick Tools toolbar. Then select the tool you want to add from the list on the left, click the right arrow button, and click OK.

4 To access commenting tools, click Comment to open the Comment pane.

3 CREATING ADOBE PDF FILES

Lesson overview

In this lesson, you'll do the following:

- Convert a TIFF file to Adobe PDF using the Create command.
- Convert a file to Adobe PDF using the authoring application's Print command.
- Combine multiple documents into a single PDF file.
- Explore the Adobe PDF settings used to convert files to Adobe PDF.
- Reduce the size of a PDF file.
- Scan a paper document into Adobe PDF.
- Convert images into searchable text.
- Convert email messages to Adobe PDF.
- Convert web pages to Adobe PDF from Acrobat and directly from Internet Explorer (Windows) or Mozilla Firefox.

 This lesson will take approximately 60 minutes to complete. Copy the Lesson03 folder onto your hard drive if you haven't already done so.

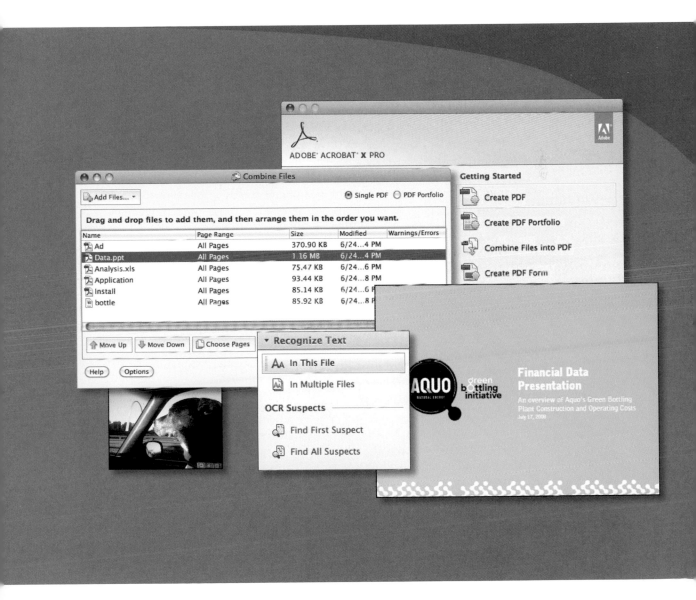

You can easily create PDF files from existing files, such as Microsoft Word documents, web pages, scanned documents, and images.

About creating Adobe PDF files

You can convert a variety of file formats to Adobe PDF, preserving all the fonts, formatting, graphics, and color of the source file, regardless of the application and platform used to create it. You can create PDFs from images, document files, websites, scanned paper documents, and clipboard content.

If the document you want to convert to PDF is open in its authoring application (for example, a spreadsheet is open in Excel), you can usually convert the file to PDF without opening Acrobat. But if Acrobat is already open, you don't have to open the authoring application to convert a file to PDF.

You also need to consider PDF file size and quality (image resolution, for example). When such factors are critical, you'll want to use a method that allows you to control conversion options. Dragging and dropping files on the Acrobat icon to create PDF files is fast and easy, but if you want more control over the process, use another method, such as using the Create button in Acrobat or the Print command in the authoring application. After you specify conversion settings, the settings apply across PDFMaker, Acrobat, and Acrobat Distiller until you change them.

● **Note:** When you're creating a PDF from within Acrobat, you must have the application that created the original file installed on your system.

Lesson 5, "Using Acrobat with Microsoft Office Files (Windows)," describes how to create Adobe PDF files directly from a variety of Microsoft Office files using PDFMaker in Windows. Lesson 13, "Using Acrobat in Professional Printing," covers the creation of press-quality PDF files.

If the security settings applied to an Adobe PDF file allow it, you can also reuse the content of the document. You can extract content for use in another authoring application, such as Microsoft Word, or you can reflow the content for use with handheld devices or screen readers. The success with which content can be repurposed or reused depends very much on the structural information contained in the PDF file. The more structural information a PDF document contains, the more opportunities you have for successfully reusing the content, and the more reliably a document can be used with screen readers. (For more information, see Lesson 4, "Reading and Working with PDF Files.")

Using the Create command

You can use the Create command in Acrobat to convert a variety of different file formats to Adobe PDF.

You'll convert a single TIFF file to an Adobe PDF file. You can use this same method to convert a variety of both image and non-image file types to Adobe PDF.

1 Start Acrobat.

2 Do one of the following:

- Click Create PDF in the Welcome screen.

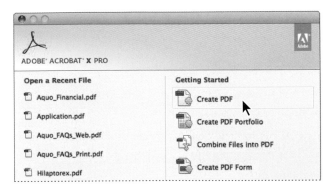

- Click the Create button on the Quick Tools toolbar, and choose PDF From File. (In Mac OS, the toolbars are available only if you already have a document open.)

- Choose File > Create > PDF From File.

3 In the Open dialog box, choose TIFF from the Files Of Type (Windows) or Show (Mac OS) menu. (The menu lists all the file types that can be converted using this method.)

4 Navigate to the Lesson03 folder on your hard drive.

5 Click Settings to open the Adobe PDF Settings dialog box.

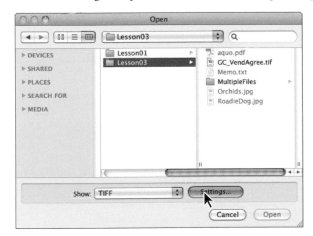

In the Adobe PDF Settings dialog box, you can choose the compression settings for color, grayscale, and monochrome images, and the color management options used when the file is converted to Adobe PDF. Resolution is determined automatically.

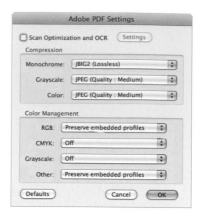

6 Click Cancel to leave the options unchanged for now.

You can also review and edit the settings used to convert your files to PDF in the Convert To PDF panel of the Preferences dialog box.

7 In the Open dialog box, select the GC_VendAgree.tif file, and click Open.

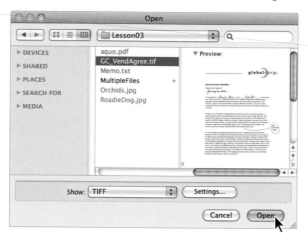

Acrobat converts the TIFF file to Adobe PDF and opens the PDF file automatically.

8 Click the Fit One Full Page button (⊞) on the Common Tools toolbar so that you can see the entire agreement.

Notice that the handwritten note that the signer of the agreement has added is preserved in the Adobe PDF file.

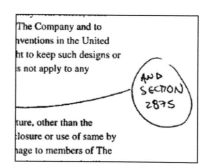

9 Choose File > Save As > PDF, name the file **GC_VendAgree1.pdf**, and save it in the Lesson03 folder. Then choose File > Close to close the PDF file.

Dragging and dropping files

You can also create Adobe PDF files from many documents simply by dragging the file onto the Acrobat icon or into the document pane in Acrobat (Windows). Acrobat uses the conversion settings you specified the last time you converted a file.

Experiment with dragging the Orchids.jpg file and the RoadieDog.jpg files into the Acrobat document pane (Windows), onto the Acrobat icon on your desktop, or onto the Acrobat icon in the Dock (Mac OS). Close any open PDF files when you are finished. You can save the newly created PDF files or close them without saving.

Creating Adobe PDFs from Microsoft Office files (Mac OS)

In Acrobat X, you convert Microsoft Office files to Adobe PDF just as you would convert any other file. You can use the Print command in Microsoft Office or the Create menu in Acrobat. Or you can drag the file onto the Acrobat icon on your desktop. Acrobat X does not offer PDFMaker for the Mac OS version of Microsoft Office. For more information, see the relevant topics in this lesson and "Creating PDFs" in Adobe Acrobat X Help.

Converting and combining different types of files

You can use the Combine Files Into A Single PDF command on the Create button menu to easily convert different types of files to Adobe PDF and combine them into one PDF file. If you're using Acrobat Pro, you can also assemble multiple documents into a PDF Portfolio. For information on creating PDF Portfolios, see Lesson 7, "Combining Files in PDF Portfolios."

Now, you'll convert a file to Adobe PDF and combine it with several other PDF files.

Assembling the files

First, you'll select the files you want to combine, and specify which pages to include. You'll combine a JPEG file with several PDF files. You'll include only a single page from one of the PDF documents.

1 In Acrobat, choose File > Create > Combine Files Into A Single PDF. Alternatively, if you're working in Windows or have a document open in Mac OS, you can click the Create button in the Quick Tools toolbar, and choose Combine Files Into A Single PDF.

Acrobat opens the Combine Files dialog box so that you can assemble your documents.

2 Click the Add Files button in the Combine Files dialog box, and choose Add Files from the menu.

Now you'll select the files that you want to convert and combine. The types of files that you can convert vary depending on whether you are working in Windows or Mac OS.

3 In the Add Files dialog box, navigate to the MultipleFiles folder in the Lesson03 folder. Make sure that All Supported Formats is selected.

4 Select the bottle.jpg file. Then Ctrl-click (Windows) or Command-click (Mac OS) to add the following files to your selection:

- Analysis.xls.pdf
- Ad.pdf
- Data.ppt.pdf
- Install.pdf
- Application.pdf

5 Click Open (Windows) or Add Files (Mac OS).

You can add these files in any order, because you can rearrange them in the Combine Files window. You can also use the Remove button to remove any unwanted files.

6 Click an empty area of the dialog box to deselect all files. Then select each file in turn, and use the Move Up and Move Down buttons to arrange the files in the following order:

- Ad
- Data.ppt
- Analysis.xls
- Application
- Install
- bottle

You can convert all pages in a file, or you can select a specific page or range of pages to convert.

7 Select the Data.ppt file in the Combine Files dialog box, and click the Choose Pages button.

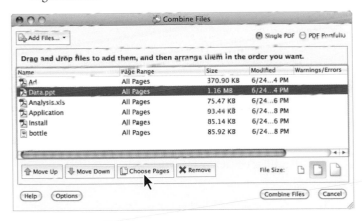

8 Use the page controls in the Preview And Select Page Range dialog box to view the pages in this document.

9 Select the Pages option, and enter **1** in the text box to include only the first page of the presentation. Click OK. Notice that the entry in the Page Range column has changed.

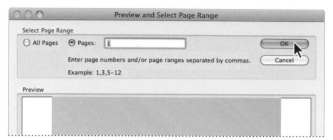 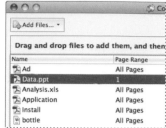

Converting and consolidating the files

You'll convert the assembled files into one PDF file.

1 Make sure that the middle icon (Default File Size) is selected for File Size in the lower-right corner of the dialog box.

The Default File Size option produces a PDF file suitable for viewing and printing business documents. The Smaller File Size option optimizes files for web distribution. Use the Larger File Size option to prepare documents for high-quality printing.

2 Click Combine Files.

Acrobat converts any native files into PDF and then consolidates all the selected files into a single file, named Binder1.pdf. The file opens automatically.

3 Use the Next Page (⬇) and Previous Page (⬆) buttons to page through your consolidated documents.

4 Choose File > Save As > PDF, and rename the file **Aquo.pdf**. Save the file to the Lesson03 folder. Click Save.

Without leaving Acrobat, you have converted a JPEG file to Adobe PDF and combined it with several other PDF files.

5 Choose File > Close to close the file.

Inserting a blank page

In Acrobat, you can insert blank pages into a PDF file, which makes it easy to create a transition page or a notes page.

1   In Acrobat, open the Aquo.pdf file you created, and navigate to page 7, the last page.

2   Open the Tools pane, and then the Pages panel.

3   Select More Insert Options in the Insert Pages area of the Pages panel, and choose Insert Blank Page.

4   In the Insert Pages dialog box, choose After from the Location menu, and make sure page 7 is selected in the Page area of the dialog box. Then click OK.

5   Click the Next Page button on the Common Tools toolbar to display the blank page.

6   Open the Content panel in the Tools pane. Select Add Or Edit Text Box. Acrobat opens the Typewriter toolbar.

7   Select the Typewriter tool in the toolbar. The pointer turns into an I-beam. Click an insertion point at the top of the page, and change the font (we used Adobe Garamond Pro Bold). Type **Notes**. Use options on the Typewriter toolbar to change text attributes, including font size and color.

8   Choose File > Save to save the document, and then close the file.

Using PDFMaker

When you install Adobe Acrobat X, the installer adds Acrobat PDFMaker buttons or menu commands to supported applications, including Microsoft Office applications (Windows only), Mozilla Firefox, Autodesk AutoCAD, and others. PDFMaker options vary from one application to another, but they always give you the ability to quickly create a PDF file from the source application file. Depending on the application, you can also use PDFMaker to add bookmarks, tag the PDF document to make it more accessible, add security features, or include layers.

For specific information about using PDFMaker in Office for Windows, see Lesson 5, "Using Acrobat with Microsoft Office Files (Windows)." To use PDFMaker in Microsoft Outlook or Lotus Notes, see "Converting email messages to PDF (Windows)" later in this lesson. To use PDFMaker in Firefox or Internet Explorer, see "Converting web pages to Adobe PDF" later in this lesson.

PDFMaker options

Acrobat PDFMaker is automatically installed with several supported applications. In each application, it includes options you can use to customize PDF files created with that application. Though most of the supported applications are in Windows, PDFMaker is also installed with Firefox for Mac OS.

Microsoft Word (Windows)

- Retain links
- Create accessible PDF files
- Retain bookmarks, headings, and styles as bookmarks
- Retain endnotes, footnotes, and other reference types
- Embed Flash in the Word document and retain it in the PDF
- Merge mail templates to Adobe PDF and, optionally, mail them to recipients
- Import comments from the corresponding PDF file back to the Word document

Microsoft Excel (Windows)

- Retain links
- Convert multiple work-sheets or a selection to PDF
- Create accessible PDF files
- Bookmark worksheets
- Retain document information and comments

Microsoft PowerPoint (Windows)

- Retain links
- Create accessible PDF files
- Retain Flash media in the PDF file
- Create bookmarks of slides
- Create PDF/A- and PDF/X-compliant files
- Create secure PDFs
- Create and send PDFs through email
- Create PDFs and send them for review

Microsoft Outlook (Windows)

- Archive email to structured PDF Portfolios, retaining folder and message information
- Create indexed archives for faster searching
- Retain attachments
- Automate archives
- Convert a document to PDF and attach it to email
- Convert a document to PDF, apply security to it, and attach it to email

Microsoft Project (Windows)

- Create secure PDFs
- Create PDF/A-compliant files
- Convert a document to PDF and attach it to email
- Convert a document to PDF and send it for review

Microsoft Publisher (Windows)

- Retain links
- Preserve spot colors, crop marks, and transparency
- Allow bleeds and print bleed marks
- Create secure PDFs
- Create bookmarks
- Convert a document to PDF and send it through email
- Convert a document to PDF and send it for review

Microsoft Access (Windows)

- Convert single reports, tables, forms, and queries to PDF
- Create a single PDF from multiple reports, with individual reports bookmarked

Microsoft Visio (Windows)

- Preserve layers, object metadata, and comments
- Select which layer or layers to preserve
- Create secure PDFs
- Create PDF/A-compliant PDF files
- Convert a document to PDF and send it through email
- Convert a document to PDF and send it for review

IBM Lotus Notes (Windows)

- Archive email to structured PDF Portfolios, retaining folder and message information
- Retain attachments
- Create indexed archives for faster searching
- Automate archives

AutoDesk AutoCAD (Windows)

- Retain links
- Convert multiple model spaces or layouts to PDF
- Retain layers
- Import comments from the corresponding PDF back to the AutoCAD document.
- Create documents compliant with PDF/E, PDF/A, and other standards
- Retain scale and document information
- Create PDF Portfolios from multiple files
- Create secure PDFs
- Convert a document to PDF and send it through email
- Convert a document to PDF and send it for review

continued on next page

continued from previous page

Microsoft Internet Explorer (Windows)		
• Create accessible PDF files	• Create bookmarks	• Convert selected areas in a web page to PDF
• Retain Flash media present in the website in the PDF	• Convert a document to PDF and send it through email	• Create a header or footer

Mozilla Firefox		
• Create accessible PDF files	• Create bookmarks	• Create a header or footer
• Retain Flash media present in the website in the PDF	• Convert a document to PDF and send it through email	

Using the Print command to create Adobe PDF files

As you saw earlier in this lesson, you can easily create Adobe PDF files using the Create command or the Create button in the toolbar. However, you can also create an Adobe PDF file from almost any application file by using the application's Print command with the Adobe PDF printer (Windows) or the Save As Adobe PDF option (Mac OS).

Printing to the Adobe PDF printer (Windows)

The Adobe PDF printer isn't a physical printer like one that might sit in your office. Rather, it is a simulated printer that converts your file to Adobe PDF instead of printing it to paper. The printer name is Adobe PDF.

You'll convert a text file to Adobe PDF using the Print command with the Adobe PDF printer. You can use this technique from almost any application, regardless of whether the application has built-in features for creating PDF files. You should be aware, however, that the Adobe PDF printer creates untagged PDF files. (A tagged structure is required for reflowing content to a handheld device and is preferable for producing reliable results with a screen reader.)

Steps may vary depending on whether you are using Windows XP, Vista, or Windows 7. These steps assume that you are using Windows 7.

1   From your desktop, navigate to the Lesson03 folder, and select the Memo.txt file.

2   Choose File > Open With > WordPad. The text file opens in WordPad, a text editor that comes with Windows.

3   In WordPad in Windows 7, click the menu button and choose Print. In Windows XP or Vista, choose File > Page Setup, and click the Printer button.

4   Choose Adobe PDF from the list of printers. You may need to scroll to see it.

To change the settings used to convert the text file to Adobe PDF, click Preferences in the Print dialog box or Properties in the Page Setup dialog box. For more information, see the "Adobe PDF Presets" sidebar later in this lesson.

5   In Windows 7, click Print. If you're using Windows Vista or XP, click OK twice to close the Page Setup dialog box and return to the memo, and then choose File > Print and click Print.

6   Save the file using the default name (Memo.pdf) in the Lesson03 folder, and click Save in the Save PDF File As dialog box.

7   If the PDF file doesn't open automatically, navigate to the Lesson03 folder, and double-click the Memo.pdf file to open it in Acrobat. When you have reviewed the file, close it and quit WordPad.

The Adobe PDF printer is an easy and convenient way to create a PDF file from almost any document. However, if you're working with Microsoft Office files, the Create Adobe PDF buttons or the Acrobat ribbon (which use PDFMaker) let you create tagged documents and include bookmarks and hypertext links.

8   Close any open files.

Printing with the Save As Adobe PDF option (Mac OS)

In Acrobat X for Mac OS, the Adobe PDF Printer has been replaced with the Save As Adobe PDF option in the PDF menu in the Print dialog box. You can use the Save As Adobe PDF option when you print from any application.

1 From your desktop, navigate to the Lesson03 folder, and double-click the Memo.txt file.

The text file opens in a text editor such as TextEdit.

2 Choose File > Print. It doesn't matter which printer is selected.

3 Click the PDF button at the bottom of the dialog box, and choose Save As Adobe PDF.

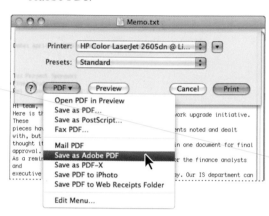

Note: If you need to create a custom PDF settings file, you can do so using Distiller. To open it in Acrobat Pro, select Acrobat Distiller in the Print Production panel in the Tools pane. For more information about creating custom PDF settings files, see Adobe Acrobat X Help.

4 In the Save As Adobe PDF dialog box, choose an Adobe PDF Settings file, and choose your version of Acrobat (Acrobat Standard or Acrobat Pro) from the After PDF Creation menu to open the PDF file in Acrobat. Click Continue.

5 In the Save dialog box, accept the default name of Memo.pdf, and save the file to the Lesson03 folder.

6 Click Save.

7 If the PDF file doesn't open automatically, navigate to the Lesson03 folder, and double-click the Memo.pdf file to open it in Acrobat. When you have reviewed the file, close it and quit the text editor application.

You have just converted a simple text document to an Adobe PDF document using the authoring application's Print command.

8 Close any open files.

Adobe PDF presets

A PDF preset is a group of settings that affect the process of creating a PDF file. These settings are designed to balance file size with quality, depending on how the PDF file will be used. Most predefined presets are shared across Adobe Creative Suite® applications, including Adobe InDesign®, Adobe Illustrator®, Adobe Photoshop®, and Acrobat. You can also create and share custom presets to meet your own needs.

Some PDF presets are not available until you move them from the Extras folder to the Settings folder; the Extras folder is installed only with Acrobat Pro. For more detailed descriptions of each preset, see Adobe Acrobat X Help.

- **High Quality Print** creates PDFs for quality printing on desktop printers and proofing devices.

- **Oversized Pages** creates PDFs suitable for viewing and printing engineering drawings larger than 200 by 200 inches.

- **PDF/A-1b: 2005 (CMYK and RGB)** is used for the long-term preservation (archival) of electronic documents.

- **PDF/X-1a (2001 and 2003)** standards minimize the number of variables in a PDF document to improve reliability. PDF/X-1a files are commonly used for digital ads that will be reproduced on a press.

- **PDF/X-3 (2003)** files are similar to PDF/X-1a files, but they support color-managed workflows and allow some RGB images.

- **PDF/X-4 (2007)** has the same color-management ICC color specifications as PDF/X-3, but it includes support for live transparency.

- **Press Quality** creates PDF files for high-quality print production (for example, for digital printing or for separations to an imagesetter or platesetter).

- **Rich Content PDF** creates accessible PDF files that include tags, hyperlinks, bookmarks, interactive elements, and layers.

- **Smallest File Size** creates PDF files for displaying on the web or an intranet, or for distribution through an email system.

- **Standard** creates PDF files to be printed to desktop printers or digital copiers, published on a CD, or sent to a client as a publishing proof.

Reducing file size

The size of a PDF file can vary dramatically depending on the Adobe PDF settings used to create it. For example, files created using the High Quality Print preset are larger than files created using the Standard or Smallest File Size presets. Regardless of the preset used to create a file, you can often reduce the file size without having to regenerate the PDF file.

You'll reduce the size of the Ad.pdf file.

1 In Acrobat, open the Ad.pdf file in the Lesson03/MultipleFiles folder.

2 Choose File > Save As > Reduced Size PDF.

3 Select Acrobat 9.0 And Later for file
compatibility, and click OK.

The newer the version of Acrobat that you
choose for compatibility, the smaller the
file will be. If you choose compatibility
with Acrobat X, however, you should be
sure that your intended audience does
indeed have Acrobat X installed.

4 Name the modified file **Ad_Reduce.pdf**. Click Save to complete the process.

It is always a good idea to save a file using a different name so that you don't over-write the unmodified file.

Acrobat automatically optimizes your PDF file, a process that may take a minute or two. Any anomalies are displayed in the Conversion Warnings window. If necessary, click OK to close the window.

5 Minimize the Acrobat window. Use Windows
Explorer (Windows) or the Finder (Mac OS)
to open the Lesson03/MultipleFiles folder and
view the size of the Ad_Reduce.pdf file. The file
size is smaller than that of the Ad.pdf file.

You can repeat steps 1-5 using different compatibility settings to see how they affect file size. Note that some settings might actually increase the file size.

6 In Acrobat, choose File > Close to close your file.

About compression and resampling

Many factors affect file size and file quality, but when you're working with image-intensive files, compression and resampling are important. PDF Optimizer gives you greater control over file size and quality.

To access PDF Optimizer, choose File > Save As > Optimized PDF.

In the PDF Optimizer dialog box, you can choose from a variety of file compression methods designed to reduce the file space used by color, grayscale, and monochrome images in your document. Which method you choose depends on the kind of images you are compressing. The default Adobe PDF presets use automatic (JPEG) compression for color and grayscale images and CCITT Group 4 compression for monochrome images.

In addition to choosing a compression method, you can resample bitmap images in your file to reduce the file size. A bitmap image consists of digital units called pixels, whose total number determines the file size. When you resample a bitmap image, the information represented by several pixels in the image is combined to make a single larger pixel. This process is also called *downsampling*, because it reduces the number of pixels in the image. (When you downsample or decrease the number of pixels, information is deleted from the image.)

Neither compression nor resampling affects the quality of text or line art.

Creating files from the clipboard

You can copy content from any type of file, and then choose File > Create > PDF From Clipboard in Acrobat to create a new PDF file. The Create PDF From Clipboard command uses Distiller to convert content to PDF, and PDF content created in this way is fully searchable; it is not an image. (In Mac OS, you can also use the PDF From Screen Capture command to convert screen shots.)

You can also easily add text and graphics that you have copied to the clipboard to an existing PDF. Open the PDF file, and then in the Pages panel in the Tools pane, choose More Insert Options > Insert From Clipboard.

Scanning a paper document

● **Note:** If Acrobat does not recognize your scanner, refer to your scanner documentation for setup instructions and troubleshooting advice.

You can scan paper documents to PDF from a broad range of scanners, add metadata while scanning, and optimize your scanned PDF. In Windows, you can choose presets for black and white, grayscale, color documents, and color images. These presets optimize the quality of your scanned document. You can also define your own conversion settings.

If you do not have a scanner connected to your system, skip this exercise.

1   Insert any one-page document into your scanner, and push the Scan button on the scanner. This automatically opens a dialog box on your system asking which program to launch to execute the scan. Choose Acrobat. Alternatively, do one of the following:

   • **In Windows:** In Acrobat, choose File > Create > PDF From Scanner, and select a preset for your document.

   • **In Mac OS:** Choose File > Create > PDF From Scanner, select options in the Acrobat Scan dialog box, and click Scan.

The scan occurs automatically.

2   When prompted, click OK to confirm that the scan is complete.

The PDF of the scanned document appears in Acrobat.

3   Choose File > Save, and save the scan in the Lesson03 folder as **Scan.pdf**.

4   In Windows, to see the settings that were used for the conversion, choose File > Create > PDF From Scanner > Configure Presets. In this dialog box, you can specify a number of options, including single- or double-sided scanning, paper size, prompt for more pages, file size, application of optical character recognition, and addition of metadata in the Document Properties dialog box. Click Cancel to exit the dialog box without making any changes.

5   Choose File > Close to close your document.

Making scanned text editable and searchable

▶ **Tip:** Acrobat can perform OCR automatically when you scan images. Just make sure Make Searchable is selected in the scanner preset (Windows) or Acrobat Scan dialog box (Mac OS) before you scan.

When you convert a file from an application such as Microsoft Word or Adobe InDesign to PDF, the text is fully editable and searchable. However, text in image files, whether scanned documents or files saved in an image format, is not editable and searchable. Using OCR (optical character recognition), Acrobat analyzes the image and replaces portions of it with discrete characters. It will identify any characters it may have analyzed incorrectly, as well.

You'll apply OCR to the TIFF file you converted earlier.

1   Choose File > Open, navigate to the Lesson03 folder, and open the GC_VendAgree1.pdf file that you saved earlier.

2   With the Selection tool selected in the Common Tools toolbar, move the pointer over text in the document. You can select areas in the document, but Acrobat does not specifically select any of the text.

3   Open the Tools pane, and click Recognize Text to open its panel.

4   Click In This File in the Recognize Text panel. Acrobat displays the Recognize text dialog box.

5   Make sure Current Page is selected in the Pages area of the dialog box. Then click Edit to edit the settings for the conversion.

6   In the Recognize Text - General Settings dialog box, choose ClearScan from the PDF Output Style menu.

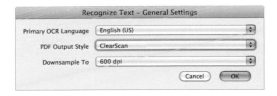

Note: By default, Acrobat converts the document into a searchable image. You can use this setting to convert documents, but ClearScan often provides more robust, accurate text conversion.

Using ClearScan converts the file to include scalable text and graphics, so that you can edit both in Acrobat.

7   Click OK to close the Recognize Text - General Settings dialog box, and then click OK again to close the Recognize Text dialog box and run ClearScan.

Acrobat converts the document.

8 With the Selection tool, select a word on the page. Acrobat has converted the image to editable, searchable text.

9 Click Find First Suspect in the Recognize Text panel. Acrobat searches the document and identifies any words that may have been converted incorrectly. If it finds any suspect words, you can examine them and correct them as needed. You may also need to use the Edit Document Text tool, found in the Content panel, to address issues with spacing.

In this **agreement** I, _Sara_
that Global Corporation (here
proprietary data and confidentia
Company. I agree to treat such
anything about who I am workir
in writing.

10 Click OK to close the Touchup dialog box, and then click Close to close the Find Element dialog box.

11 Choose File > Save As > PDF. Navigate to the Lesson03 folder, and save the file as **GC_VendAgree_OCR.pdf**. Then close the file.

Converting email messages to PDF (Windows)

You can convert email messages from any application using the Print command, but you have additional flexibility if you use Acrobat PDFMaker in Microsoft Outlook or Lotus Notes (Windows only). You'll use your own email files in this exercise. If you don't use either of these applications, you can skip this exercise.

It can be useful to save email messages in a form that is independent of your email application, either for archival purposes or just for the convenience of having a more portable and easily searchable file. PDFMaker adds buttons and commands to the Outlook and Lotus menus and toolbars that convert individual messages or email folders to Adobe PDF.

If you don't see the Acrobat button or commands in Outlook or Lotus Notes, consult "Show or activate PDFMaker in Microsoft Office and LotusNotes" in Adobe Acrobat X Help.

Converting email folders (Acrobat Pro)

At the completion of any personal or business project, you'll often have a folder or several folders full of project-related email messages. With Acrobat Pro, you can easily convert these folders to a fully searchable Adobe PDF file that is completely independent of your email application.

Each email message in the folder is converted as a separate file and saved by default in a PDF Portfolio.

1 Select a folder. In Outlook
2010, click Selected Folders on
the Adobe PDF ribbon, and
choose Create New PDF. In
earlier versions of Outlook,
click Create Adobe PDF From
Folders. In Notes, click Convert Selected Folder(s) To Adobe PDF in the toolbar.

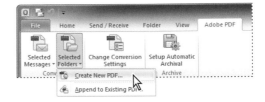

To save time, select folders that don't contain many messages for this exercise.

2 In Outlook, in the Convert Folder(s) To
PDF dialog box, you can select additional
folders that you want to convert. Use
the Convert This Folder And All Sub
Folders option to automatically include
all subfolders. Alternatively, expand the
folder and manually select the required
subfolders. We selected the Inbox folder
and left the Convert This Folder And All
Sub Folders option unselected. Click OK.

3 In the Save Adobe PDF File As dialog box, click Save to save the PDF file in the
Lesson03 folder under the email folder name (Inbox.pdf). You may need to
allow access to the email application program.

Your converted email messages open automatically in a PDF Portfolio in Acrobat.

Setting up automatic archiving

Automatically backing up your email messages is easy with Acrobat.

1 In Outlook 2010, click Setup
Automatic Archival in the
Adobe PDF ribbon. In earlier
versions of Outlook, choose
Adobe PDF > Setup Automatic
Archival. In Lotus Notes,
choose Actions > Setup
Automatic Archival.

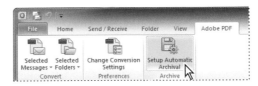

2 In the Acrobat PDFMaker dialog box, click the Automatic Archival tab, and select Enable Automatic Archival.

Now you'll specify how often the backup operation will run. You'll set the options to back up your email weekly on Saturday at 12:00 PM.

3 For Frequency, select Weekly, and choose Saturday from the adjacent menu.

4 For Run At, choose 12:00 PM. Use the arrow keys to change the time increments, or you can type new values for the hours, minutes and AM/PM entries. You'll leave the other options at their default values.

5 Click Add to select the folders to archive.

▶ **Tip:** The Embed Index For Faster Search option, on the Settings tab, is useful when you archive folders containing many messages. This option creates an index for the entire email collection. Searching this index is faster than searching PDF files one by one.

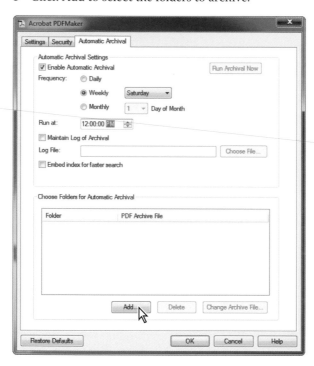

6 If you're using Acrobat Pro, select the Settings tab, and then select Output Adobe PDF Portfolio When Creating A New PDF File to merge the files into a PDF Portfolio. Deselect this option to merge the pages into a single PDF.

7 In the Convert Folder(s) To PDF dialog box, select the folders to be archived. We selected the Inbox folder, the Outbox folder, and the Sent Items folder. Expand any folders that have subfolders (indicated by a plus sign next to the folder name) to verify that you want to convert all the subfolders.

If you select the Convert This Folder And All Sub Folders option, you will automatically archive any and all folders in the Inbox. If you don't want to convert all subfolders, you must deselect this option and then manually deselect subfolders that you don't want to convert.

8 When you have finalized your selection, click OK, and enter a name for the archive file in the Save PDF Archive File As dialog box. (We saved the archive file in the Lesson03 folder using the name EmailArc.) Then click Open.

9 Click OK to finish. Your email files in the specified folders will be automatically archived every Saturday at 12:00 PM.

Be aware that this archiving process will overwrite the archive file from the previous week.

In order to see what the archive file looks like, you can run an archive operation now.

10 Choose Adobe PDF > Setup Automatic Archival. In the Acrobat PDFMaker dialog box, click the Automatic Archival tab, and click Run Archival Now. Your PDF files are automatically created and stored in the named file.

At any time, you can add or remove folders from the automatic archival process using the Add and Delete buttons in the Automatic Archival tab of the Acrobat PDFMaker dialog box. You can change the name and/or location of the archive file using the Change Archival File button in this same dialog box.

11 When you are finished, close any open PDF files, and close Outlook or Lotus Notes.

Converting web pages to Adobe PDF

You can convert or "capture" an entire web page or several levels of a multipage website. From Internet Explorer, you can also capture only selected content on a web page. You can define a page layout, set display options for fonts and other visual elements, and create bookmarks for web pages that you convert to Adobe PDF. The HTML file and all associated files—such as JPEG images, cascading style sheets, text files, image maps, and forms—are included in the conversion process, so the resulting PDF behaves much like the original web page.

Because converted web pages are in Adobe PDF, you can easily save them, print them, email them to others, or archive them for your own use.

Setting Acrobat preferences

You can set the Acrobat Internet preferences to determine how Acrobat converts web pages.

1 In Acrobat, choose Edit > Preferences (Windows) or Acrobat > Preferences (Mac OS), and select Internet from the categories on the left. By default, several Internet preference options are automatically selected.

- Display PDF In Browser displays any PDF document opened from the web inside the browser window. If this option is not selected, PDF documents open in a separate Acrobat window.

- Display In Read Mode By Default displays PDF files without toolbars or panes, so that all that appears is a semi-transparent floating toolbar when you move your mouse over the lower area of the PDF file. If you deselect this option, PDF files open with toolbars and panes.

- Allow Fast Web View downloads PDF documents for viewing on the web one page at a time. If this option is not selected, the entire PDF file downloads before it is displayed.

- Allow Speculative Downloading In The Background enables a PDF document to continue downloading from the web, even after the first requested page displays. Downloading in the background stops when any other task, such as paging through the document, is initiated in Acrobat.

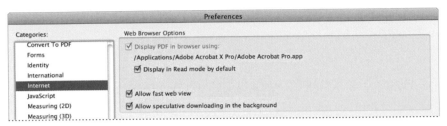

2 When you have finished reviewing your Internet settings, click OK in the Preferences dialog box to apply any changes you have made, or click Cancel to exit the dialog box without making any changes.

Setting options for converting web pages

Before you download and convert the pages, you may want to check the options that control the structure and appearance of your converted web pages. To modify these settings, choose File > Create > PDF From Web Page, and then click Settings to open the Web Page Conversion Settings dialog box.

Click Settings in the Conversion Settings area of the dialog box to open the HTML Conversion Settings dialog box. To convert Chinese, Japanese, and Korean (CJK) language web pages to PDF on a Roman (Western) system in Windows, you must have installed the CJK language support files while installing Acrobat. You should also select an appropriate encoding option from the Default Encoding menu. Click OK or Cancel to close the dialog boxes.

Converting web pages from within Acrobat

Because web pages are updated on a regular basis, when you visit the web pages described in this lesson, the content of the pages may have changed, and you may have to use links other than those described here. However, you should be able to apply the steps in this lesson to virtually any links on any website. If you are working inside a corporate firewall, for example, you might find it easier to complete this exercise substituting an internal site for the Adobe Press site or the Peachpit site.

Before you can download and convert web pages to Adobe PDF, you must be able to access the web. If you need help with setting up an Internet connection, talk to your Internet Service Provider (ISP).

Now you'll enter a URL in the Create PDF From Web Page dialog box and convert some web pages.

1 If the Create PDF From Web Page dialog box is not open, choose File > Create > PDF From Web Page.

2 For URL, enter the address of the website you'd like to convert. (We used the Adobe Press website at http://www.adobepress.com.)

3 Click the Capture Multiple Levels button.

You control the number of converted pages by specifying the levels of site hierarchy you wish to convert, starting from your entered URL. For example, the top level consists of the page corresponding to the specified URL, the second level consists of pages linked from the top-level page, and so on. Consider the number and complexity of pages you may encounter when downloading more than one level of a website at a time. A complex site can take a very long time to download. Therefore, we don't recommend selecting Get Entire Site for most websites. In addition, downloading pages over a dial-up modem connection will usually take much longer than downloading them over a high-speed connection.

4 Make sure that the Get Only option is selected, and that 1 is selected for the number of levels.

5 Select Stay On Same Path to convert only pages that are subordinate to the URL you entered.

6 Select Stay On Same Server to download only pages on the same server as the URL you entered.

7 Click Create. The Download Status dialog box displays the status of the download in progress. When downloading and conversion are complete, the converted website appears in the Acrobat document window, with bookmarks in the Bookmarks panel.

If Acrobat cannot download any linked material, it returns an error message. Click OK to clear any error message.

8 Click the Fit One Full Page button (⊞) on the Common Tools toolbar to fit the view of the converted web page to your screen.

9 Use the Next Page (⬇) and Previous Page (⬆) buttons to move through the pages.

10 Choose File > Save As > PDF, name the file **Web.pdf**, and save it in the Lesson03 folder.

In Windows, if you're downloading more than one level of pages, the Download Status dialog box moves to the background after the first level is downloaded.

The converted website is navigable and editable just like any other PDF document. Acrobat formats the pages to reflect your page-layout conversion settings, as well as the look of the original website.

Downloading and converting linked pages

When you click a web link in the Adobe PDF version of the web page that links to an unconverted page, Acrobat downloads and converts that page to Adobe PDF.

1 Navigate through the converted website until you find a web link to a page that wasn't included in your original conversion. We used a link below the AdobePress title bar. (The pointer changes to a pointing finger when positioned over a web link, and a tool tip displays the URL of the link.)

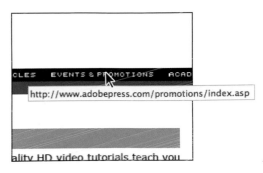

2 Right-click (Windows) or Control-click (Mac OS) the link, and choose Append To Document from the context menu.

The Download Status dialog box appears again. When the download and conversion are complete, Acrobat displays the linked page and adds a bookmark for the page to the Bookmarks list.

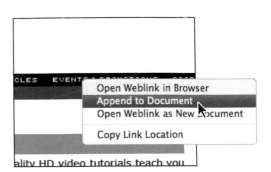

3 Choose File > Save As > PDF, rename the file **Web1.pdf**, and save it in the Lesson03 folder.

4 When you're finished looking at your converted web pages, quit Acrobat.

Now you'll convert web pages directly from Internet Explorer or Firefox.

Converting web pages in a web browser

If you've ever had the frustrating experience of printing a web page from your browser only to discover portions of the page missing, you'll appreciate the Acrobat feature that lets you create and print an Adobe PDF version of the web page without ever leaving your browser. You can use PDFMaker in Internet Explorer (Windows) or Firefox (Windows or Mac OS) to convert the currently displayed web page to an Adobe PDF file. When you print a converted web page from Acrobat, the page is reformatted to a standard page size, and logical page breaks are added.

First you'll set the preferences used to create Adobe PDF pages from your web pages, and then you'll convert a page.

1 Open Firefox or Internet Explorer, and navigate to a favorite web page. We opened the Peachpit Press home page at http://www.peachpit.com.

2 In Firefox or Internet Explorer, click the arrow next to the Convert button (🔁), and choose Preferences from the menu. These preferences are described in "Setting options for converting web pages" earlier in this lesson.

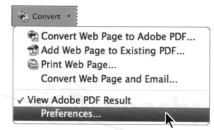

If you don't see the Convert button in Internet Explorer, choose View > Toolbars > Adobe PDF. In Firefox, choose View > Toolbars > Adobe Acrobat - Create PDF.

3 Click Cancel to exit the dialog box without making any changes.

Now you'll convert the web page to Adobe PDF.

4 Click the arrow next to the Convert button on the Acrobat toolbar to display the menu, and choose Convert Web Page To Adobe PDF.

5 In the Convert Web Page To Adobe PDF dialog box, navigate to the Lesson03 folder. Enter a filename (we used **PeachpitHome.pdf**). Then click Save.

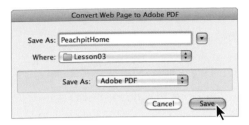

The default filename used by Acrobat is the text used in the HTML tag <TITLE>. Any invalid characters in the web page filename are converted to an underscore when the file is downloaded and saved.

Your selected text is converted to PDF, and the file automatically opens in Acrobat.

6 When you are finished, close the browser, Acrobat, and any open PDF files.

You can also convert a web page to Adobe PDF and email it automatically using the Convert Web Page And Email command in the Convert button menu. (For more information, see Adobe Acrobat X Help.)

Review questions

1 How can you find out which file types can be converted to Adobe PDF using the Create PDF From File command?

2 If you're working with a file type that isn't supported by the Create PDF From File or From Multiple Files command, how can you create a PDF file?

3 Why would you use PDFMaker to create PDF files?

4 How can you convert an image file to searchable text?

Review answers

1 Choose File > Create > PDF From File. Open the Files Of Type (Windows) or Show (Mac OS) menu in the Open dialog box to view the supported file types.

2 You can create a PDF file from almost any application by using the Print command in the source application. In Windows, select the Adobe PDF printer. In Mac OS, click the Create PDF button in the Print dialog box, and then choose Save As Adobe PDF. When you click the Print button, Acrobat creates an Adobe PDF file rather than sending your file to a desktop printer.

3 When you install Acrobat, it adds buttons or menu commands to supported applications to let you create PDF files easily from those applications using PDFMaker. PDFMaker includes options that let you customize PDF files from different applications. For example, you can create bookmarks, preserve layers, add security features, or tag documents using PDFMaker in some applications.

4 To convert an image file to searchable text, click In This File or In Multiple Files in the Recognize Text panel in the Tools pane. Then select the options you want to apply, such as whether to use ClearScan or to save the document as a searchable image.

4 READING AND WORKING WITH PDF FILES

Lesson overview

In this lesson, you'll do the following:

- Navigate an Adobe PDF document using tools, page thumbnails, and bookmarks.

- Change how an Adobe PDF document scrolls and displays in the document window.

- Search a PDF document for a word or phrase.

- Fill out a PDF form.

- Print all or a portion of a PDF document.

- Explore the accessibility features that make it easier for users with vision and motor impairments to use Acrobat.

- Add tags and Alt text to a PDF document.

- Share a document with others electronically.

 This lesson will take approximately 60 minutes to complete. Copy the Lesson04 folder onto your hard drive if you haven't already done so.

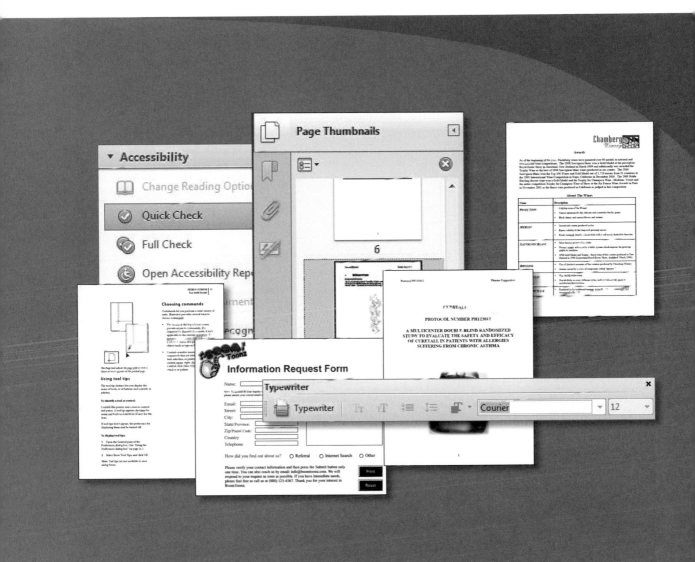

Get the most out of the PDF documents you create
and read using navigational aids, accessibility features,
search tools, and more.

Changing the opening view

You'll open a PDF file and look at the initial view settings, and then you'll change those settings to reflect your personal preferences.

1   In Acrobat, choose File > Open, navigate to the Lesson04 folder, and select the Protocol.pdf file. Click Open.

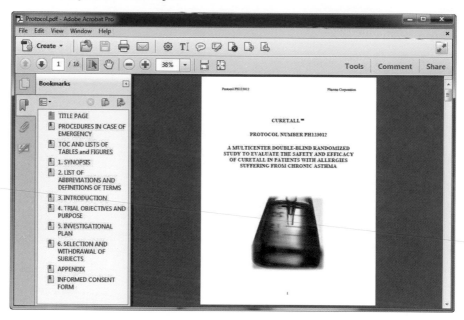

Acrobat displays the cover page with the Bookmarks panel open.

2   Choose File > Properties. Then, in the Document Properties dialog box, click the Initial View tab.

In the Layout And Magnification area, you see that the creator of this document set the file to open to page 1, with one page filling the document pane, and with the Bookmarks panel open.

Now you'll experiment with some different opening views.

3 Choose Page Only from the Navigation Tab pop-up menu to hide the Bookmarks panel when the document opens. Change the Page Layout to Two-Up (Facing), and change the Magnification to Fit Visible. Click OK to exit the dialog box.

You need to save, close, and then reopen the file for these settings to take effect.

4 Choose File > Save As > PDF, and save the file as **Protocol1.pdf** in the Lesson04 folder. Then choose File > Close to close the document.

5 Choose File > Open, and double-click the Protocol1.pdf file to open it. Now Acrobat displays two pages, and the Bookmarks panel is hidden.

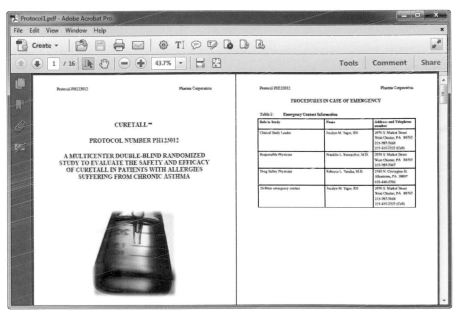

You can use the initial view settings to determine how viewers initially see documents that you create and distribute.

6 Close your file and reopen the original work file, Protocol.pdf.

About the onscreen display

► **Tip:** To see the printed size of your page, move your pointer into the lower-left area of the document pane.

Take a look at the magnification field in the Common Tools toolbar at the top of the document window. The magnification does not refer to the printed size of the page, but rather to how the page is displayed onscreen. Acrobat determines the onscreen display of a page by treating the page as a 72 ppi (pixels-per-inch) image. For example, if your page has a print size of 2-by-2 inches, Acrobat treats the page as if it were 144 pixels wide and 144 pixels high (72 x 2 = 144). At 100% view, each pixel in the page is represented by one screen pixel on your monitor.

How big the page appears onscreen depends on your monitor size and resolution setting. For example, when you increase the resolution of your monitor, you increase the number of screen pixels within the same monitor area. This results in smaller screen pixels and a smaller displayed page, since the number of pixels in the page itself stays constant.

Reading PDF documents

Acrobat provides a variety of ways for you to move through and adjust the onscreen magnification of a PDF document. For example, you can scroll through the document using the scroll bar at the right side of the window, or you can turn pages as in a traditional book using the Next Page and Previous Page buttons in the Common Tools toolbar. You can also jump to a specific page.

Using Read mode

As you saw in Lesson 1, Read mode maximizes the screen space available to a document in Acrobat so you can read it more comfortably.

1 Choose View > Read Mode. In Read mode, all elements of the work area are hidden except the document pane and the menu bar.

2 Use the Page Up, Page Down, or arrow keys on your keyboard, or use the scroll bar to move through the document.

3 Move the mouse over the lower area of the document. The semi-transparent floating toolbar appears, so that you can easily move to a different page or change the magnification.

4 When you're done reading, choose View > Read Mode again to restore the work area.

Browsing the document

You can move to different pages in a document using a variety of navigation methods.

1 If you're not on the first page of the document, enter **1** in the page number box on the Common Tools toolbar, and press Enter or Return.

2 Choose View > Zoom > Fit Width or click the Scrolling Mode button (▤) on the Common Tools toolbar to resize your page to fit the width of your screen.

3 Select the Hand tool (✋) from the Common Tools toolbar, and then position your pointer over the document. Hold down the mouse button. Notice that the pointer changes to a closed hand when you hold down the mouse button.

4 Drag the closed hand up and down in the window to move the page on the screen. This is similar to moving a piece of paper around on a desktop.

5 Press Enter or Return to display the next part of the page. You can press Enter or Return repeatedly to view the document from start to finish in screen-sized sections.

6 Choose View > Zoom > Zoom To Page Level, or click the Fit One Full Page button (⊞). Click the Previous Page button (●) as many times as necessary to return to page 1.

7 Position the pointer over the down arrow in the scroll bar or click in any empty portion of the scroll bar, and click once.

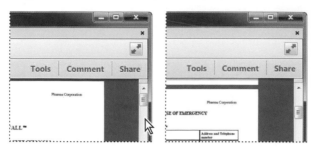

The document scrolls automatically to display all of page 2. In the next few steps, you'll control how Acrobat scrolls and displays PDF pages.

You can also access the Actual Size, Zoom To Page Level, Fit Width, and Fit Visible commands by clicking the arrow to the right of the magnification pop-up menu in the Common Tools toolbar.

8 Click the Scrolling Mode button in the Common Tools toolbar, and then use the scroll bar to scroll to page 3 of 16.

The Scrolling Mode option displays pages end to end, like frames in a filmstrip.

9 Choose View > Page Navigation > First Page to go back to the beginning of the document.

10 Click the Fit One Full Page button (⊞) to return to the original page layout.

You can use the page number box in the Common Tools toolbar to move directly to a specific page.

11 Click in the page box so that the pointer changes to an I-beam, and then highlight the current page number.

12 Type **15** to replace the current page number, and press Enter or Return.

Acrobat displays page 15.

The scroll bar also lets you navigate to a specific page.

13 Begin dragging the scroll box upward in the scroll bar. As you scroll, a page preview box appears. When page 3 of 16 appears in the preview box, release the mouse.

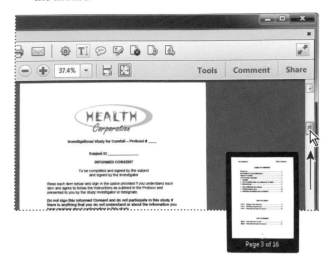

The table of contents is displayed.

Browsing with page thumbnails

Page thumbnails are miniature previews of document pages that are displayed in the Page Thumbnails panel of the navigation pane. You used page thumbnails in Lesson 2 to navigate a PDF document.

Now, you'll gain more experience with page thumbnails, as you use them to change the view of pages. In Lesson 6, "Enhancing and Editing PDF Documents," you'll learn how to use page thumbnails to reorder pages in a document.

1 Choose View > Zoom > Fit Width, or click the Scrolling Mode button to view the full width of the page. You should still be looking at page 3.

2 Click the Page Thumbnails button (🔲) in the navigation pane to open the Page Thumbnails panel.

Acrobat automatically displays page thumbnails for every page in the document in the navigation pane. The page thumbnails represent both the content and page orientation of the pages in the document. Page-number boxes appear beneath each page thumbnail.

3 Click the page 7 thumbnail to go to page 7. You may need to scroll down through the thumbnails to see the one for page 7.

The page number for the page thumbnail is highlighted, and a full-width view of page 7 appears in the document window.

Take a look at the page 7 thumbnail. The rectangle inside the page thumbnail, called the page-view box, represents the area displayed in the current page view. You can use the page-view box to adjust the area and magnification of the page being viewed.

4 Position the pointer over the lower-right corner of the page-view box. The pointer turns into a double-headed arrow.

5 Drag to shrink the page-view box, and release the mouse button. In the Common Tools toolbar, the magnification level has changed to represent the smaller area.

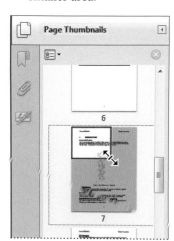 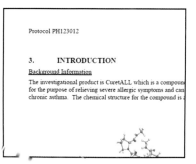

6   Position the pointer over the bottom border of the page-view box. The pointer changes to a hand.

7   Drag the page-view box within the page thumbnail, and watch the view change in the document window.

8   Drag the page-view box down to focus your view on the graphic in the middle of the page.

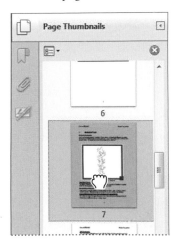 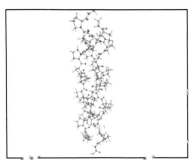

Page thumbnails provide a convenient way to monitor and adjust your page view in a document.

9   Click the Page Thumbnails button to hide the panel.

Changing the page view magnification

You can change the magnification of the page view using controls in the Common Tools toolbar.

1   Choose View > Zoom > Fit Width, or click the Scrolling Mode button. A new magnification appears.

2   Click the Previous Page button (◉) as many times as necessary to move to page 3. Notice that the magnification remains the same.

3   Choose View > Zoom > Actual Size to return the page to a 100% view.

4 Click the arrow to the right of the magnification text box to display the preset magnification options. Choose 200%.

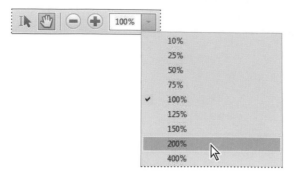

You can also type in a specific value for the magnification in the text box.

5 Click the arrow to the right of the magnification box, and choose Actual Size to display the page at 100% again.

Next, you'll use the Zoom In button to magnify the view.

6 Select the page number, type **7**, and press Enter or Return to go to page 7.

7 Click the Zoom In (⊕) button once.

8 Click the Zoom In button again to increase the magnification further.

Each click on a Zoom button increases or decreases the magnification by a set amount.

9 Click the Zoom Out button (⊖) twice to return the view to 100%.

Now you'll use the Marquee Zoom tool to magnify the image. The Marquee Zoom tool is hidden by default, so you'll add it to the Common Tools toolbar.

10 Choose View > Show/Hide > Toolbar Items > Select & Zoom > Marquee Zoom to display the Marquee Zoom tool in the Common Tools toolbar.

11 Select the Marquee Zoom tool (⊕). Position the pointer near the upper-left of the image, and drag down to the lower-right corner.

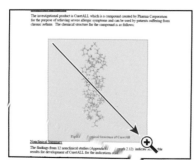 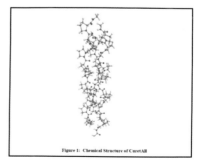

Figure 1: Chemical Structure of CuretAll

The view zooms in on the area you enclosed. This is called marquee-zooming.

12 Choose View > Zoom > Zoom To Page Level.

Tip: You can show or hide other tools in the Common Tools toolbar by choosing View > Show/Hide > Toolbar Items, selecting a category, and then selecting the tool you want to display or hide.

Using the Dynamic Zoom tool

The Dynamic Zoom tool lets you zoom in or out by dragging the mouse up or down.

1 Choose View > Show/Hide > Toolbar Items > Select & Zoom > Dynamic Zoom to add the Dynamic Zoom button to the Common Tools toolbar, if it's not already there.

2 Select the Dynamic Zoom tool (🔍).

3 Click in the document pane. Drag upward to increase the view, and drag down to reduce it.

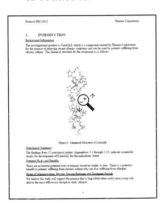
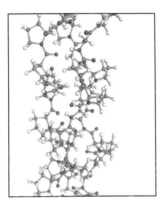

4 When you're finished, select the Hand tool, and then click the Fit One Full Page button (🗎).

Following links

In a PDF document, you don't have to view pages in sequence. You can jump immediately from one section of a document to another using custom navigational aids such as links.

One benefit of working with electronic documents is that you can convert traditional cross-references into links, which users can use to jump directly to the referenced section or file. For example, you can make each item under the Contents list into a link that jumps to its corresponding section in the document. You can also use links to add interactivity to traditional book elements such as glossaries and indexes.

First you'll add some navigational tools to the Common Tools toolbar.

1   Choose View > Show/Hide > Toolbar Items > Page Navigation > Show All Page Navigation Tools.

Now you'll use an existing link to move to a specific area in the document.

2   Click the First Page button (⤒) in the Common Tools toolbar to return to the first page, and then click the Next Page button (⤓) twice to move to the Table of Contents page (page 3).

3   Move the pointer over the "3. Introduction" heading in the Table of Contents. The Hand tool changes to a pointing finger, indicating the presence of a link. Click to follow the link.

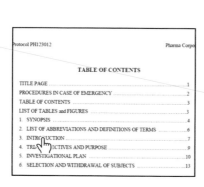 

This entry links to the Introduction.

4   Click the Previous View button (◉) to return to your previous view of the Table of Contents.

You can click the Previous View button at any time to retrace your viewing path through a document. The Next View button reverses the action of your last Previous View.

You have learned how to page through a PDF document, change the magnification and page layout mode, and follow links.

5   To restore the default toolbar configuration, choose View > Show/Hide > Toolbar Items > Reset Toolbars. Click OK to confirm that you want to restore the defaults.

Searching PDF documents

You can quickly search through a PDF document, looking for a word or a phrase. If, for example, you didn't want to read through this Protocol document but simply wanted to find occurrences of the term *adverse event*, you can use either the Find feature or the Search feature to locate that information. The Find feature locates a word or phrase in the active document. The Search feature locates a word or phrase in one document, across a selection of documents, or in a PDF Portfolio. Both features search text, layers, form fields, and digital signatures.

First you'll run a simple Find operation on the open document.

1 Choose Edit > Find. In the text box in the toolbar that appears in the upper-right corner of the application window, type **adverse event**.

To see the options available with the Find feature, click the arrow to the right of the text box. You can use these options to refine your search, looking for whole words only or specifying uppercase or lowercase letters, and you can also include bookmarks and comments in the search. An option is in effect (on) when there is a check mark next to its name.

2 Press Enter or Return to start the Find operation.

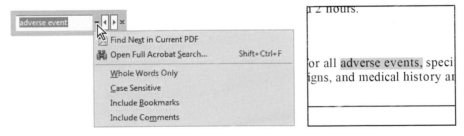

The first occurrence of *adverse event* is highlighted on page 5 of the document.

3 Click the Find Next button (▶) in the toolbar to find the next occurrence of the phrase.

Next, you'll perform a more sophisticated search of the Protocol document using the Search feature. In this exercise, you'll search only the Protocol document, but you can use the Search feature to search all documents in a folder as well as all documents in a PDF Portfolio. You can even search non-PDF files in a PDF Portfolio.

4 Choose Edit > Advanced Search.

5 To search only the open document, select In The Current Document.

In this search, we'd like to find references to adverse events that are significant.

6 In the Search text box, enter **adverse events sign**.

7 Click the Show More Options link at the bottom of the Search pane.

8 From the Return Results Containing pop-up menu, choose Match Any Of The Words. This ensures that the search will return all results for "adverse," "events," and derivatives of "sign."

9 Click Search.

▶ **Tip:** You can also save your search results in Acrobat X. To do so, click the Save icon next to the New Search button in the Search pane, and then choose either Save Results To PDF or Save Results To CSV.

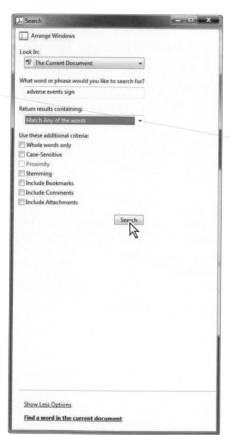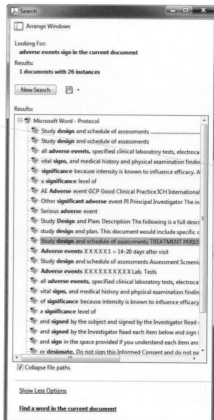

The search results are displayed in the Search pane.

10 Click any search result to go to the page that contains that information.

You can check any of the other search results in the Search pane by clicking them.

11 When you're finished, close the Search pane.

The Search feature searches object data and image XIF (extended image file format) metadata. When you search multiple PDF documents, Acrobat also looks at the document properties and XMP metadata. If any of your PDF documents have attachments, you can also include those attachments in the search. If you include a PDF index in your search, Acrobat searches indexed structure tags. To search an encrypted document, you must first open the document.

Printing PDF documents

Many of the options in the Acrobat Print dialog box are similar to those you'd find in the Print dialog boxes of other popular applications. For example, you can select a printer and set up parameters such as paper size and orientation. However, Acrobat also gives you the flexibility to print only the current view (that is, what is displayed on the screen at that moment), a specific page, selected pages, or a range of pages within the PDF file.

You'll instruct Acrobat to print pages you select in the Page Thumbnails panel, a particular view, and noncontiguous pages from Acrobat.

1   In the Protocol.pdf document, click the Page Thumbnails button in the navigation pane. Then, click the thumbnails that correspond with the pages you want to print. You can Ctrl-click (Windows) or Command-click (Mac OS) page thumbnails to select contiguous or non-contiguous pages.

2   Choose File > Print. Select the name of the printer you want to print to. Because you selected pages in the Page Thumbnails panel, the Selected Pages option is selected automatically in the Print dialog box.

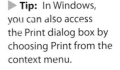 **Tip:** In Windows, you can also access the Print dialog box by choosing Print from the context menu.

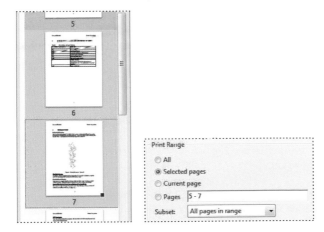

3   Click OK or Print to print your selected pages. Click Cancel if you want to abort the printing operation.

If you need help troubleshooting a printing issue, click Printing Tips in the Print dialog box to go to the Adobe website for the latest printing tips and information.

4 After the pages print (or the Print dialog box closes, if you opted not to print), deselect any thumbnails, and then close the Page Thumbnails panel.

5 Go to page 7 of the document.

6 Zoom in to 200%, and then use the Hand tool to shift the page so that you see only the diagram.

7 Choose File > Print, and select the name of the printer you want to print to.

8 Select Current View. The preview changes to represent what is actually visible in the document pane. If you print with Current View selected, Acrobat prints only the contents of the document pane.

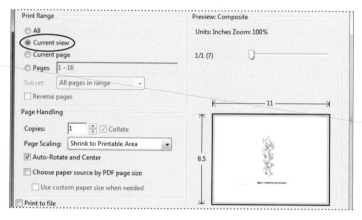

9 Select Pages. The preview changes to display the first page of the document again.

10 In the Pages text box, type **1, 3-5, 7-9**. If you click OK or Print now, Acrobat will print pages 1, 3, 4, 5, 7, 8, and 9. You can enter any set of noncontiguous pages or ranges of pages, using commas, in this text box.

11 If you want to print the pages you've selected, click OK. If you don't want to print, click Cancel.

12 Choose File > Close to close the Protocol document.

For information on printing comments, see Lesson 9, "Using Acrobat in a Review Cycle."

If your PDF file contains odd-sized pages, you can use the Page Scaling options in the Print dialog box to reduce, enlarge, or divide pages. The Fit To Printable Area option scales each page to fit the printer page size; pages in the PDF file are magnified or reduced as necessary. The Tiling options print oversize pages on several pages that can be assembled to reproduce the oversize image.

Printing booklets

If your printer supports duplex printing, you can print a 2-up, saddle-stitched booklet from Acrobat. Booklets comprise multiple pages that are arranged so that they can be folded to present the correct page order. In a 2-up, saddle-stitched booklet, two side-by-side pages, printed on both sides, are folded once and fastened along the fold. The first and last pages print on the same sheet, the second and next-to-last pages print on the same sheet, and so on. When you collate, fold, and staple the double-sided pages, you create a single book with correct pagination.

To print a booklet from Acrobat:

1 Choose File > Print, and select your printer.

2 In the Page Handling area of the Print dialog box, choose Booklet Printing from the Page Scaling menu.

3 In the Print Range area, specify which pages to print.

4 Choose additional page-handling options. You can auto-rotate pages, specify the first and last sheet to print, and select the binding edge. The Preview image changes as you specify options. For information about the options, see "Printing booklets" in Adobe Acrobat X Help.

Filling out PDF forms

PDF forms can be interactive or noninteractive. Interactive PDF forms have built-in form fields and behave in much the same way as most forms that you encounter on the web or that are sent to you electronically. You enter data using the Selection tool or Hand tool in Acrobat or Adobe Reader. Depending on the settings applied by the person who created the form, users of Adobe Reader may or may not be able to save a copy of the completed form before they return it.

Noninteractive PDF forms (flat forms) are pages that have been scanned to create a facsimile of a form. These pages do not contain actual form fields; they contain only the images of form fields. Traditionally you would print out these forms, fill them out by hand or using a typewriter, and then mail or fax the hard copy. With Acrobat, you can fill out these noninteractive or flat forms online using the Typewriter tool.

For information on creating and managing interactive forms, see Lesson 10, "Working with Forms in Acrobat."

You'll fill out fields in an interactive form, and then add information where there is no field using the Typewriter tool.

1 Choose File > Open, and navigate to the Lesson04 folder. Select the MusicForm.pdf file, and click Open.

2 With the Hand tool selected, click in the Name field. Enter your name. The text appears in the font and type size chosen by the form creator.

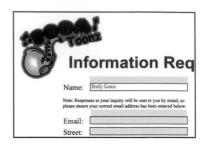

3 Complete another field.

Some fields, such as Street and Email, require you to type in text, while check boxes and radio buttons require you only to click to select them. The Print and Reset buttons perform actions when you click them.

The person who created this form forgot to create an interactive field for the telephone number. You'll use the Typewriter tool to enter the data.

4 In the Tools pane, open the Content panel. Then click Add Or Edit Text Box.

Acrobat opens the Typewriter toolbar.

5 Move your pointer over the tools in this toolbar and take a moment to read the tool tips. You can use these tools to increase or decrease the size of the text you enter, or to increase or decrease the space between lines of text that you enter.

6 Select the Typewriter tool ( ). The pointer icon changes to an I-beam.

7 Position the pointer over the Telephone field, and click to create an insertion point. Then type in any phone number.

You can use the Typewriter tool to add text to any PDF file, unless security applied to the document prohibits it.

8 Choose File > Save As > PDF, and save a copy of the form in the Lesson04 folder, using the filename **MusicForm_complete.pdf**.

You can open the saved file if you wish to verify that all your data was saved.

9 Click the close button to hide the Typewriter toolbar.

10 Choose File > Close to close the order form.

About flexibility, accessibility, and structure

The accessibility and flexibility of your Adobe PDF files determine how easily vision- and motion-impaired users and users of hand-held devices can access, reflow, and, if you allow it, reuse the content of your files. You control the accessibility and flexibility of your Adobe PDF files through the amount of structure you build into the source file and the method you use to create the Adobe PDF file.

By making your PDF documents more accessible to users, you can broaden your readership and better meet government standards for accessibility. Accessibility in Acrobat falls into two categories:

- Accessibility features that help authors create accessible documents from new or existing PDF documents. These features include simple methods for checking accessibility and adding tags to PDF documents. With Acrobat Pro, you can also correct accessibility and reading-order problems in PDF files by editing the PDF file structure.

- Accessibility features that help readers who have motion or vision limitations to navigate and view PDF documents more easily. Many of these features can be adjusted by using a wizard, the Accessibility Setup Assistant.

For Adobe PDF files to be flexible and accessible, they must have structure. Adobe PDF files support three levels of structure—tagged, structured, and unstructured. Tagged PDF files have the most structure. Structured PDF files have some structure, but are not as flexible or accessible as tagged PDF files. Unstructured PDF files have no structure. (As you will see later in this lesson, you can add limited structure to unstructured files.) The more structure a file has, the more efficiently and reliably its content can be reused.

Structure is built into a document when, for example, its creator defines headers and columns, adds navigational aids such as bookmarks, and adds alternate text descriptions for graphics. In many cases, documents are automatically given logical structure and tags when they are converted to Adobe PDF.

When you create PDFs from Microsoft Office files or from files created in later versions of Adobe FrameMaker®, InDesign, or Adobe PageMaker®, or when you create Adobe PDF files from websites, the resulting PDF files are tagged automatically.

In Acrobat Pro, if your PDF documents don't reflow well, you can correct most problems using the Accessibility panel or the TouchUp Reading Order tool. However, this is not as easy as creating a well-structured document in the first place. For an in-depth guide to creating accessible PDF documents, visit http://access.adobe.com.

Working with accessible documents

You'll examine a tagged PDF document and see how easy it is to reflow the document and extract content.

Checking for accessibility

It's always a good idea to check the accessibility of any Adobe PDF document before you distribute it to users. The Acrobat Quick Check feature tells you right away if your document has the information necessary to make it accessible. At the same time, it checks for protection settings that would prohibit access.

First you'll look at the accessibility and flexibility of a tagged PDF file that was created from a Microsoft Word file.

1 Choose File > Open, navigate to the Lesson04 folder, and double-click the Tag_ Wines.pdf file.

▶ **Tip:** By default, Acrobat displays only some of the panels in the Tools pane. To select which panels appear in the list, click the menu button at the top of the Tools pane, and then select or deselect individual panels.

2 Choose File > Save As > PDF, and save the file as **Tag_Wines1.pdf** in the Lesson04 folder.

3 In the Tools pane, open the Accessibility panel. If the Accessibility panel isn't listed, choose View > Tools > Accessibility to open it.

4 In the Accessibility panel, select Quick Check.

Acrobat quickly checks the document for accessibility issues, and displays the message that it didn't identify any issues in the document.

5 Click OK to close the message box.

 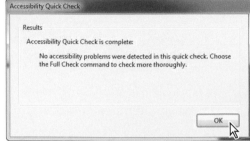

6 Close the Tools pane.

You can add security to your PDF files and still make them accessible. The 128-bit encryption offered by Acrobat X prevents users from copying and pasting text from a PDF file while still supporting assistive technology. You can also use the Enable Text Access For Screen Reader Devices For The Visually Impaired option to modify security settings in older PDF documents (Acrobat 3 and later) to make them accessible without compromising security. This option is in the Password Security Settings dialog box. (See Lesson 08, "Adding Signatures and Security" for more about adding security.)

Reflowing a flexible PDF file

Now you'll take a quick look at how flexible a tagged PDF file is. You'll reflow the PDF file, and then you'll save the contents of the PDF file as accessible text.

First, you'll adjust the size of your document window to mimic the smaller screen of a hand-held device.

1 Choose View > Zoom > Actual Size to display the document at 100%.

2 Resize the Acrobat window to about 50% of the full-screen display. In Windows, click the Maximize/Restore Down button if the window is currently maximized; if the window isn't maximized, drag a corner of the application window to reduce it. In Mac OS, resize the document pane by dragging a corner.

Your goal is to resize the Acrobat window so that the ends of the sentences in the document pane are cut off.

3 Choose View > Zoom > Reflow.

The content of the document is reflowed to accommodate the smaller document screen, and you can now read an entire line of text without using the horizontal scroll bar.

When you reflow text, artifacts such as page numbers and page headers often drop out because they are no longer relevant to the page display. Text is reflowed one page at a time. You cannot save the document in the reflowed state.

Now you'll examine how the display changes when you change the magnification.

4 Choose 400% from the magnification pop-up menu.

5 Scroll down the page to see how the text reflows. Again, because the text is reflowed, you don't have to use the horizontal scroll bar to move back and forth across the page to read the enlarged text. The text is automatically contained within the document pane.

6 When you've finished viewing the reflowed text, restore the Acrobat document window to its usual size, and close the file.

> **Awards**
>
> As of the beginning of the year, Chamberg

You can save the contents of a tagged document in a different file format for reuse in another application. For example, if you save this file as accessible text, you'll see that even the contents of the table are saved in an easy-to-use format.

With Acrobat, you can even make some unstructured documents more readily accessible to all types of users. You can add tags to a PDF document using the Add Tags To Document command in any version of Acrobat. However, to correct tagging and order errors, you must be using Acrobat Pro.

Making files flexible and accessible

Some tagged Adobe PDF documents may not contain all the information necessary to make their contents fully flexible or accessible. For example, your file may not contain alternate text for figures, language properties for portions of the text that use a different language than the default language for the document, or expansion text for abbreviations. (Designating the appropriate language for different text elements ensures that the correct characters are used when you reuse the document for another purpose, that the word can be pronounced correctly when read out loud, and that the document will be spell-checked with the correct dictionary.)

If you're using Acrobat Pro, you can add alternate text and multiple languages using the Tags panel. (If only one language is required, it is easier to choose the language in the Document Properties dialog box.) You can also add alternate text using the TouchUp Reading Order tool.

Now you'll look at the accessibility of a page of a user guide. This document was designed to be printed, so no attempt was made to make it accessible.

1 Choose File > Open, and open the AI_UGEx.pdf file in the Lesson04 folder.

2 Open the Tools pane. Then, in the Accessibility panel, click Quick Check. The message box indicates that the document has no logical structure. Click OK to clear the message box.

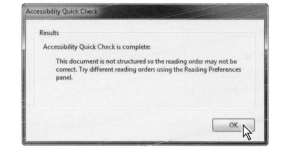

Now you'll see how this page reflows.

3 Choose View > Zoom > Actual Size to display the document at 100%.

4 Close the Tools pane.

5 Reduce the size of the document pane: In Windows, click the Maximize/Restore Down button if the window is maximized; if it isn't, drag a corner of the window. In Mac OS, drag a corner of the document pane to resize it. Resize the Acrobat window small enough that the width of a full page cannot be displayed on the screen (at 100%).

6 Choose View > Zoom > Reflow.

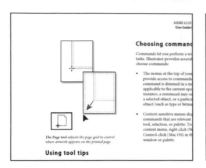

The text reflows well, despite the lack of structure.

7 Choose View > Zoom > Zoom To Page Level. Resize the Acrobat window to its usual size.

Acrobat is able to reflow even this unstructured document relatively well. However, the lack of structure in the document makes it inaccessible. You can add tags to improve the flexibility and accessibility of the page.

Adding tags

You can add tags to a PDF document in Acrobat. When you add tags to a document, Acrobat adds a logical tree structure to the document that determines the order in which page content is reflowed and read by screen readers and the Read Out Loud feature. On relatively simple pages, the Add Tags To Document command can work well. On more complex pages—pages that contain irregularly shaped columns, bulleted lists, text that spans columns, and so on—the Add Tags To Document command may not be sufficient.

You'll add tags to this document to make it more accessible.

1 Open the Tools pane. In the Accessibility panel, click Add Tags To Document.

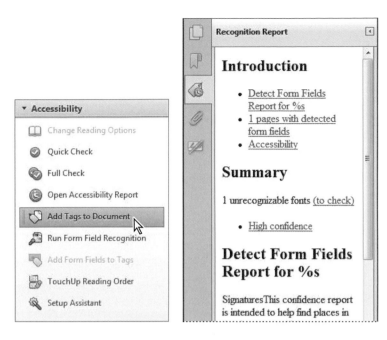

Acrobat adds tags to the document and opens a Recognition Report in the navigation pane.

2   Scroll through the Recognition Report. Notice that the Accessibility section indicates that the document does not include Alt text. If you're using Acrobat Pro, you can use the TouchUp Reading Order tool to add it.

3   Click the Tags button to open the Tags panel in the navigation pane. (If the Tags button isn't displayed, choose View > Show/Hide > Navigation Panes > Tags.) Click the arrow next to Tags to view the tags Acrobat has added to the document.

While Acrobat can track the structure of most page elements and tag them appropriately, pages with complex layouts or unusual elements may not always result in successfully tagged PDF documents and may require editing. When you tag a PDF file using Acrobat, the Recognition Report lists pages where problems were encountered and suggestions for fixing them.

Tip: The Recognition Report is a temporary file and can't be saved. The Full Check feature generates an accessibility report that you can save.

It's a good idea to check these items in the PDF document to determine what corrections, if any, need to be made. Use the report to navigate to the problem areas of your PDF document by clicking the links for each error. Then, if you're using Acrobat Pro, use the TouchUp Reading Order tool to correct the problem.

4 If you're using Acrobat Standard, close the document and skip the next exercise.

Adding Alt text (alternate text)

Non-text elements in your document, such as figures and multimedia elements, won't be recognized by a screen reader or Read Out Loud feature unless they are accompanied by alternate text. When you reviewed the Recognition Report, you noticed that the figure is missing Alt text. Using Acrobat Pro, you'll add alternate text now. First, though, you'll close the Tags panel.

1 Click the Tags button to close the Tags panel.

Tip: If the Show Tables And Figures option is selected in the TouchUp Reading Order panel, the Alt text will be displayed in a label in the document pane.

2 In the Accessibility panel, click TouchUp Reading Order. Acrobat opens the TouchUp Reading Order panel.

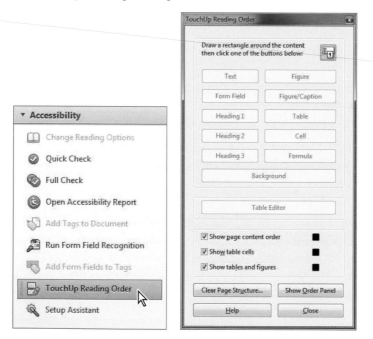

You could use this panel to create tags: Simply drag a rectangle around an area of content and then click the tag you want to apply. For example, drag around a heading, and then click Heading 1 to apply that tag. However, you've already added tags in this document, so you don't need to use the TouchUp Reading Order panel.

3 Right-click (Windows) or Control-click (Mac OS) the figure in the document pane, and choose Edit Alternate Text from the context menu.

4 In the Alternate Text dialog box, enter **Figure shows Hand tool being used to drag the artboard across the Illustrator window**. Then click OK.

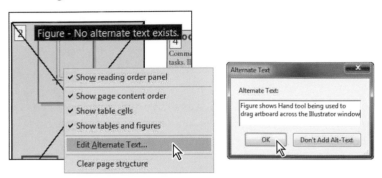

5 Click Close to close the TouchUp Reading Order panel.

6 To check your alternate text, choose View > Read Out Loud > Activate Read Out Loud. Then choose View > Read Out Loud > Read This Page Only. You'll hear your alternate text. To stop the reading, press Ctrl+Shift+E (Windows) or Command+Shift+E (Mac OS).

Notice that both the alternate text and the caption are read. If you want only the alternate text to be read, combine the figure and caption elements using the TouchUp Reading Order panel.

7 Choose File > Close to close your work without saving your changes.

For an in-depth guide to creating accessible PDF documents, visit http://access.adobe.com.

Using the Acrobat accessibility features

Many people with vision and motor impairments use computers, and Acrobat has a number of features that make it easier for these users to work with Adobe PDF documents. These features include:

- Automatic scrolling

- Keyboard shortcuts

- Support for several screen-reader applications, including the text-to-speech engines built into Windows and Mac OS platforms

- Enhanced onscreen viewing

Using the Accessibility Setup Assistant

Both Acrobat X and Adobe Reader include an Accessibility Setup Assistant that launches automatically the first time the software detects a screen reader, screen magnifier, or other assistive technology on your system. (You can also launch the Assistant manually at any time by selecting Setup Assistant in the Accessibility panel in Acrobat, or by choosing Edit > Accessibility > Setup Assistant in Reader.) The Accessibility Setup Assistant walks you through setting the options that control how PDF documents appear onscreen. You can also use it to set the option that sends print output to a Braille printer.

A full explanation of the options you can set in the Accessibility Setup Assistant is available in the Adobe Acrobat X Help. The options available depend on the type of assistive technology you have on your system. The first panel of the Accessibility Setup Assistant requires you to identify the type of assistive technology that you are using:

*   Select Set Options For Screen Readers if you use a device that reads text and sends output to a Braille printer.

*   Select Set Options For Screen Magnifiers if you use a device that makes text appear larger on the screen.

*   Select Set All Accessibility Options if you use a combination of assistive devices.

*   Select Use Recommended Settings And Skip Setup to use the settings Adobe recommends for users with limited accessibility. (Note that the preferred settings for users with assistive technology installed are not the same as the default Acrobat settings for users who are not using assistive technology.)

In addition to the options you can set using the Accessibility Setup Assistant, you can select a number of options in the Acrobat or Adobe Reader preferences that control automatic scrolling, reading-out-loud settings, and reading order. You may want to use some of these options even if you don't have assistive technology on your system. For example, you can set your Multimedia preferences to show available descriptions for video and audio attachments.

If you opened the Accessibility Setup Assistant, click Cancel to exit the dialog box without making any changes.

About automatic scrolling

When you're reading a long document, the automatic scrolling feature saves a lot of keystroke and mouse actions. You can control the speed of scrolling, scroll backward and forward, and exit automatic scrolling with a single keystroke.

Now you'll test the automatic scroll feature.

1 Choose File > Open, and open the Protocol.pdf file. If necessary, resize the Acrobat window to fill your desktop, and select the Hand tool (✋).

2 Choose View > Page Display > Automatically Scroll.

 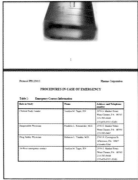 

3 You can set the rate of scrolling using the number keys on your keyboard. The higher the number, the faster the rate of scrolling. Try pressing 9, and then pressing 1, for example, to change the rate of scrolling. To exit automatic scrolling, press the Esc key.

About keyboard shortcuts

Before keyboard shortcuts are available, you may have to change your General preferences (see Lesson 2, "Exploring the Work Area").

For some common commands and tools, the keyboard shortcut is displayed next to the command or tool name if you have the preferences set to use single-key accelerators. A list of keyboard shortcuts is available in Adobe Acrobat X Help.

You can also use the keyboard to control Acrobat within Microsoft Internet Explorer in Windows. If the focus is on the web browser, any keyboard shortcuts you use act according to the web browser settings for navigation and selection. Pressing the Tab key shifts the focus from the browser to the Acrobat document and application, so navigation and command keystrokes function normally. Pressing Ctrl+Tab shifts the focus from the document back to the web browser.

Changing the background color

Now you'll experiment with changing the color of the background. Note that these changes affect only the onscreen display on your own system; they do not affect the printed document, nor are they saved with the document for display on systems other than your own.

1 Choose Edit > Preferences (Windows) or Acrobat > Preferences (Mac OS), and select Accessibility from the list of categories on the left.

2 Select the Replace Document Colors option.

3 Select Custom Color.

4 Click the Page Background color square to open the color picker.

5 You can select a color from the color picker or you can select a custom color. We chose pale gray.

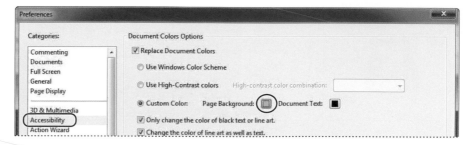

6 Click OK to apply your changes.

7 View the PDF file in Acrobat. The background color of the page has changed to the color you specified.

8 When you are finished, leave your background color as it is, select a different color, or return it to white.

You can also change the background color of form fields, and the color of form fields displayed when your pointer moves over them, in the Forms preferences. You can change the background color for full-screen presentations in the Full Screen preferences. You can change the underline color used in the spell-check feature to identify misspelled words in the Spelling preferences.

Smoothing text

You can smooth text, line art, and images to improve onscreen readability, especially with larger text sizes. If you use a laptop or if you have an LCD screen, you can also choose a Smooth Text option to optimize your display quality. Set the options to smooth text in the Page Display preferences.

Magnifying bookmark text

You can increase the text size used in bookmark labels.

1 Click the Bookmarks button to display the Bookmarks panel, if it's not already open.

2 Choose Text Size > Large from the options menu of the Bookmarks panel.

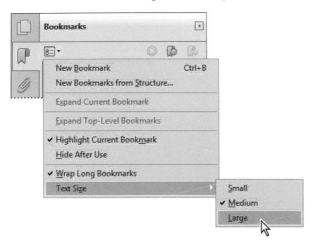

3 Restore your bookmark text size to medium.

You may want to experiment with screen-display options and other accessibility controls to find a combination that best suits your needs.

4 When you are finished, choose File > Close. You need not save your work.

Setting screen reader and reading-out-loud preferences

After you have installed your screen reader or similar application and set it up to work with Acrobat, you can set the screen reader preferences in Acrobat. You set these preferences in the same panel in which you set the Read Out Loud feature preferences that control the volume, pitch, and speed of the speech; the nature of the voice; and the reading order preferences.

Newer systems (both Windows and Mac OS) have built-in text-to-speech engines. Although the Read Out Loud feature can read the text of a PDF file out loud, it is not a screen reader. Not all systems support the Read Out Loud feature.

In this exercise, you'll look at the preferences that affect how Adobe PDF documents are read out loud. Unless you have text-to-speech software on your system, you do not need to set these preferences.

1 Choose File > Open, and open the Tag_Wines.pdf file.

2 If your system has text-to-speech software, choose View > Read Out Loud > Activate Read Out Loud. (You may not need to activate the Read Out Loud function, depending on how much of the lesson you completed.)

3 After you have activated the Read Out Loud feature, choose View > Read Out Loud > Read This Page Only. Acrobat reads the page that is currently displayed. To stop the reading, press Shift+Ctrl+E (Windows) or Shift+Command+E (Mac OS).

You can experiment with the reading options.

4 Choose Edit > Preferences (Windows) or Acrobat > Preferences (Mac OS), and select Reading from the list on the left. Experiment, if you like.

You can control the volume, pitch, speed, and voice used. If you use the default voice, you cannot change the pitch and speed of delivery.

If your system has limited memory, you may wish to reduce the number of pages Acrobat reads before data is delivered page by page. The default value is 50 pages.

5 Click OK in the Preferences dialog box to apply any changes that you make. Or click Cancel to exit the Preferences dialog box without making any changes.

6 To test the settings you changed, choose View > Read Out Loud > Read This Page Only.

7 To stop the reading, press Ctrl+Shift+E (Windows) or Command+Shift+E (Mac OS).

Sharing PDF files

You can share a PDF document with other people by posting it on a website, burning it to a disc, or sending it as an email attachment. Acrobat makes it easy to distribute a PDF document to others using Adobe SendNow Online or by attaching the document to an email message.

Adobe SendNow Online uploads a document to Acrobat.com, a free, secure web service. It sends email to the recipients you specify so that they can read the file online or download it. You need a free Adobe ID to upload files to Acrobat.com.

1 With the Protocol.pdf file open, click Share to open the Share pane.

2 In the Share pane, select Use Adobe SendNow Online. Acrobat automatically adds the active document.

If you want to upload a different file, clear the filename, click Add File, select the file you want to share, and click Open (Windows) or Add (Mac OS) to add it.

3 Enter the email addresses of people you want to notify about the document, separating the addresses with semicolons or returns. For this exercise, enter your own email address.

4 Enter a subject and a simple message, and then click Send Link.

5 Sign in with your Adobe ID and password, if prompted. If you don't have an Adobe ID, follow the onscreen instructions to create one.

Acrobat uploads the document and then sends email to recipients with a link to the uploaded file.

To send a PDF file as an attachment, select Attach To Email in the Share pane, add a file, and then click Attach. Acrobat attaches the document to a blank email message in your email application.

6 Close any open documents, and quit Acrobat.

Review questions

1 Name three methods you can use to navigate to a different page.

2 Name two ways to change the view magnification.

3 How can you determine whether a file is accessible?

4 How can you print discontiguous pages?

Review answers

1 You can move to a different page by clicking the Previous Page or Next Page button in the Page Navigation toolbar; dragging the scroll box in the scroll bar; entering a page number in the page box in the Page Navigation toolbar; or clicking a bookmark, page thumbnail, or link that jumps to a different page.

2 You can change the view magnification by choosing View > Zoom, and then choosing a view; dragging the Marquee Zoom tool; choosing a preset magnification from the magnification pop-up menu; or entering a specific percentage in the magnification text box.

3 Select Quick Check in the Accessibility panel to determine whether a PDF file is accessible.

4 To print discontiguous pages, either select the page thumbnails, and then choose File > Print, or, in the Print dialog box, select Pages, and then enter the page numbers or ranges you want to print, separated by commas.

5 USING ACROBAT WITH MICROSOFT OFFICE FILES (WINDOWS)

Lesson overview

In this lesson, you'll do the following:

- Convert a Microsoft Word file to Adobe PDF.

- Convert Word headings and styles to PDF bookmarks and Word comments to PDF notes.

- Change the Adobe PDF conversion settings.

- Convert a Microsoft PowerPoint presentation to Adobe PDF.

- Convert a Microsoft Excel file to Adobe PDF and send it for review.

- Save PDF files as Word documents.

- Copy PDF tables to Excel spreadsheets.

 This lesson will take approximately 45 minutes to complete. Copy the Lesson05 folder onto your hard drive if you haven't already done so.

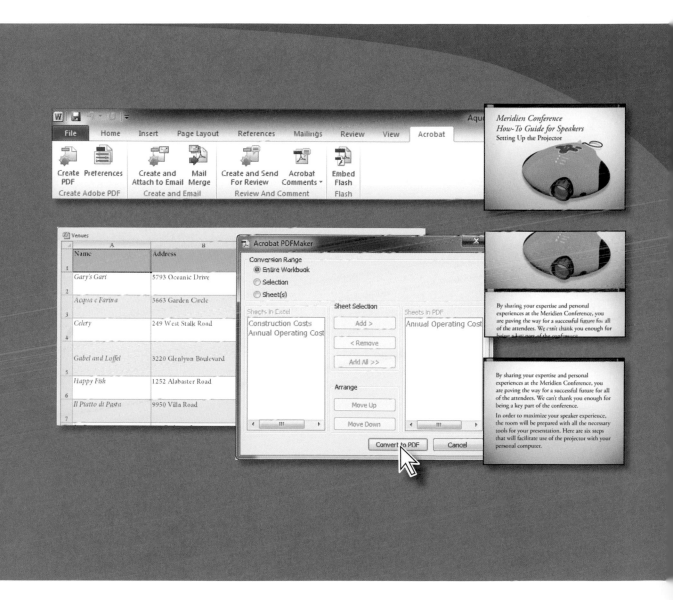

Using Acrobat PDFMaker, you can easily convert Microsoft Office documents to PDF. And with Acrobat X, you can go the other direction—saving PDF files as Word documents and extracting charts from PDF files to Excel spreadsheets.

Getting started

This lesson is designed for Windows users who have Microsoft Office applications such as Microsoft Word, Microsoft PowerPoint, and Microsoft Excel installed on their computers. You need to have one or more of these applications installed on your system to use this lesson. If you do not use these Microsoft Office applications, skip this lesson. Visit the Adobe website (www.adobe.com) to see which versions of Microsoft Office are supported.

This lesson assumes you are using Microsoft Office 2010, but the steps are the same in Office 2007.

For information on converting Microsoft Outlook files to PDF, see Lesson 3.

About Acrobat PDFMaker

Acrobat PDFMaker makes it easy to convert Microsoft Office documents to PDF. When you install Acrobat in Windows, it automatically installs PDFMaker for any Microsoft Office applications it finds on the system. In Microsoft Office 2007 and 2010 applications, PDFMaker options are on the Acrobat ribbon. In earlier versions of Office, Acrobat adds a PDFMaker toolbar and an Adobe PDF menu to the application. You can control the settings used in the PDF conversion, automatically email the PDF file, and set up an email review process without ever leaving the Microsoft application. PDFMaker can also attach your Office source file to the PDF file.

PDF files are often substantially smaller than their source files. (Complex Excel files may be an exception.) You can also create PDF/A-compliant files from any Office files. (Note, however, that PDFMaker does not support the PDF/A standard for Microsoft Publisher.)

For Office 2007 and 2010 applications, if you don't see the Acrobat ribbon, choose Add-Ins from the Options dialog box, and select Acrobat PDFMaker Office COM Addin. For Office 2003 and earlier, choose Help > About [application name], click Disabled Items, select Adobe PDF from the list, and click Enable. Then close and restart your Microsoft application.

Acrobat installs essentially the same buttons and commands in Word, PowerPoint, and Excel. There are, however, some application-specific differences.

Converting Microsoft Word files to Adobe PDF

Word is a popular authoring program that makes it easy to create a variety of types of documents. Word documents often include text styles and hyperlinks, and they may contain comments added during a review process. When you create an Adobe PDF document from your Word document, you can convert text using specific Word styles, such as headings, to Acrobat bookmarks, and you can convert comments to Acrobat notes. Hyperlinks in a Word document are preserved when it is converted to PDF. Your Adobe PDF file will look just like your Word file and retain the same functionality, but it will be equally accessible to readers on all platforms, regardless of whether or not they have the Word application. (PDF files created from Word files are tagged, making the content easy to repurpose and improving accessibility.)

Converting Word headings and styles to PDF bookmarks

If your Word document contains headings and styles that you want to convert to linked bookmarks in Adobe PDF, you must identify these headings and styles in the Acrobat PDFMaker dialog box. (Word Heading 1 through Heading 9 styles are converted automatically.) You'll convert a statement of work document that was formatted using custom styles. You'll need to make sure that the styles used are converted to linked bookmarks when you create the Adobe PDF file.

1 Start Microsoft Word.

2 In Word, choose File > Open. Navigate to the Lesson05 folder, select the SOW draft.doc file, and click Open. Choose File > Save As, rename the file **SOW draft_final.doc**, and save it in the Lesson05 folder.

First, you'll change the PDF settings to create bookmarks based on the styles used in the document.

3 In Word 2007 or 2010, click Preferences in the Acrobat ribbon. In earlier versions of Word, choose Adobe PDF > Change Conversion Settings.

The Acrobat PDFMaker dialog box contains the settings that control the PDF conversion. There are different tabs available, depending on the application. In Word, the dialog box includes a Word tab and a Bookmarks tab.

4 Click the Bookmarks tab to select which styles are used to create bookmarks.

5 Scroll down the list and select the box next to each of the following styles, so that a check mark appears in it: Second Level, Third Level, Title, and Top Level. These are the styles you want to use to create bookmarks.

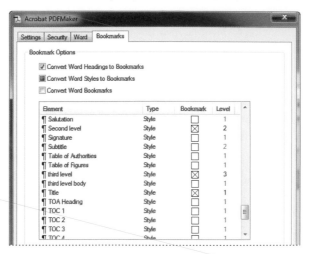

An X appears next to each style, indicating that a bookmark will be created for it. Notice that the level for Title and Top Level is automatically set to 1, Second Level is set to 2, and Third Level is set to 3. These are the hierarchical levels of PDF bookmarks. To change the level setting for a style, click its level number, and then choose a new level from the pop-up menu.

Any settings that you make in the Bookmarks tab apply only to the conversion of Word documents.

Converting Word comments to PDF notes

You needn't lose any comments that have been added to your Word document when you convert the document to Adobe PDF. You can convert them to PDF notes. There are three comments in this document that need to remain available in the PDF.

1 Click the Word tab in the Acrobat PDFMaker dialog box, and select Convert Displayed Comments To Notes In Adobe PDF.

The Comments area displays information about the comments that will be included. Make sure that the box in the Include column is selected.

2 To change the color of the note in the Adobe PDF document, click repeatedly on the icon in the Color column to cycle through the available color choices. We chose blue.

3 To have the note automatically open in the PDF document, select the Notes Open option. You can always close the note in the PDF document later if you wish.

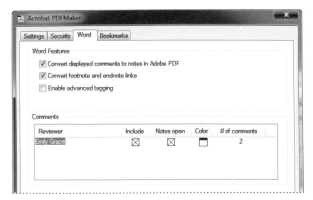

Any settings that you make in the Word tab apply only to the conversion of Word documents.

Specifying the conversion settings

In every Office application, PDFMaker includes the Settings tab, which is where you can select the conversion settings that determine how the PDF file is created. For most purposes, the predefined settings files (or presets) work well. However, if you need to customize the conversion settings, click Advanced Settings, and then make the changes appropriate for your file.

You'll convert this document using the Standard settings file.

1 Click the Settings tab.

2 From the Conversion Settings menu, choose Standard.

3 Verify that View Adobe PDF Result is selected. When this option is selected, Acrobat automatically displays the Adobe PDF file you create as soon as the conversion is complete.

4 Make sure that Create Bookmarks is selected.

5 Make sure that Enable Accessibility And Reflow With Tagged Adobe PDF is selected. Creating tagged PDF makes your files more accessible.

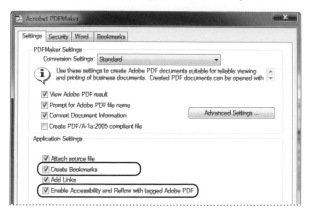

For more information on making your PDF files accessible, see Lesson 4, "Reading and Working with PDF Files."

● **Note:** Acrobat PDFMaker will use these conversion settings for converting Word documents until you change them.

6 Select Attach Source File to attach the Word document to the PDF file. This option can be useful if you want the viewer to have access to the original for editing purposes.

7 Click OK to apply your settings.

8 Choose File > Save to save your work so far.

Converting your Word file

Now that you've defined the settings to be used for the conversion, you're ready to convert your Word file to Adobe PDF.

1 In Word 2007 or 2010, click the Create PDF button (⬛) on the Acrobat ribbon. In earlier versions of Word, click the Convert To Adobe PDF button (⬛) on the Acrobat PDFMaker toolbar.

2 In the Save Adobe PDF As dialog box, name the file **SOWdraft.pdf**, and save it in the Lesson05 folder.

PDFMaker converts the Word document to Adobe PDF. The status of the conversion is shown in the Acrobat PDFMaker message box.

Because you selected View Adobe PDF Result, Acrobat automatically displays your converted file. Notice that the Word comment has been converted to an open Adobe PDF note.

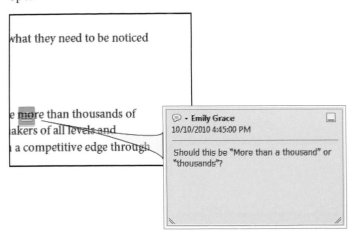

3 Scroll if necessary to see the first note. After you have read the sticky note, click the close box on the sticky note.

4 Click the Bookmarks button (📑)in the navigation pane, and view the bookmarks that were created automatically.

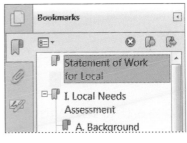

In Acrobat X, when you select a bookmark in the navigation pane, the link takes you directly to the heading, not the top of the page that contains the heading.

5 Click the Attachments button (📎) in the navigation pane to verify that your original Word file is attached.

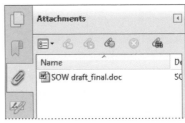

6 When you have finished reviewing the file, close it.

7 Choose File > Exit to quit Acrobat.

8 Quit Microsoft Word.

▶ **Tip:** In Acrobat X, you can edit headers and footers in PDF files created from Office 2007 and 2010 files.

▶ **Tip:** If you simply want to convert your Microsoft Office file to Adobe PDF using the current PDFMaker conversion settings, drag the Office file onto the Acrobat X icon on your desktop or into an empty document pane in the Acrobat work area.

Converting Excel documents and starting a review

When you convert Excel documents to PDF, you can easily select and order the worksheets to include, as well as retaining all links and creating bookmarks.

You'll create an Adobe PDF file from an Excel document, and then start a formal review process in which the PDF file is emailed to selected reviewers. In addition to managing the email process, Acrobat also offers powerful file-management and comment-management tools to facilitate the review.

Converting the entire workbook

You can choose to convert an entire workbook, a selection, or selected sheets to PDF. In this exercise, you'll convert an entire workbook.

1 Start Microsoft Excel.

2 Choose File > Open, navigate to the Lesson05 folder, select the Financial2008.xls file, and click Open. Then choose File > Save As, rename the file **Financial2008_final.xls**, and save it in the Lesson05 folder.

This Excel file includes two worksheets. The first lists construction costs, and the second shows operating costs. You'll need to convert both these sheets to include them in the PDF. You'll start by changing the PDF conversion settings.

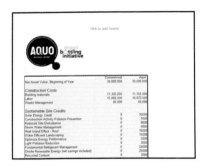 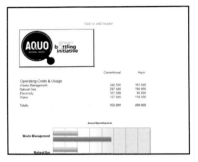

3 Click Preferences in the Acrobat ribbon. If you're using Excel 2003 or earlier, choose Adobe PDF > Change Conversion Settings.

4 In the Settings tab of the Acrobat PDFMaker dialog box, choose Smallest File Size from the Conversion Settings menu, because you're going to be emailing the PDF file.

5 Select the Fit Worksheet To A Single Page option.

6 Make sure that the Enable Accessibility And Reflow With Tagged Adobe PDF option is selected. When you create tagged PDF, you can more easily copy tabular data from PDF files back into spreadsheet applications. Creating tagged PDF also makes your files more accessible.

7 Select the Prompt For Selecting Excel Sheets option to open a dialog box at the beginning of the file conversion process that allows you to specify which sheets to include and in what order.

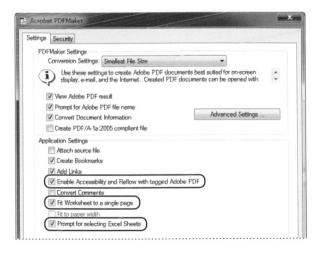

PDFMaker will use these conversion settings when converting Excel documents to PDF until you change the settings.

8 Click OK to apply your settings.

In Acrobat, you can convert an oversized worksheet to a PDF that is one sheet wide and several sheets long. In the Settings tab of the Acrobat PDFMaker dialog box, the Fit Worksheet To A Single Page option adjusts the size of each worksheet so that all the entries on that worksheet appear on the same page of the PDF. The Fit To Paper Width option adjusts the width of each worksheet so that all the columns on that worksheet appear on one page in the PDF.

Starting an email-based review

You can email a file for review using the Create And Send For Review button on the Acrobat ribbon (Excel 2007 or 2010) or the Convert To Adobe PDF And Send For Review button (earlier versions). The recipient will receive an email with instructions for how to participate in the review and return comments using Acrobat.com.

You can also use the Tracker feature in Acrobat to invite additional reviewers to join the process or to send reminders to reviewers. You can also invite users of Adobe Reader to participate in the review. For more information on using Acrobat in review processes, see Lesson 9, "Using Acrobat in a Review Cycle."

1   In Excel 2007 or 2010, click the Create And Send For Review (🖼) button in the Acrobat ribbon. In Office 2003 or earlier, choose Adobe PDF > Convert To Adobe PDF And Send For Review.

2   In the Acrobat PDFMaker dialog box, select Entire Workbook.

This is the dialog box where you'd select specific material or worksheets, if you wanted to.

3   Click Convert To PDF.

4   In the Save Adobe PDF File As dialog box, click Save to save the file as **Financial2008_final.pdf** in the Lesson05 folder.

The Send For Shared Review dialog box opens to guide you through the process.

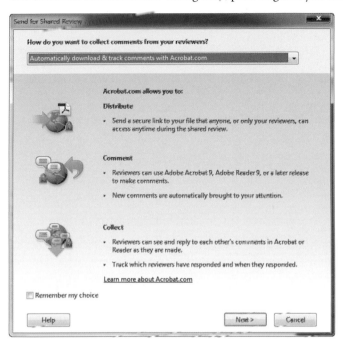

5   From the pop-up menu, choose whether to use Acrobat.com or your own
    internal server for the review process. Click Next.

The steps vary depending on how you choose to collect data from your reviewers.

6   When you have completed the steps in the wizard and emailed your file, close
    the PDF file and quit Microsoft Excel.

Though you can walk through the steps alone using multiple email addresses for
yourself, you cannot fully experience the email review feature without the help of
at least one other participant. We encourage you to experiment with this feature
when you have a document to review with colleagues.

Using the spreadsheet split view

When you work with spreadsheets, it is often useful to be able to keep the column or row names in view while scrolling up and down columns or across rows. The Spreadsheet Split command in Acrobat lets you do this.

1   In Acrobat, choose File > Open. Navigate to the Lesson05 folder and open the GE_Schedule.pdf file.

This schedule is difficult to read onscreen because the type size is small if you have the view set to Fit Page. You'll use the Spreadsheet Split command to look more closely at some of the data. First you'll change the view of the page.

2   Choose Window > Spreadsheet Split to divide the document pane into four quadrants.

You can drag the splitter bars up, down, left, or right to resize the panes.

In Spreadsheet Split view, changing the zoom level changes the zoom level in each quadrant. (In Split Window view, you can have a different zoom level in each of the two windows.)

3   Drag the vertical splitter bar to the left so that the categories fill the left pane.

4   Drag the horizontal splitter bar up so that it is directly below the column headings.

5   Use the vertical scroll bar to scroll down through the categories. Because the column headers remain visible, it is easy to evaluate the schedule for each task.

6   When you are finished exploring the Spreadsheet Split view, close the GE_Schedule.pdf file without saving your work.

Converting PowerPoint presentations

You can convert Microsoft PowerPoint presentations to PDF in the same way that you convert Microsoft Word documents. However, there are additional options available to help you preserve the look and feel of the presentation. You'll convert a simple presentation and preserve its slide transitions.

1 Start PowerPoint. Choose File > Open, navigate to the Lesson05 folder, and select the Projector Setup.ppt file. Click Open.

A Push transition has been applied to the slides in this file.

2 Click Preferences in the Acrobat ribbon (PowerPoint 2007 or 2010) or choose Adobe PDF > Change Conversion Settings (earlier versions).

3 Select the Settings tab, and then select Convert Multimedia and Preserve Slide Transitions. Make sure View Adobe PDF Result is selected, too.

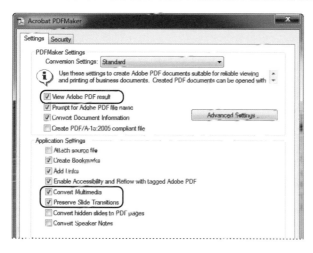

4 Click OK.

You can include speaker's notes and hidden slides, and specify other settings.

5 Click Create PDF in the Acrobat ribbon (PowerPoint 2007 or 2010) or choose Adobe PDF > Convert to Adobe PDF (earlier versions). Click Save in the Save Adobe PDF dialog box. Acrobat opens the PDF file after conversion.

6 In Acrobat, choose View > Full Screen Mode. Then press the arrow keys to move through the presentation. The Push slide transitions remain in the PDF file. Close the PDF file and PowerPoint.

About Adobe Presenter (Acrobat Suite)

Adobe Presenter, included with Acrobat Suite, is an addition to PowerPoint that produces rich media files for use in presentations, training, and education. Presenter slide shows can include video, voice-over narration, interactive quizzes, and other dynamic content to enhance their appeal. Publishing your Presenter slide show to PDF preserves all of the slide show content. It also reduces the file size and allows users to view it offline. Users need Adobe Reader 9 or later or Acrobat 9 or later to open Presenter PDFs.

Converting web pages from Internet Explorer

Acrobat X adds a button and a menu to the toolbar of Internet Explorer 6 or later that let you convert the currently displayed web page or portion of a web page to an Adobe PDF file, convert and print it, or convert and email it in one easy operation. When you print a web page that you have converted to an Adobe PDF file, the page is reformatted to a standard printer page size and logical page breaks are added. You can be sure that your print copy will have all the information on the web page that you see onscreen.

For more information on converting web pages from within Internet Explorer, see Lesson 3, "Creating Adobe PDF Files."

Saving PDF files as Word documents

You can save PDF files as Word documents (either .docx or .doc files)—no matter what application the document originated in. You'll save a speaker registration form as a Word document.

1 In Acrobat, choose File > Open. Navigate to the Lesson05 folder, and select the Speaker Reg.pdf file. Click Open.

2 Choose File > Save As > Microsoft Word > Word Document. (If you're using Word 2003 or earlier, choose Word 97-2003 Document, which saves a .doc file.)

3 In the Save As dialog box, click Settings.

4 In the Save As DOC Settings or Save As DOCX Settings dialog box, select Retain Page Layout. Make sure the other options are all selected. Then click OK.

5 Click Save to save the file.

Acrobat displays the status of the conversion process as it works. When you save complex PDF documents, the conversion to Word may take longer.

6 In Windows Explorer, navigate to the Lesson05 folder, and open the Speaker Reg.doc or Speaker Reg.docx file in Word.

7 Scroll through the document to confirm that the text and images have been saved appropriately.

In most cases, Acrobat saves PDF files as Word documents with impressive integrity. However, depending on the way the document was created, you may need to adjust spacing or make minor corrections. Always carefully review a document in Word after you've saved it from Acrobat.

8 Close the PDF file in Acrobat, and then quit Word.

Extracting PDF tables as Excel spreadsheets

You can export tables from a PDF document as Excel worksheets. You'll export a list of restaurants from a PDF document to a new Excel file.

1 In Acrobat, choose File > Open. Navigate to the Lesson05 folder, and select Venues.pdf. Click Open.

The PDF document includes a table of restaurants in the fictitious city of Meridien. You'll export that table to an Excel file.

2 Select the Selection tool (I) in the Common Tools toolbar.

3 Drag from the upper-left corner of the table to the lower-right corner, so that the entire table is selected.

4 Right-click in the selected table, and choose Export Selection As.

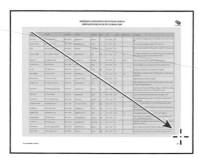 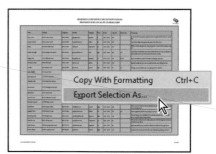

5 In the Export Selection As dialog box, choose Excel Workbook (*.xlsx) from the Save As Type menu. Name the file **Venues.xlsx**. Then click Save.

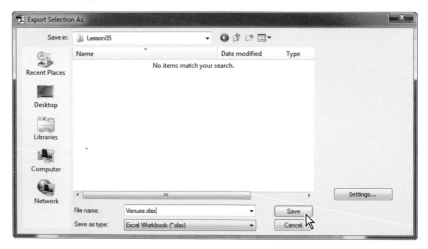

Acrobat reports its progress.

6 When Acrobat has finished exporting the document, open Excel, choose File > Open, navigate to the Lesson05 folder, and open the Venues.xlsx file. Acrobat appropriately converted the fields in the table.

	A	B	C	D	E
	Name	Address	Telephone	Website	Category
1					
2	Gary's Gari	5793 Oceanic Drive	490 65 8569	garysgari.mer	Japanese
3	Acqua e Farina	3663 Garden Circle	490 32 3880	acquaefarina.mer	Italian
4	Celery	249 West Stalk Road	490 52 4798	celery.mer	Vegeteria
5	Gabel and Loffel	3220 Glenlyon Boulevard	490 46 8997	gabeandloffel.mer	Café
6	Happy Fish	1252 Alabaster Road	490 27 9435	happyfish.mer	Japanese
7	Il Piatto di Pasta	9950 Villa Road	490 32 3880	ilpiatto.mer	Italian

7 Close any open documents, Office applications, and Acrobat.

Review questions

1 How can you be sure that Word styles and headings are converted to Acrobat bookmarks when you convert Word documents to Adobe PDF using PDFMaker?

2 How can you convert a PDF document to a Word document?

3 Can you retain slide transitions when you save a PowerPoint presentation to PDF?

Review answers

1 If you want Word headings and styles to be converted to bookmarks in Acrobat, select them for conversion in the Acrobat PDFMaker dialog box. In Microsoft Word, click Preferences in the Acrobat ribbon (choose Adobe PDF > Change Conversion Settings in earlier versions of Word), and click the Bookmarks tab. Make sure that the required headings and styles are selected.

2 To save a PDF file as a Word document, choose File > Save As > Microsoft Word > Word Document (or Word 97-2003 Document).

3 Yes. To retain slide transitions, click Preferences in the Acrobat ribbon (or choose Adobe PDF > Change Conversion Settings in earlier versions of PowerPoint), and then make sure Preserve Slide Transitions is selected. PDFMaker uses those settings until you change them.

6 ENHANCING AND EDITING PDF DOCUMENTS

Lesson overview

In this lesson, you'll do the following:

- Rearrange pages in a PDF document.

- Rotate and delete pages.

- Insert pages into a PDF document.

- Edit links and bookmarks.

- Renumber pages in a PDF document.

- Insert video and other multimedia files into a PDF.

- Copy text and images from a PDF document.

- Set document properties and add metadata to a PDF.

 This lesson will take approximately 45 minutes to complete. Copy the Lesson06 folder onto your hard drive if you haven't already done so.

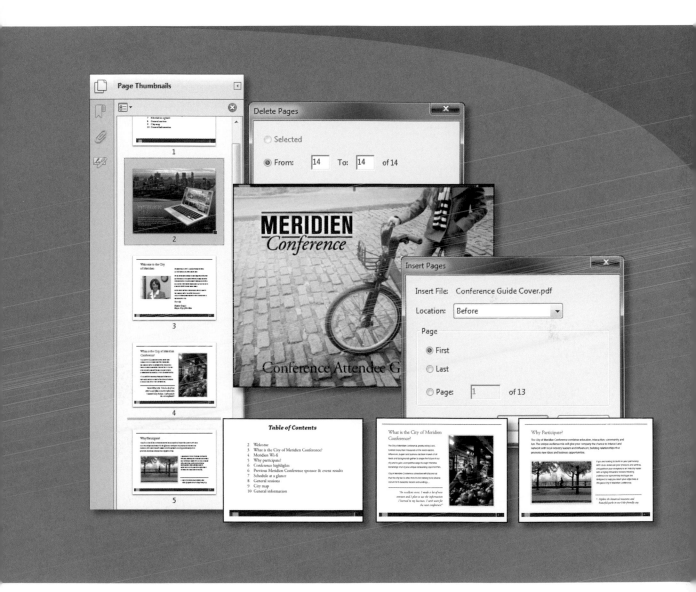

You can modify PDF documents by rearranging, cropping, deleting, or inserting pages; editing text or images; or adding multimedia files. You can also repurpose content by copying it for other uses.

Examining the work file

You'll work with conference materials for the fictitious Meridien Conference. The presentation has been designed both for print and for online viewing. Because this online presentation is in the developmental phase, it contains a number of mistakes. You'll use Acrobat to correct the problems in this PDF document and to enhance it with a video file.

1 Start Acrobat.

2 Choose File > Open. Navigate to the Lesson06 folder, select Conference Guide.pdf, and click Open. Then choose File > Save As > PDF, rename the file **Conference Guide_final.pdf**, and save it in the Lesson06 folder.

3 Click the Bookmarks button (📑) in the navigation pane. The Bookmarks panel opens, revealing several bookmarks that have already been created. Bookmarks are links to specific points in the document. They can be generated automatically from the table-of-contents entries of documents created by most desktop publishing programs or from formatted headings in applications such as Microsoft Word. You can also create bookmarks in Acrobat. You can specify the appearance of bookmarks and add actions to them.

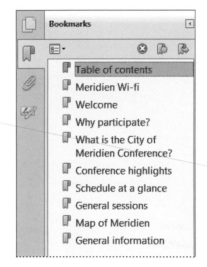

4 Use the Next Page button (⊙) to page through the document.

Notice that the bookmark icon that corresponds to the page that you are viewing is highlighted as you move through the pages. (There are a couple of bookmark errors that you'll correct later.)

5 With the Hand tool () or the Selection tool (), click the icon for the Table of contents bookmark to return to the first page of the presentation.

6 In the document pane, move the pointer over the items listed under contents. Notice that the items in the list have already been linked, indicated by the hand changing to a pointing finger.

7 Click the Meridien Wi-fi entry in the document pane to follow its link. (Be sure to click the entry in the table of contents, not the bookmark in the Bookmarks panel.)

Notice that the page number on the page displayed in the document pane is 2, though the page number in the table of contents showed the page as being page 4. The page is out of order.

8 Choose View > Page Navigation > Previous View to return to the table of contents.

Moving pages with page thumbnails

Page thumbnails offer convenient previews of your pages. In Lesson 2, you used page thumbnails to navigate a document. Now you'll use them to quickly rearrange pages in a document.

1 Click the Page Thumbnails button (⬜) in the navigation pane.

The Meridien Wi-fi page is out of place. According to the table of contents, it should follow the page titled "What is the City of Meridien Conference?"

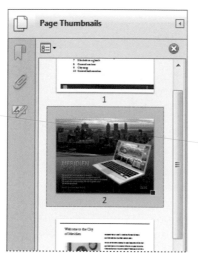

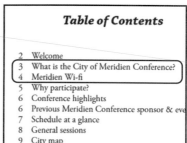

2 Click the page 2 thumbnail to select it.

3 Drag the selected thumbnail image down until the insertion bar appears between the thumbnails of pages 4 and 5.

4 Release the mouse button to insert the page at its new position.

The Meridien Wi-fi page now follows the "What is the City of Meridien Conference?" page, and it precedes the "Why participate?" page.

5 To check the sequence of pages, choose View > Page Navigation > First Page to go to the first page of the document, and then use the Next Page button (⊙) to page through the presentation.

6 When you're satisfied that the pages are in the correct order, close the Page Thumbnails panel. Then choose File > Save to save your work.

Editing Adobe PDF pages

If you look at the first page of the presentation (page 1 of 13), you'll notice that the first page, the Table of Contents page, is rather plain. To make the presentation more attractive, you'll add a cover page, which you'll then rotate to match the other pages in the presentation.

Inserting a page from another file

▶ **Tip:** If you insert a page that is larger than the other pages in a document, you can use the Crop tool to crop out unnecessary areas of the page. The Crop tool is in the Pages panel.

You'll start by inserting the cover page.

1 Open the Tools pane, and then expand the Pages panel.

2 In the Insert Pages area of the panel, select Insert From File.

3 Navigate to the Lesson06 folder, and select Conference Guide Cover.pdf. Click Select.

4 In the Insert Pages dialog box, choose Before from the Location menu, and then select First in the page area. Then click OK. You want to insert this PDF file before any of the pages in your document.

The cover document appears as page 1 in the Conference Guide_final.pdf document.

5 Choose File > Save to save your work.

Rotating a page

The cover page is now in the conference document, but it has the wrong orientation. You'll rotate the new page to match the rest of the document.

1 In the Pages panel, select Rotate.

 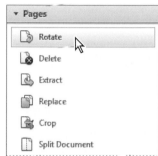

2 From the Direction menu, choose Counterclockwise 90 Degrees.

3 Select Pages, and make sure the rotation will affect only page 1 to 1. Then click OK.

▶ **Tip:** If you want to rotate all the pages in a file for viewing purposes only, choose View > Rotate View > Clockwise or Counterclockwise. When you close the file, the pages revert to their original rotation.

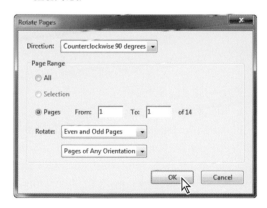 

Acrobat rotates the page so that it matches the rest of the document. To ensure that only the first page was rotated, click the Next Page button in the Common Tools toolbar to page through the document.

Deleting a page

The last page in the document doesn't quite fit with the others, and the conference committee has decided to distribute it separately. You'll delete it from the document.

1 Go to the last page in the document (page 14).

2 In the Pages panel, select Delete.

3 In the Delete Pages dialog box, make sure From is selected, and that you're deleting only page 14. Then click OK.

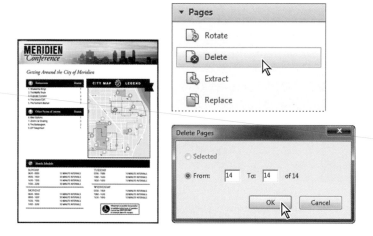

4 Click Yes to confirm that you want to delete page 14.

The page is deleted from the Conference Guide_final.pdf file.

5 Choose File > Save, and save your work.

Renumbering pages

You may have noticed that the page numbers on the document pages do not always match the page numbers that appear below the page thumbnails and on the toolbar. Acrobat automatically numbers pages with Arabic numerals, starting with page 1 for the first page in the document, and so on. However, you can change the way Acrobat numbers pages. You'll give the title page a roman numeral, so that the contents page is page 1.

1 Click the Page Thumbnails button (▯) in the navigation pane to display the page thumbnails.

2 Click the page 1 thumbnail to go to the cover page.

You'll renumber the first page of the document—the cover page—using lowercase roman numerals.

3 Click the options button at the top of the Page Thumbnails panel, and choose Number Pages.

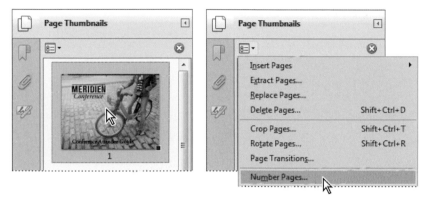

4 For Pages, select From and enter from **1** to **1** of 13. For Numbering, select Begin New Section, choose "i, ii, iii" from the Style menu, and enter **1** in the Start text box. Click OK.

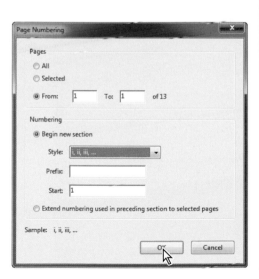

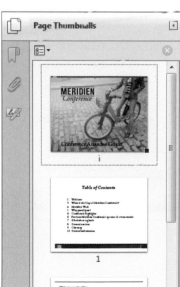

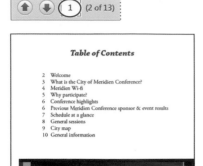

(2 of 13)

5 Choose View > Page Navigation > Page. Enter **1**, and click OK.

Notice that the number 1 in the page number text box is now assigned to the contents page of the document.

6 Close the Page Thumbnails panel.

7 Choose File > Save to save your changes.

▶ **Tip:** You can physically add page numbers to the pages of your Adobe PDF document using the Add Headers & Footers command. You can also add Bates numbering.

Editing links

▶ **Tip:** To quickly return to your previous view, use the Previous View button. You can add it to the toolbar by choosing View > Show/ Hide > Toolbar Items > Page Navigation > Previous View.

Now you'll correct the broken links on the contents page, and add a missing link.

1 Go to page 1, the table of contents page, if you're not there already.

2 Click the links for each of the table of contents entries to identify problems. The link for page 3 and the second link for page 6 go to the wrong pages. There is no link for the last entry.

First, you'll correct the links that go to the wrong pages.

3 Open the Content panel in the Tools pane, and select the Link tool. Acrobat outlines the links on the page.

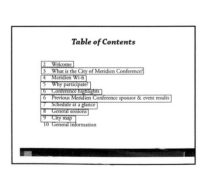

4 Double-click the link for page 3, "What is the City of Meridien Conference?"

5 In the Link Properties dialog box, click the Actions tab. The action associated with this link is to go to page 3. Click Edit.

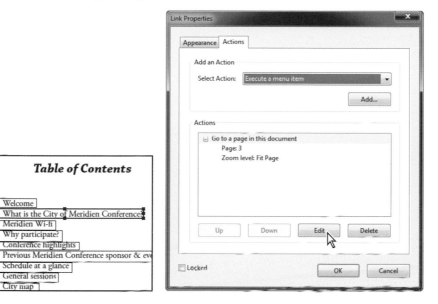

6 In the Go To A Page In This Document dialog box, select Use Page Number, and enter **3** in the Page box. Click OK.

The listed action now goes to page 4. Remember that you renumbered the pages, so page 3 is actually the 4th page in the PDF file.

7 Click OK.

8 Select the Selection tool, and click the link for page 3. It goes to the appropriate page now. Return to the table of contents page.

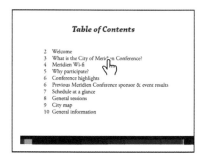 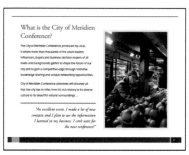

9 Follow steps 3–7 to make the same change for the link to the previous event results, changing the linked page number to page 6.

Now you'll create a link for the last entry.

10 Go to page 1, if you're not there already, and select the Link tool in the Content panel.

11 Drag a link box around the final contents entry, "10 General information."

12 In the Create Link dialog box, choose Invisible Rectangle for the Link Type, and select Go To A Page View in the Link Action area. Then click Next.

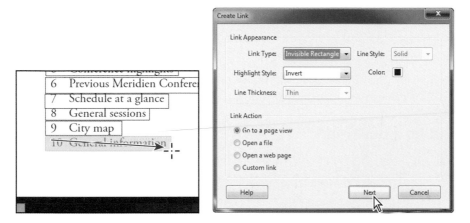

13 Scroll to page 10. When the General Information page is on the screen, click Set Link. Acrobat returns you to the contents page.

14 Select the Selection tool, and then click the link you just created to test it.

15 Choose File > Save to save your work.

Working with bookmarks

A bookmark is simply a link represented by text in the Bookmarks panel. While bookmarks that are created automatically by many authoring programs are generally linked to headings in the text or to figure captions, you can also add your own bookmarks in Acrobat to create a custom outline of a document or to open other documents.

Additionally, you can use electronic bookmarks as you would paper bookmarks—to mark a place in a document that you want to highlight or return to later.

Adding a bookmark

First, you'll add a bookmark for the second topic on page 6, the section titled "Previous Meridien Conference sponsor and event results."

1 Go to page 6 in the document, so that you can see the event results.

2 Open the Bookmarks panel, and then click the Conference highlights bookmark. The new bookmark will be added directly below the selected bookmark.

3 Click the New Bookmark button (📑) at the top of the Bookmarks panel. A new, untitled bookmark appears.

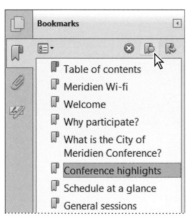 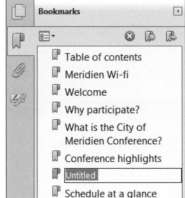

4 In the text box of the new bookmark, type **Previous conference results**. Press Enter or Return to accept the name.

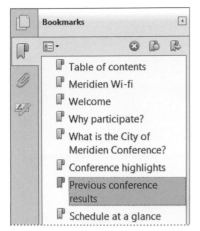 

Changing a bookmark destination

A couple of bookmarks link to the wrong pages. You'll change those now.

1 In the Bookmarks panel, click the Why participate? bookmark. The document pane displays the "What is the City of Meridien Conference?" page.

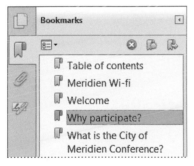 

2 Click the Next Page button (⊙) twice to go to page 5 (6 of 13) of the document, which is the page you want the bookmark to link to.

3   From the options menu at the top of the Bookmarks panel, choose Set Bookmark Destination. Click Yes in the confirmation message to update the bookmark destination.

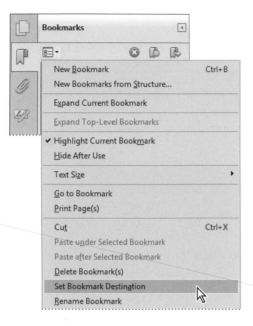

4   Repeat the process to correct the destination of the "What is the City of Meridien Conference?" bookmark, which should be linked to page 3 (4 of 13).

5   Choose File > Save to save the Conference Guide_final.pdf file.

Naming bookmarks automatically

You can create, name, and automatically link a bookmark by selecting text in the document pane.

1   Select the Selection tool in the toolbar.

2   Drag the I-beam to highlight the text that you want to use as your bookmark.

Be sure to have the magnification of the page at the required level. Whatever magnification is used will be inherited by the bookmark.

3   Click the New Bookmark button at the top of the Bookmarks panel. A new bookmark is created in the bookmarks list, and the highlighted text from the document pane is used as the bookmark name. By default, the new bookmark links to the current page view displayed in the document window.

Moving bookmarks

After creating a bookmark, you can easily drag it to its proper place in the Bookmarks panel. You can move individual bookmarks or groups of bookmarks up and down in the Bookmarks list, and you can nest bookmarks.

Some of the bookmarks are out of order in the current document. You'll rearrange them now.

1   In the Bookmarks panel, drag the icon for the Welcome bookmark directly below the icon for the Table of contents bookmark.

2   Drag the other bookmarks so that they appear in the same order as the entries in the table of contents.

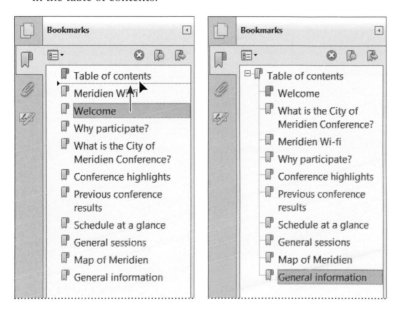

3   Choose File > Save to save your work.

Adding multimedia files

With Acrobat, you can easily transform your PDF files into exciting multidimensional communication tools by inserting video, audio, and Flash animations. These multimedia components require only Acrobat or Reader X to run in Windows or Mac OS.

When you add a multimedia file to a PDF, you can set launch behaviors and other options that determine how the file appears and plays in the PDF document. You'll add a video to your PDF document, set its launch behaviors, and specify how the poster will be created.

Adding a video file to a PDF file

Using the Video tool in Acrobat, you can easily add an FLV file to a PDF. The file is completely embedded within the PDF document, so anyone can view it using Adobe Reader; you do not need QuickTime or Adobe Flash Player to view videos in the PDF file.

1 Go to page 5 (6 of 13) in the Conference Guide_final.pdf file.

2 Open the Content panel in the Tools pane, select Multimedia, and then choose Video. The pointer becomes a cross-hair.

3 Drag a video box over the image on the page. That's where you want the video to appear.

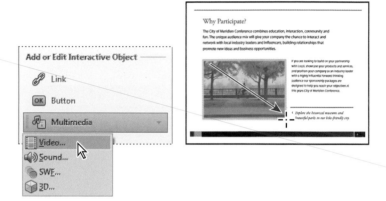

4 In the Insert Video dialog box, click Choose. Navigate to the Lesson06 folder, and select the Welcome Video.flv file. Click Open.

5 Select Show Advanced Options to expand the Insert Video dialog box.

6 Select the Launch Settings tab. From the Enable When menu, choose The Content Is Clicked.

7 From the Disable When menu, choose The Page Containing The Content Is Closed. For Playback Style, choose Play Content On Page.

8 In the Poster Image area, select Retrieve Poster From Media. The poster is the image that appears when the video is not playing, and it's what prints when you print the page.

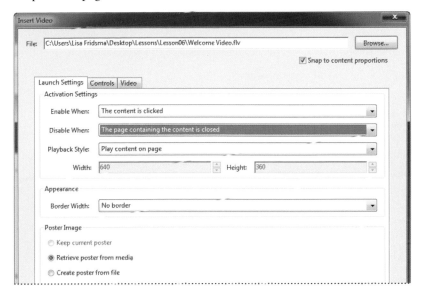

9 Select the Controls tab. From the Skin menu, choose Play, Stop, Seek, Mute, And Volume. The skin determines the controls viewers use to interact with the video and how those controls appear on the page.

10 When you're satisfied with the options you've chosen, click OK.

The video appears on the page where you dragged the box. If you want to change the placement, change the size or shape of the video box, or change the video options, select the Video tool again. Then drag new boundaries for the video box or double-click the video to open the Edit Video dialog box.

11 Click the Play button to play the video. To change the volume or stop playing the video, move the pointer over the video until you see the video controls.

12 Choose File > Save to save your work.

Adding a Flash animation

You can also add Flash animations (SWF files) to Adobe PDFs. To insert a SWF file, choose Multimedia > SWF in the Content panel, and then drag a box on the page for the animation. Select the file you want to import, and then specify launch settings, including the poster setting, just as you would when importing a video file.

Setting up presentations

Generally, when you make a presentation to a group of people, you want the document to take over the entire screen, hiding distractions such as the menu bar, toolbars, and other window controls.

You can set up any PDF file to display in Full Screen mode, and you can set a variety of transition effects to play as you move between pages. You can even set the speed at which pages "turn." You can also convert presentations that you've prepared in other programs, such as PowerPoint, to Adobe PDF, preserving many of the authoring program's special effects. For more information, see Adobe Acrobat X Help.

Editing text

Though you wouldn't want to reconsider entire paragraphs of prose, you can easily make simple text edits in PDF documents in Acrobat. You can edit the text itself, and you can make changes to text attributes such as spacing, point size, and color. You can insert or replace text if the font used for that text is installed on your system; if the font is embedded or a subset is included in the PDF, you can change text attributes.

You may have noticed a few typos or other embarrassing errors in the conference guide. You'll make some corrections to the text now.

1   Go to page 6 (7 of 13). The heading "Conference Highlights" has an extra letter in it.

2   Open the Content panel in the Tools pane, and select the Edit Document Text tool. Acrobat loads system fonts, which may take a moment.

▶ **Tip:** There are other errors in the document, including a few apostrophes that shouldn't be there. If you want more text-editing practice, you can make changes on other pages, too.

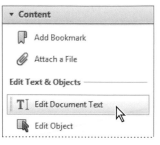

3   Select the word "Hightlights."

4   Type **Highlights**, and then click elsewhere on the page to deselect the text.

5   Go to page 1 (2 of 13), the table of contents page. To spice it up a little, you'll change the color of the title.

6   Select the Edit Document Text tool again, and then select the heading "Table of Contents."

7   Right-click (Windows) or Control-click (Mac OS) the text, and choose Properties.

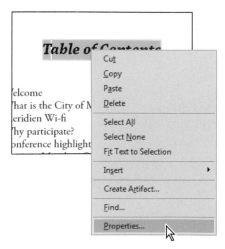

8 In the TouchUp Properties dialog box, select the Text tab.

9 Click the Fill color box, and then click Other Color.

10 In the color dialog box, select a color that matches a color in the bar across the bottom of the page. (We used a dark red.) Click OK, and then click Close to make the change.

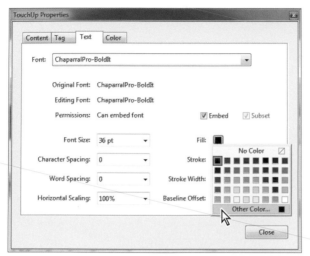

11 Choose File > Save to save your work.

● **Note:** You can save a PDF file as a Microsoft Word document. For information, see Lesson 5, "Using Acrobat with Microsoft Office Files (Windows)."

Copying text and images from a PDF file

Even if you no longer have access to the source file for a PDF document, you can reuse the text and images in other applications. For example, you might want to add some of the text or images to a web page. You can copy the text out of the PDF file in rich text format (RTF) or as accessible text so you can import it into a different authoring application for reuse. You can save images in the file in JPEG, TIF, or PNG format.

If you want to reuse only small amounts of text or one or two images, copy them to the clipboard or to an image format file using the Selection tool. (If the Copy, Cut, and Paste commands are unavailable, the creator of the PDF may have set restrictions on editing the content of the document.)

A marketing director has asked to use text from the conference guide in an email campaign. You'll copy the text for her.

1   Go to page 3 (4 of 13), and then select the Selection tool (I) in the Common Tools toolbar.

2   Move the pointer over the text on the page. Notice that the pointer changes when it is in text-selection mode.

3   Drag the Selection tool across the header and first two paragraphs to select the text.

4   Right-click or Control-click the text, and choose Copy With Formatting, which preserves the column layout.

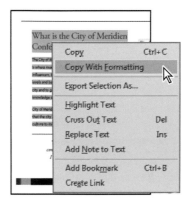

● **Note:** If you're unable to select text in a PDF file, the text may be part of an image. You can convert image text to text that can be selected by using the Recognize Text panel. For more information about text recognition, see Lesson 3.

5   Minimize the Acrobat window, open a new or existing document in an authoring application such as a text editor or Microsoft Word, and then choose Edit > Paste.

Your text is copied into the document in your authoring application. You can edit and format the text as you wish. If a font copied from a PDF document is not available on the system displaying the copied text, Acrobat substitutes the font.

You can copy individual images for use in another application using the Snapshot tool.

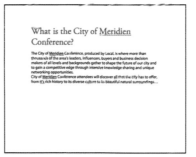

6   In the Acrobat document pane, click outside any selected text to deselect it.

7   Choose Edit > Take A Snapshot.

The Snapshot tool allows you to copy both text and images. However, the resulting image is in bitmap format, and any text it copies is not editable.

8   Drag to select the image of the woman selecting fruit. The image is copied to your clipboard. Click OK to clear the message box.

If you click anywhere on the page instead of dragging a marquee with the Snapshot tool selected, the entire page is copied to the clipboard.

9 Choose File > Create > PDF From Clipboard. Acrobat pastes the image into a new PDF file.

Note: You can export all the images in a PDF file to JPEG, PNG, TIFF, or JPEG2000 format by selecting Export All Images in the Document Processing panel. Each image is saved in a separate file.

10 Close any open documents in other applications, and your new PDF file, which you do not need to save. Leave Conference Guide_final.pdf open.

Editing images and other objects

In Acrobat Pro, you can use the Edit Object tool to make last-minute corrections to images and objects in an Adobe PDF document. For major revisions, use your original authoring application, and then regenerate the PDF document.

You can use the Edit Object tool context menu to perform some editing tasks on images without starting an external editing application. To open the context menu, right-click (Windows) or Control-click (Mac OS) the text using the TouchUp Object tool. Using the TouchUp Object tool, you can change how a document reflows and can affect accessibility. For example, changing the location of an object affects the order in which that object (or its alternate text) is read by a screen reader.

To edit an image or object with the Edit Object tool, select Edit Object in the Content panel. Then select an object, and right-click (Windows) or Control-click (Mac OS) the object, and then choose a command.

- Delete Clip deletes objects that are clipping the selected object. For example, if you scale text and the resulting characters are clipped, selecting this option shows you the complete characters.

- Create Artifact removes the object from the reading order so it isn't read by a screen reader or the Read Out Loud command.

- Edit Image, which appears when a bitmap image is selected, opens an editing program such as Adobe Photoshop.

- Edit Object, which appears when a vector object is selected, opens an editing program such as Adobe Illustrator.

- Properties lets you edit properties for the content, tag, and text, such as adding alternate text (Alt text) to an image to make it accessible.

Setting document properties and metadata

You're nearly done with this conference guide. To finish it off, you'll set the initial view, which determines what people see when they first open the file, and add metadata to the document.

1 Choose File > Properties.

2 In the Document Properties dialog box, click the Initial View tab.

3 From the Navigation Tab menu, choose Bookmarks Panel And Page. When the viewer opens the file, both the page and the bookmarks will be visible.

4 Select the Description tab.

The document's author has already entered some metadata for the file, including some keywords. Metadata is information about the document itself, and you can use it to search for documents. You'll add some more keywords.

5 In the Keywords field, after the existing keywords, type **; map; vendors**. Keywords must be separated by commas or semicolons.

6 Click OK to accept changes to the Document Properties dialog box.

7 Choose File > Save to save your work, and then close all open files and quit Acrobat.

Review questions

1 How can you change the order of pages in a PDF document?

2 How do you insert an entire PDF file into another PDF file?

3 How can you insert a video file into a PDF document?

4 What kinds of text attributes can you change from within Acrobat?

5 How do you copy text from a PDF file?

Review answers

1 You can change the page order by selecting the page thumbnails corresponding to the pages you want to move, and dragging them to their new locations in the Page Thumbnails panel.

2 To insert all the pages from a PDF file before or after any page in another PDF file, select Insert From File in the Pages panel, and then select the file you wish to insert.

3 To insert a video file, select Multimedia > Video in the Content panel, and then drag a video box on the page. Select the file you want to insert and specify any settings, such as when it plays and how viewers access controls.

4 You can use the Edit Document Text tool to change text formatting—font, size, color, letter spacing, and alignment—or to change the text itself.

5 If you're copying a couple of words or sentences, use the Selection tool to copy and paste the text into another application.

7 COMBINING FILES IN PDF PORTFOLIOS

Lesson overview

In this lesson, you'll do the following:

- Quickly and easily combine files of different types into one PDF Portfolio (Acrobat Pro only).

- Customize the look and feel of a PDF Portfolio.

- Share a PDF Portfolio.

- Search a PDF Portfolio.

- Modify an existing PDF Portfolio.

- Combine files into a single PDF file without creating a PDF Portfolio.

 This lesson will take approximately 45 minutes to complete. Copy the Lesson07 folder onto your hard drive if you haven't already done so.

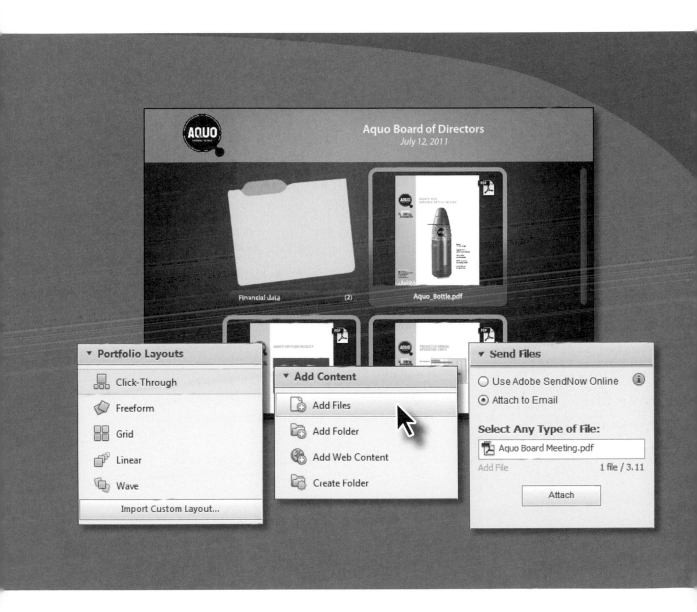

A PDF Portfolio brings together multiple documents—
in PDF or other formats—into a coherent document.
You can customize how the documents are presented
to viewers.

About PDF Portfolios

In Acrobat X Pro, you can assemble multiple files into an integrated PDF Portfolio. You can combine files of different formats, created in different applications, without converting them to PDF. For example, you could assemble all the documents for a specific project, including text documents, email messages, spreadsheets, CAD drawings, and PowerPoint presentations. The original files retain their individual identities, but are still part of the PDF Portfolio file. Each component file can be opened, read, edited, and formatted without affecting the other documents in the PDF Portfolio.

PDF Portfolios offer several advantages over files merged into an ordinary PDF file:

- You can add and remove component documents easily.

- You can quickly preview component files without having to pause for Open or Save dialog boxes.

- You can edit individual files within the PDF Portfolio without affecting the other files. You can also edit non-PDF files in their native applications from within a PDF Portfolio; any changes you make are saved to the file within the PDF Portfolio.

- You can share the PDF Portfolio with others and be sure they receive all the component parts.

- You can sort component files by categories that you can customize.

- You can print one, all, or any combination of components in the PDF Portfolio.

- You can search individual component documents or the entire PDF Portfolio, including non-PDF component files.

- You can add non-PDF files to an existing PDF Portfolio without converting them to PDF.

- You can make changes to component files without affecting the original source files, and the source files of a PDF Portfolio are not changed when you create the PDF file.

Creating a PDF Portfolio

In this lesson, you'll create a PDF Portfolio of documents for the board meeting of a fictitious beverage company. The PDF Portfolio will include a Microsoft Excel spreadsheet, a Microsoft Word document, a Microsoft PowerPoint presentation, and several PDF files. Later, you'll customize the PDF Portfolio with a header and a company logo.

1 Start Acrobat Pro.

2 In the Welcome screen, click Create PDF Portfolio.

The Create PDF Portfolio dialog box appears.

3 Select Linear for the Portfolio layout.

Acrobat Pro displays a preview and description of the selected layout. The Linear layout presents documents in the order you set. You can select other layouts to see how they present documents, and then select Linear again.

4 Click Add Files at the bottom of the dialog box.

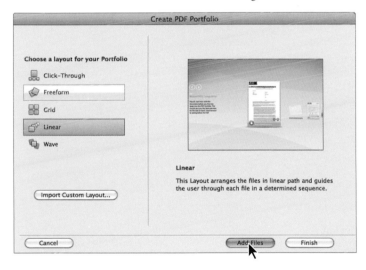

5 Navigate to the Lesson07 folder.

The folder contains an Excel spreadsheet, a PowerPoint presentation, a Word document, and several PDF files.

6 Select the Aquo_Bottle.pdf file, and click Open (Windows) or Finish (Mac OS).

Acrobat creates and opens the Portfolio1.pdf file, with Aquo_Bottle.pdf centered in the window.

The Acrobat application window changes to display options specific to working with PDF Portfolios.

7 Click Add Files in the Add Content panel in the Layout pane on the right side of the application window.

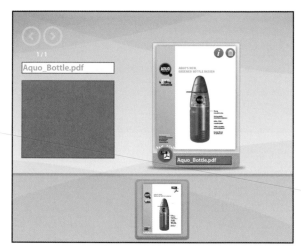
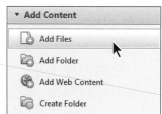

8 Navigate to the Lesson07 folder, and then Ctrl-click (Windows) or Command-click (Mac OS) to select the following files:

- Aquo_Building.pdf
- Aquo_Costs.pdf
- Aquo_Fin_Ana.xls
- Aquo_Fin_Data.pptx
- Aquo_Mkt_Summ.doc
- Aquo_Overview.pdf

9 Click Open to add the selected files to the PDF Portfolio.

When you add a file to a PDF Portfolio, a copy of the original document is included in the PDF file. Some file formats, such as TIFF, are natively supported by Acrobat and Reader. However, to see files in some formats, viewers need to have an application installed that supports the format. Which formats require supporting applications depends on the operating system the viewer is using. For example, if you include a PowerPoint presentation in your portfolio, a viewer using Windows XP must have PowerPoint installed to see it, but one using Windows Vista can view the presentation without having PowerPoint installed.

Organizing files in folders

You can add an entire folder to a PDF Portfolio, or you can combine existing files in a new folder. You'll create a folder for the financial data.

1 Select Create Folder in the Add Content panel.

2 Name the new folder **Financial data**, and click OK.

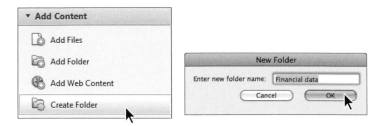

3 Click Details to open the Details pane. Acrobat displays the PDF Portfolio files in a table format, so you can see each file, in order, with its properties.

4 Drag the Aquo_Fin_Ana.xls and Aquo_Fin_Data.pptx files into the new folder.

▶ **Tip:** When you view a PDF Portfolio, double-click a component to preview it, and then click Open File in the upper-right corner to open the file itself.

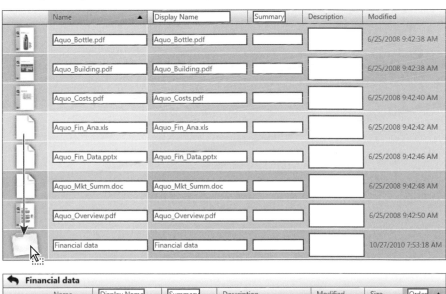

5 Choose File > Save As > PDF Portfolio. Name the PDF Portfolio **Aquo Board Meeting,** and click Save.

Adding descriptions to component files

You can add descriptions to files and folders in the PDF Portfolio to help viewers find the files they want.

1 Click in the Description column for the Financial data folder to create an insertion point.

2 Type **Financial analysis spreadsheet and financial presentation** in the description box.

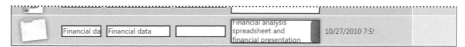

You'll move the folder to the top of the list to display it first in the PDF Portfolio.

3 Drag the Financial Data folder to the top of the list.

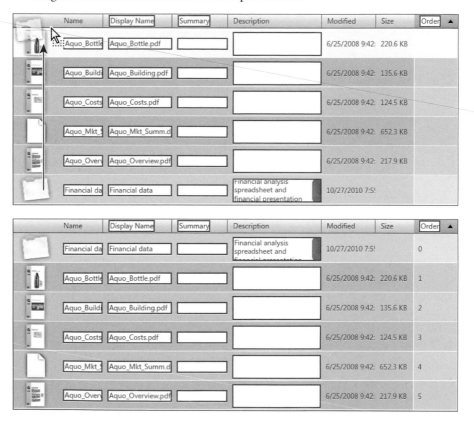

4 Click Layout to view the PDF Portfolio in the Linear layout again.

5 Click the information button (ⓘ) next to the folder name. Acrobat Pro displays information about the folder, including the description.

 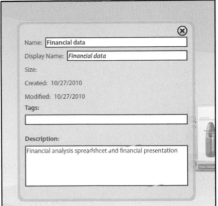

6 Close the information box to return to the main layout.

Customizing your PDF Portfolio

Acrobat Pro provides several options for customizing the look and feel of your PDF Portfolio. You'll choose a layout and select a color scheme to create a more professional-looking document. You'll also add a header with the company's logo to finish the look.

▶ **Tip:** To edit an existing PDF Portfolio, open it, and then click Edit in the PDF Portfolio toolbar.

Selecting a layout

Acrobat X Pro includes several layout options for PDF Portfolios. The layouts determine how component documents are displayed on the home page of the PDF Portfolio, and how the viewer navigates through the content. By default, the Click-Through layout is applied. You selected the Linear layout when you created the PDF Portfolio, but you can change your mind at any time. You'll preview the available layouts and choose one for this PDF Portfolio.

1 Select Click-Through in the Portfolio Layouts panel.

In the Click-Through layout, documents are displayed one at a time, in order, with a mini-navigator at the bottom of the screen that lets you select any document.

2 Click Preview at the top of the application window to see how the layout appears to someone viewing the PDF Portfolio. Use the arrows to navigate through the documents.

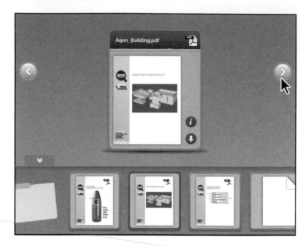

3 Click Edit in the PDF Portfolio toolbar at the top of the window to return to edit mode.

4 Select each of the other layouts, clicking Preview each time, to see how they display the documents in this PDF Portfolio.

5 Select Grid as the layout for this project. In the Grid layout, all the documents are visible in a grid.

Selecting a visual theme

You can further customize a PDF Portfolio by selecting which colors to use for text, backgrounds, and the cards that display component data. You'll select a theme that is appropriate for the board-meeting packet.

1 Open the Visual Themes panel. Modern is selected by default.

2 Select each theme to see how it changes the look of the PDF Portfolio.

3 Select Tech Office for this PDF Portfolio.

4 Open the Color Palettes panel. Click each palette to view it applied to the PDF Portfolio. Select the one you like best. We selected the first one.

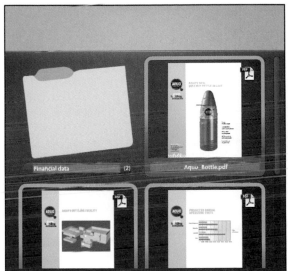

5 Choose File > Save Portfolio.

Adding a header

You can also add a header to your PDF Portfolio. The header appears at the top of the layout. You can include text and a graphic in the header. You'll add the company logo and the type and date of the meeting to the header.

1 Click the empty area at the top of the PDF Portfolio. The Header Properties panel appears at the bottom of the Layout pane.

2 From the Templates menu, choose Text And Image.

There are several header templates, including different text and graphic configurations.

3 Click Add Image in the Header Items area of the Header Properties panel.

4 Navigate to the Lesson07 folder, select Logo.gif, and click Open. The logo appears in the upper-left corner of the PDF Portfolio.

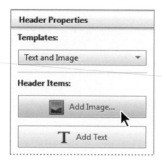
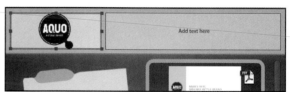

5 Double-click the Add Text Here panel on the right side of the header.

6 Type **Aquo Board of Directors**.

7 Press Enter or Return, and type **July 12, 2011**.

8 Select "Aquo Board of Directors." In the Textfield Properties panel, change the font size to 22, click the Bold button; then click the color swatch, and select white for the text color.

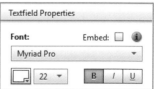

9 Select "July 12, 2011," increase the font size to 18 points, click the Italic button, and select white for the text color.

10 Click Preview to see the header at the top of the PDF Portfolio.

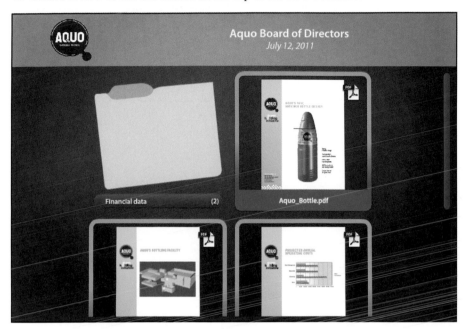

11 Choose File > Save Portfolio to save the file.

Viewing file details

The File Details view lists PDF Portfolio component files in table format, with columns such as file descriptions, size, and modification dates. To customize the columns that appear in the File Details view, select columns in the Details pane while in edit mode.

Sharing your PDF Portfolio

● **Note:** Recipients must have an Adobe ID (available free) to download a file from Acrobat.com. For details about uploading a PDF Portfolio file to Acrobat.com, see Adobe Acrobat X Help.

A PDF Portfolio is a PDF file, so you can share it any way you'd share any other PDF. You can simply save the file and transfer it to a recipient by email, on removable media such as a CD or DVD, or by uploading it to a server or website. However, Acrobat makes it even easier to share PDF Portfolios by email or by posting them to Acrobat.com, a secure web-based service. In this lesson, you'll email the PDF Portfolio to yourself.

1 Click Share to open the Share pane.

2 In the Share pane, choose Attach To Email.

3 Confirm that the Aquo Board Meeting.pdf file is listed as the file to send.

4 Click Attach. Your default email application opens, with a new message open. The PDF Portfolio file is included as an attachment.

5 Type your email address in the To line, and add a brief message and subject line.

6 Send the message.

Searching a PDF Portfolio

● **Note:** Acrobat can search any document in a PDF Portfolio as long as it can access the document on that computer. If you cannot preview a PDF Portfolio component because there is no supporting application installed, you also cannot search the component.

You can search for specific words in all the components of a PDF Portfolio, even those that aren't PDF files. You'll search for a quote by a particular person.

1 Click in the Search box on the right side of the PDF Portfolio toolbar.

2 Type **Schneider** to find a quote by the vice president of the company.

3 Click the binoculars icon (🔍).

The search results appear below the search box.

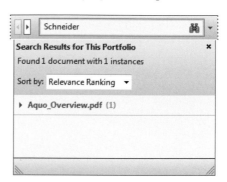

4 Click the listed document to expand it, and then click the instance that includes the name "Schneider" to open the document and highlight the word.

5 Close the PDF Portfolio and any other open files.

Combine files in a single PDF

Sometimes you may want to combine files into a single PDF file without creating a PDF Portfolio. In a merged PDF file, all documents are converted into PDF files and then merged into a single PDF file as sequential pages.

To create a merged PDF file:

1 Choose File > Create > Combine Files Into A Single PDF.

2 In the upper-right corner of the Combine Files dialog box, make sure that Single PDF is selected.

3 Click Add Files, and then select Add Files or Add Folders.

4 Select the files or folders you want to include, and click Open (Windows) or Add Files or Add Folders (Mac OS).

5 Arrange the files in the order you want them to appear in the merged PDF file. To reposition a file, select it and click Move Up or Move Down, or drag it into position.

6 If you want to include only some of the pages of a document, select the file, and click Choose Pages. Then select the pages you want to include.

7 Click Options to specify conversion settings, including whether to add bookmarks or enable accessibility features.

8 Specify a file size by clicking a page icon.

The Small File Size option uses compression and resolution settings that are appropriate for onscreen display. The Default File Size option creates PDF files for business printing and viewing onscreen. The Larger File Size option uses High Quality Print conversion settings.

9 Click Combine Files.

A status dialog box shows the progress of the file conversions. Some source applications may start and close automatically during the process.

Review questions

1   Name three advantages to creating a PDF Portfolio.

2   Do you need to convert documents to PDF to include them in a PDF Portfolio?

3   How can you edit an existing PDF Portfolio?

4   True or False: You can search all documents in a PDF Portfolio, even non-PDF components.

Review answers

1   PDF Portfolios provide several advantages:

   - You can add and remove component documents easily, including non-PDF files.

   - You can preview component files quickly.

   - You can edit individual files within the PDF Portfolio independently.

   - PDF Portfolios contain all their components, so you can share them easily.

   - You can sort component files by categories and arrange them in the order you want.

   - You can print one, all, or any combination of components in the PDF Portfolio.

   - You can search the entire PDF Portfolio, including non-PDF component files.

   - You can make changes to component files without affecting the original source files, and the source files of a PDF Portfolio are not changed when you create the PDF file.

2   No. You can combine any documents in a PDF Portfolio, and they remain in their original format.

3   To edit a PDF Portfolio, click Edit in the PDF Portfolio toolbar.

4   True. Acrobat can search any document in a PDF Portfolio, as long as an application that can open the file is present on the computer.

8 ADDING SIGNATURES AND SECURITY

Lesson overview

In this lesson, you'll do the following:

- Use Adobe Reader in Protected Mode (Windows only).

- Apply password protection to a file to restrict who can open it.

- Apply a password to prevent others from printing or changing a PDF file.

- Certify a document.

- Create a digital ID that includes an image.

- Digitally sign documents.

 This lesson will take approximately 45 minutes to complete. Copy the Lesson08 folder onto your hard drive if you haven't already done so.

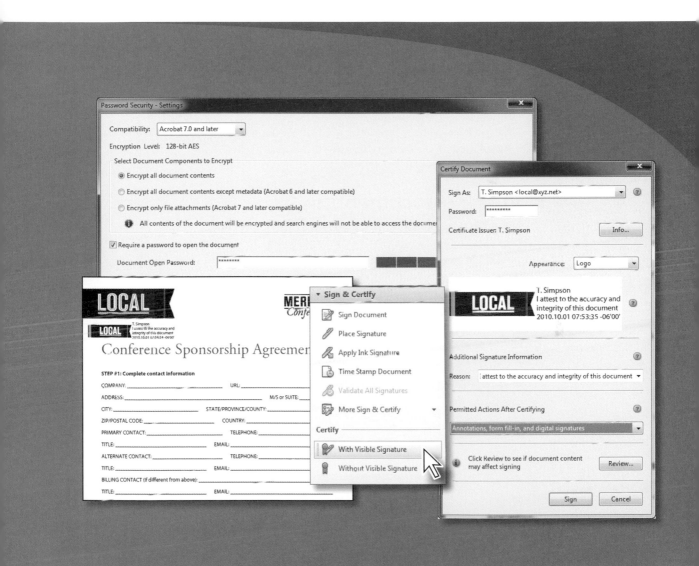

You can keep your PDF documents secure through password protection, certification, and digital signatures.

Getting started

Acrobat X provides several tools to help you secure your PDF documents. You can use passwords to prevent unauthorized users from opening, printing, or editing PDF files. You can use a certificate to encrypt PDF documents so that only an approved list of users can open them. You can also digitally sign a PDF document to indicate your approval, or certify a PDF document to approve its contents. If you want to save security settings for later use, you can create a security policy that stores security settings. In Acrobat Pro, you can also permanently remove sensitive content from your PDF documents using the Redaction feature (see Lesson 12, "Using the Legal Features").

First you'll learn about Protected Mode in Adobe Reader for Windows, and then you'll work with the security features in Acrobat itself.

Viewing documents in Protected Mode (Windows only)

By default, Adobe Reader X for Windows opens PDF files in Protected Mode (known as "sandboxing" to IT professionals). In Protected Mode, Reader confines any processes to the application itself, so that potentially malicious PDF files do not have access to your computer and its system files.

1 Open Adobe Reader X in Windows.

2 Choose File > Open, and navigate to the Lesson08 folder.

3 Select Travel Guide.pdf, and click Open.

The Travel Guide.pdf file opens in Adobe Reader. You can access all of the Reader menus and tools. However, the PDF file cannot make calls to your system outside the Reader environment.

4 Choose File > Properties.

5 In the Document Properties dialog box, click the Advanced tab.

6 View the Protected Mode status at the bottom of the dialog box. It's On by default.

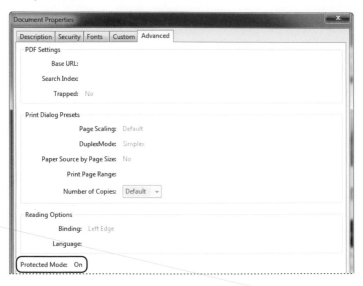

You can always confirm that a document is open in Protected Mode by viewing the Document Properties dialog box.

7 Click OK to close the Document Properties dialog box. Then, close the Travel Guide.pdf file, and quit Reader.

Adobe strongly recommends that you use Adobe Reader in Protected Mode. However, accessibility features may not work in Adobe Reader in Windows XP when Protected Mode is enabled. Additionally, some third-party plug-ins may not work in Protected Mode. If you need to disable Protected Mode, choose Edit > Preferences, select General from the list of categories, and deselect Enable Protected Mode At Startup. You'll need to restart Adobe Reader for the changes to take effect.

About security

You can secure a PDF using any of the following security methods:

• Add passwords and set security options to restrict opening, editing, and printing PDFs.

• Encrypt a document so that only a specified set of users has access to it.

- Save the PDF as a certified document. Certifying a PDF adds a certifying signature (which may be visible or invisible) that lets the document author restrict changes to the document.

- Apply server-based security policies to PDFs (for example, using Adobe LiveCycle Rights Management). Server-based security policies are especially useful if you want others to have access to PDFs for a limited time.

You can also use security envelopes to protect your PDF documents in transit, as outlined in the "Exploring on your own" section at the end of this lesson.

Securing PDFs in FIPS mode (Windows)

Acrobat and Reader (version 8.1 and later) provide a FIPS mode to restrict data protection to Federal Information Processing Standard (FIPS) 140-2 approved algorithms using the RSA BSAFE Crypto-C 2.1 encryption module.

The following options are not available in FIPS mode:

- Applying password-based security policies to documents. You can use public key certificates or Adobe LiveCycle Rights Management to secure the document, but you cannot use password encryption to secure the document.

- Creating self-signed certificates. In FIPS mode, you cannot create self-signed certificates. In FIPS mode, you can open and view documents that are protected with non-FIPS compliant algorithms, but you cannot save any changes to the document using password security. To apply security policies to the document, use either public key certificates or LiveCycle Rights Management

Viewing security settings

When you open a document that has restricted access or some type of security applied to it, you'll see a Security Settings button (🔒) in the navigation pane to the left of the document window.

1 Start Acrobat. Then choose File > Open, navigate to the Lesson08 folder, and open the Sponsor_secure.pdf file. If the Acrobat Security Settings dialog box appears, click Cancel.

2 Open the Sign & Certify panel in the Tools pane, and notice that the commands are dimmed.

3 Open the Annotations panel in the Comment pane, and notice that the commenting and text markup tools are also unavailable.

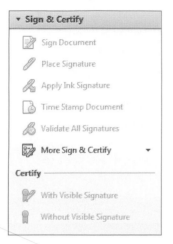

4 Click the Security Settings button (🔒) in the navigation pane to view the security settings. Click the Permission Details link to view more detail.

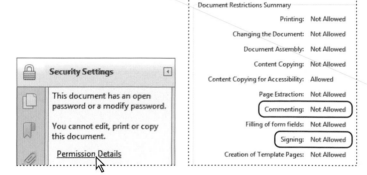

The Document Properties dialog box lists each action and whether it is allowed. As you read down the list, you'll see that signing and commenting are not allowed, which is why the related tools are dimmed.

5 When you have finished reviewing the information, click Cancel to close the Document Properties dialog box.

6 Choose File > Close to close the Sponsor_secure.pdf file.

Adding security to PDF files

You can add security to your Adobe PDF files when you first create them, or you can add it later. You can even add security to files that you receive from someone else, unless the creator of the document has limited who can change security settings.

Now, you'll add password protection to limit who can open your document and who can change the security settings.

Adding passwords

You can add two kinds of passwords to protect your Adobe PDF documents. A Document Open password allows only users who enter the password to open the document. A Permissions password allows only users who enter the password to change the permissions for the document, so that they can print or modify the document or perform other changes you've restricted.

You'll add protection to a logo file so that no one can change its contents and so that unauthorized users can't open and use the file.

1   Choose File > Open, navigate to the Lesson08 folder, and open the Local_Logo.pdf file.

There is no Security Settings button in the navigation pane, because no security has been applied to this document.

2   Choose File > Save As > PDF, name the file **Local_Logo1.pdf,** and save it in the Lesson08 folder.

3   Open the Protection panel in the Tools pane.

4   In the Protection panel, click Encrypt, and choose 2 Encrypt With Password. Click Yes when Acrobat asks whether you want to add security to the document.

The Password Security – Settings dialog box opens automatically.

First you'll set the compatibility level. The default compatibility level is compatibility with Acrobat 7.0 or later. If you're sure that all your viewers have Acrobat 7.0 or later, use that setting. If you think that some of your viewers may still be using earlier versions of Acrobat, select an earlier version. Be aware, however, that this may use a lower encryption level.

5   Choose Acrobat 7.0 And Later from the Compatibility menu, if it's not already selected.

6 Select the Require A Password To Open The Document option, and then type **Logo1234;^bg** for the password.

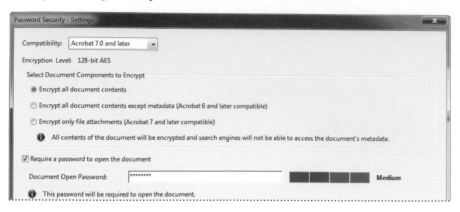

Tip: Always record your passwords in a secure location. If you forget your password, you can't recover it from the document. You might also want to store an unprotected copy of the document in a secure location.

Acrobat rates the password's strength. Stronger passwords include both uppercase and lowercase letters, numbers, punctuation marks, and symbols. Longer passwords also tend to be harder to guess. If it's critical that a document remain confidential, use a strong password. You'll share this password with anyone who you want to allow to open the document. Remember that passwords are case-sensitive.

Now you'll add a second password that controls who is allowed to change printing, editing, and security settings for the file.

7 Under Permissions, select Restrict Editing And Printing Of The Document, and type **Logo5678;^bg** as a second password. Your open password and permissions password can't be the same.

8 From the Printing Allowed menu, choose Low Resolution (150 dpi). You can prohibit printing, allow only low-resolution printing, or allow high-resolution printing.

9 From the Changes Allowed menu, choose Commenting, Filling In Form Fields, And Signing Existing Signature Fields to allow users to comment on the logo. You can prohibit all changes, some changes, or only prohibit viewers from extracting pages.

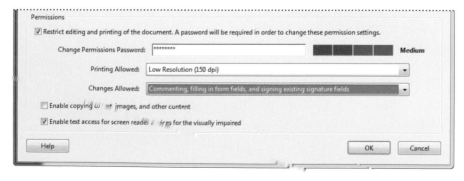

10 Click OK to apply your changes.

11 In the first dialog box, re-enter the Open Password, **Logo1234;^bg**. Then click OK, and click OK again to clear the alert box.

12 In the next dialog box, re-enter the Permissions Password, **Logo5678;^bg**. Then click OK, and click OK again to clear the alert box.

Notice that the security changes don't take effect until you save the file.

13 Choose File > Save to save the security changes.

14 Click the Security Settings button (🔒) in the navigation pane, and then click the Permission Details link. The limitations you set are in effect.

15 Click OK to close the Document Properties dialog box, and then choose File > Close to close the Local_Logo1.pdf file.

Document Restrictions Summary

Printing:	Allowed
Changing the Document:	Not Allowed
Document Assembly:	Not Allowed
Content Copying:	Not Allowed
Content Copying for Accessibility:	Allowed
Page Extraction:	Allowed
Commenting:	Allowed
Filling of form fields:	Allowed
Signing:	Allowed
Creation of Template Pages:	Allowed

Opening password-protected files

Now you'll check the security that you've added to your file.

1 Choose File > Open, and open the Local_Logo1.pdf file in the Lesson08 folder.

Acrobat prompts you to enter the required password to open the file.

2 Enter the password (**Logo1234;^bg**), and click OK.

Notice that "(SECURED)" has been appended to the filename at the top of the application window.

Now you'll test the permissions password.

3 Click the Security Settings button (🔒) in the navigation pane and click the Permission Details link.

4 In the Document Properties dialog box, try changing the Security Method from Password Security to No Security.

Acrobat prompts you to enter the Permissions password.

5 Enter the password (**Logo5678;^bg**), and click OK, and then click OK again.

All restrictions are now removed from the file.

6 Click OK to close the Document Properties dialog box.

7 Choose File > Close, and close the file without saving the changes. Because you aren't saving your changes, the passwords remain in effect next time you open the file.

About digital signatures

A digital signature, like a conventional handwritten signature, identifies the person signing a document. Unlike a handwritten signature, a digital signature is difficult to forge because it contains encrypted information that is unique to the signer and easily verified.

Signing a document electronically offers several advantages, not least of which is that you can email the signed document rather than having to fax it or send it by courier. Although digitally signing a document doesn't necessarily prevent people from changing the document, it does allow you to track any changes made after the signature is added and revert to the signed version if necessary. (You can prevent users from changing your document by applying appropriate security to the document.)

To sign a document, you must obtain a digital ID from a third-party provider or create a digital ID (self-signed digital ID) for yourself in Acrobat. The digital ID contains a private key that is used to add the digital signature and a certificate that you share with those who need to validate your signature.

For information about Adobe security partners that offer third-party digital IDs and other security solutions, visit the Adobe website at www.adobe.com.

Creating digital signatures

For this lesson, you'll use a self-signed digital ID, which is often adequate for signing documents within a corporate environment. You can set the appearance of your digital signature, select your preferred signing method, and determine how digital signatures are verified in the Security preferences. You should also set your preferences to optimize Acrobat for validating signatures before you open a signed document.

Adding images to your digital signatures

First you'll add the company logo to your signature block.

1 Choose Edit > Preferences (Windows) or Acrobat > Preferences (Mac OS), and select Security from the categories on the left.

2 In the Digital Signatures area of the dialog box, click New to open the Configure Signature Appearance dialog box.

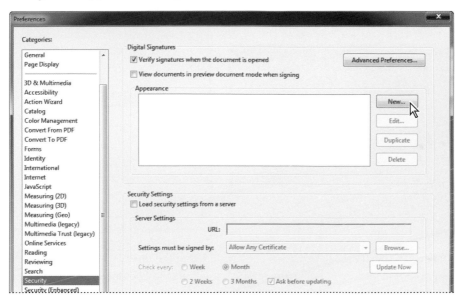

This is where you can personalize your digital signature by adding a graphic and specifying which information appears. The Preview pane shows the default digital signature appearance, which is text-based.

First you'll name the appearance of your signature and then add a corporate logo to the signature block.

3 In the Title text box, type **Logo**. When you name a signature appearance, use a name that is easy to associate with the contents of the appearance. You can create several digital signatures for yourself.

4 In the Configure Graphic section of the dialog box, select Imported Graphic, and click File.

5 In the Select Picture dialog box, click Browse, navigate to the Lesson08 folder, and select the Local_Logo.pdf file. Supported file types are listed in the Files Of Type (Windows) or Show (Mac OS) menu. Click Open (Windows) or Select (Mac OS), and then click OK to return to the Configure Signature Appearance dialog box.

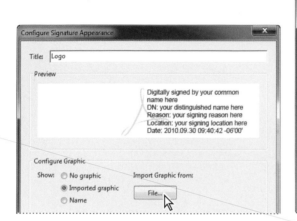

Now you'll specify the information to be included in the text block of your signature. You'll include your name, the reason for signing the document, and the date.

6 In the Configure Text area of the Configure Signature Appearance dialog box, leave Name, Date, and Reason selected. Deselect all the other options.

7 When you're happy with the preview of your signature block, click OK.

8 In the Preferences dialog box, select View Documents In Preview Document Mode When Signing.

9 Click Advanced Preferences, and click the Creation tab. Select the Show Reasons When Signing option, and click OK.

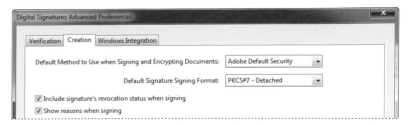

Signing in Preview Document mode

Use the Preview Document mode when you want to analyze a document for content that may alter the appearance of the document after you sign it. Such content may include transparency, scripts, fonts, and other dynamic content that can alter a document's appearance. The Preview Document mode suppresses this dynamic content, allowing you to view and sign the document in a static and secure state.

When you view a PDF in Preview Document mode, a document message bar lets you know whether the PDF complies with the PDF/SigQ Level A or Level B specification. Level A indicates that the document contains no dynamic content that can alter its appearance. Level B indicates that the document contains dynamic content that can be suppressed during signing. If the document doesn't comply with Level A or B, you may want to refrain from signing the document and contact the document author about the problem.

Acrobat automatically runs the Document Integrity Checker, which checks for Qualified Signatures conformance, before entering Preview Document mode.

You opt to use the Preview Document mode in the Security preferences.

Selecting a signing method

Now you'll specify a default signing method.

1 Click the Advanced Preferences button in the Security preferences dialog box again.

In the Verification tab of the Digital Signatures Advanced Preferences dialog box, notice that the Require Certificate Revocation Checking To Succeed Whenever Possible During Signature Verification option is selected. This ensures that certificates are always checked against a list of excluded certificates during validation.

2 Make sure Use The Document-Specified Method. Prompt If It is Not Available. (the first option) is selected. You'll be prompted if you don't have the necessary software when you try to open a document.

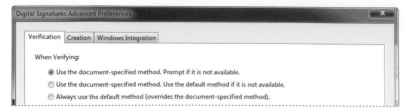

Also in the Verification tab is a pop-up menu enabling you to choose the default method for verifying signatures. This menu is dimmed unless you change the method used for verification by selecting a different radio button. You set the default method to be used when signing and encrypting documents in the Creation tab.

3 Click the Creation tab and make sure that Adobe Default Security is selected from the Default Method To Use When Signing And Encrypting Documents menu.

In Windows, the Windows Integration tab contains options for specifying whether identities from Windows Certificates can be imported and whether all root certificates in the Windows Certificates can be trusted. We recommend that you leave the default settings in this tab.

4 Click OK, and click OK again to close the Preferences dialog box.

Creating digital IDs

A digital ID is similar to a driver's license or passport. It proves your identity to people with whom you communicate electronically. A digital ID usually contains your name and email address, the name of the company that issued your digital ID, a serial number, and an expiration date.

A digital ID lets you create a digital signature or decrypt a PDF document that has been encrypted. You can create more than one digital ID to reflect different roles in your life. For this exercise, you'll create a digital ID for T. Simpson, an employee of *the* fictitious *Local Magazine*.

First, you *ll open* the draft of the travel guide document that you'll be signing.

1   Choose File > Open. Navigate to the Lesson08 folder, select Travel Guide.pdf, and click Open. Then choose File > Save As > PDF, rename the file **Travel Guide1.pdf**, and save it in the Lesson08 folder.

2   Open the Protection panel in the Tools pane.

3   Click More Protection, and then choose Security Settings.

4   In the Security Settings dialog box, select Digital IDs in the left pane. Then click the Add ID button ().

You'll create a self-signed digital ID. With a self-signed ID, you share your signature information with other users using a public certificate. (A certificate is a confirmation of your digital ID and contains information used to protect data.) While this method is adequate for most unofficial exchanges, a more secure approach is to obtain a digital ID from a third-party provider.

5   In the Add Digital ID dialog box, select A New Digital ID I Want To Create Now. Then click Next.

If you're working in Mac OS, skip to step 7. If you're working in Windows, you'll choose where to store your digital ID. The PKCS#12 Digital ID File option stores the information in a file that you can share with others. A Windows Default Certificate Digital ID is stored in the Windows Certificate Store. Because you want to easily share your digital ID with colleagues, you'll use the PKCS#12 option.

6   Make sure that New PKCS#12 Digital File ID is selected, and click Next.

Now you'll enter your personal information.

7   Enter the name you want to appear in the Signatures tab and in any signature field that you complete, and enter a corporate or organization name (if necessary) and an email address. We entered **T. Simpson** for the name, **Local Magazine** for the Organization Name, and **local@xyz.net** for the email address. Make sure that you select a Country/Region. We used the default US - United States.

8 Choose 1024-bit RSA from the Key Algorithm menu to set the level of security. Although 2048-bit RSA offers more security protection, it is not as universally compatible as 1024-bit RSA.

Now you'll specify what the encryption applies to. You can use the digital ID to control digital signatures, data encryption (security), or both. When you use a digital ID to encrypt a PDF document, you specify a list of recipients from your Trusted Identities, and you define the recipient's level of access to the file—for example, whether the recipients can edit, copy, or print the files. You can also encrypt documents using security policies.

For this exercise, you'll choose digital signatures.

9 From the Use Digital ID For menu, choose Digital Signatures, and then click Next.

Now you'll save and safeguard your information.

10 Accept the default location for the digital ID file. Then enter **Local1234;^bg** as the password. Re-enter your password to confirm it. Remember that the password is case-sensitive. Be sure to make a note of your password and keep it in a safe place. You cannot use or access your digital ID without this password.

11 Click Finish to save the digital ID file in the Security folder.

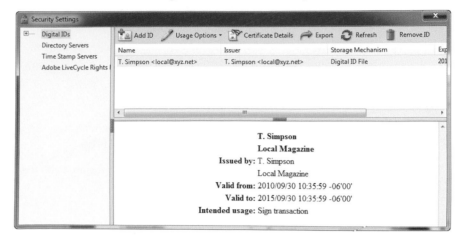

Your new digital ID appears in the Security Settings dialog box. In Windows, select the digital ID to see its details. In Mac OS, double-click it to view the certificate details. When you've finished checking your digital ID, close the dialog box.

Sharing certificates with others

Your digital ID includes a certificate that others require to validate your digital signature and to encrypt documents for you. If you know that others will need your certificate, you can send it in advance to avoid delays when exchanging secure documents. Businesses that use certificates to identify participants in secure workflows often store certificates on a directory server that participants can search to expand their list of trusted identities.

If you use a third-party security method, you usually don't need to share your certificate with others. Third-party providers may validate identities using other methods or these validation methods may be integrated with Acrobat. See the documentation provided by the third-party provider.

When you receive a certificate from someone, their name is added to your list of trusted identities as a contact. Contacts are usually associated with one or more certificates and can be edited, removed, or associated with another certificate. If you trust a contact, you can set your trust settings to trust all digital signatures and certified documents created with their certificate.

You can also import certificates from a certificate store, such as the Windows certificate store. A certificate store may contain numerous certificates issued by different certification authorities.

Signing a document digitally

Because you want the graphic designers to know that the changes to this document are approved and you want them to be sure that no additional changes have been made since the time you approved it, you'll create a visible signature field and sign the document.

1 Open the Sign & Certify panel in the Tools pane.

2 Select Sign Document in the Sign & Certify panel. Acrobat reminds you that you need to create a signature field. Click OK to close the alert box.

3 Drag to create a signature field. We dragged a signature field in the area above the map.

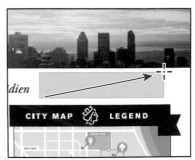

Acrobat automatically switches into Preview mode, which analyzes the document for content that may alter the document's appearance and then suppresses that content, enabling you to view and sign the document in a static and secure state.

4 In the preview toolbar across the top of the document window, click Sign Document.

5 In the Sign Document dialog box, enter the password associated with the ID in the Sign As text box, **Local1234;^bg**.

6 Choose Logo from the Appearance menu.

7 Choose I Am Approving This Document from the Reason pop-up menu.

8 Click Sign to apply your signature, and click Save to save the signed file. Click Yes or Replace when prompted to replace the original file.

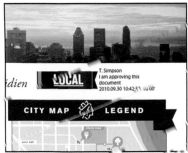

The recipient of the signed document will need your signer's certificate to validate the digital signature.

Modifying signed documents

Now you'll add a comment to the signed document to show how the digital signature information changes. But first you'll look at the signatures panel to see what a valid signature looks like.

1 Click the Signatures button in the navigation pane to display the Signatures panel. If necessary, drag the right margin of the Signatures panel so that you can see all the signature information. Expand the signature line, and expand the Signature Details entry.

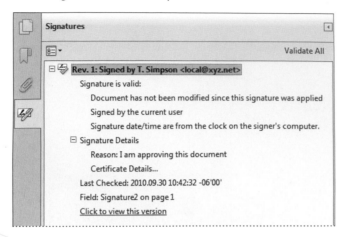

Now you'll add a note to the document and see how the addition changes the digital signature.

2 Select the Sticky Note tool (💬) in the Quick Tools toolbar.

3 Click anywhere on the document page to add a note. In the note, type **Good work.**

▶ **Tip:** Use the Signature panel to review the change history of a document or to track changes when a document is signed using multiple digital signature IDs.

Expand the signature again in the Signatures pane. The signature status has changed with the addition of a note .

Now you'll validate the signature.

4 Right-click (Windows) or Control-click (Mac OS) the signature box in the document pane, and choose Validate Signature.

5 The alert box explains that although the signature is valid, a change has been made. Click Close to close the warning box.

6 Right-click (Windows) or Control-click (Mac OS) the signature box in the document pane, and choose View Signed Version.

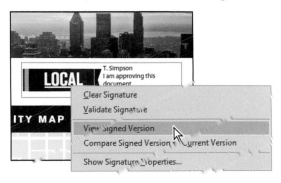

Tip: Right-click (Windows) or Control-click (Mac OS) the signature box in the document pane, and choose Show Signature Properties to resolve any issues with the signature

The View Signed Version option recovers the unchanged file. If a document has signatures on multiple versions of the document, for example, you can view any previously signed version of the document by selecting the signature in the Signatures pane and then choosing View Signed Version from the options menu.

7 Close both open PDF files. You do not need to save your work.

Certifying PDF files

▶ **Tip:** Before you distribute a document that you intend others to sign or fill in, you should enable usage rights for Adobe Reader users (choose File > Save As > Reader Extended PDF > Enable Additional Features).

You can also certify the contents of a PDF document. Certifying a document rather than signing it is useful if you want the user to be able to make approved changes to a document. When you certify a document and a user makes approved changes, the certification is still valid. You can certify forms, for example, to guarantee that the content is valid when the user receives the form. As the creator of the form, you can specify what tasks the user can perform. For example, you can specify that readers can fill in the form fields without invalidating the document. However, if a user tries to add or remove a form field or a page, the certification will be invalidated.

Now you'll certify a form to be sent to sponsors of a conference. By certifying the form, you are sure that the sponsors fill out the form as you designed it, with no additions or deletions to the form fields.

1   Choose File > Open, navigate to the Lesson08 folder, and open the Sponsor.pdf file.

For information on the Forms message bar, see Lesson 10, "Working with Forms in Acrobat."

2   Choose File > Properties, and click the Security tab.

The information in the Document Properties dialog box shows that no security and no restrictions have been applied to the document.

3   Click Cancel to close the Document Properties dialog box without making any changes.

4   Open the Sign & Certify panel in the Tools pane, and then select With Visible Signature in the Certify area of the panel.

5   Click Drag New Signature Rectangle. Click OK in the Save As Certified Document dialog box, and then click OK in the informational dialog box.

You'll use the digital ID that you created earlier in the lesson to certify the file.

6   Drag anywhere in the document to create a signature field. We created a signature field in the upper-left corner, below the Local logo.

7 Click the Sign Document button on the document message bar.

8 In the Certify Document dialog box, if you have created more than one digital ID, select the digital ID to use. We selected T. Simpson.

9 Enter the password, **Local1234;^bg**.

10 Choose Logo from the Appearance pop-up menu.

11 From the Reason menu, choose I Attest To The Accuracy And Integrity Of This Document.

12 From the Permitted Actions After Certifying menu, choose Annotations, Form Fill-In, And Digital Signatures.

13 Click Sign to complete the certification process.

14 Save your file as **Sponsor_Cert.pdf**.

15 Click the Signatures button (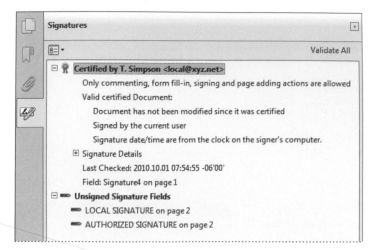) in the navigation pane to open the Signatures panel, and review which actions the certification allows. You may need to expand the certification entry.

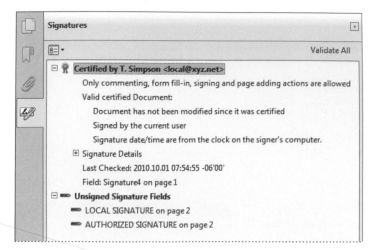

16 When you've finished reviewing the certification information, close the Signatures panel.

Signing certified documents

Now you'll sign the document that you just certified to verify that filling in a signature field doesn't invalidate the certification.

1 Go to page 2 in the document.

2 With the Hand tool selected, click in the Local Signature box at the bottom of the document. Then click the Sign Document button on the document message bar.

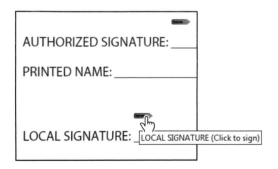

3 In the dialog box, if you have more than one digital ID defined, select your digital ID. We selected T. Simpson.

4 Enter the password, **Local1234;^bg**.

5 Leave the other values, click Sign, and save the file in the Lesson08 folder using the same filename. Click Yes or Replace to replace the original file.

6 Click the Signatures button in the navigation pane, and expand the certification entry marked with the blue ribbon icon.

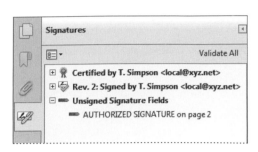 

Notice that the certification is still valid even though a signature has been added.

7 Choose File > Close.

Exploring on your own: Using security envelopes

In Acrobat, you can attach files to a PDF document and encrypt only the file attachments. In this case, the PDF document in which the file attachments are embedded functions as a security envelope. Anyone can open the security envelope and view the cover page and even a list of contents, but the attachments can only be opened as defined by the security you apply. When the attachments are opened and saved, they are identical to the original. No encryption is applied.

Suppose that you want to send a copy of the travel guide draft to a satellite office. The draft is confidential at this point, so you want to be sure that no unauthorized person intercepts and opens it. To ensure this, you'll create a security envelope, attach the document to it, and apply security. You'll use the wizard to walk you through the process; however, you can also create security envelopes manually.

1 In Acrobat, open the Travel Guide.pdf file.

2 Open the Protection panel in the Tools pane.

3 In the Protection panel, click More Protection, and then choose Create Security Envelope

4 In the Create Security Envelope dialog box, the Travel Guide.pdf file is listed. Select it, and then click Next.

If you wanted to add files, you could click the Add File To Send button. In the Files To Enclose dialog box, browse to select the file or files to add. Note that you can add non-PDF files and that you can add more than one file. If you want to experiment with adding non-PDF files, try adding some of the lesson files from the Lesson03 folder.

5 Select the eEnvelope With Date Stamp template from the list of available templates. Then click Next.

6 For the delivery method, select Send The Envelope Now. Click Next, and then click Yes to close the message box.

7 In the Security Policy dialog box, first select Show All Policies. The policies available to you are listed. Select Encrypt With Password. Click Next.

8 Complete the Identity panel, and click Next, if you haven't already established an identity.

9 Click Finish.

Now you'll choose your security settings.

10 In the Password Security - Settings dialog box, use the default setting for the compatibility level and the document contents to encrypt, and set a password requirement for opening the documents.

11 Click OK, and re-enter the password when prompted.

After you complete this process, Acrobat launches your default email program and creates an email message with the security envelope attached. Send the email to yourself to see what the finished product looks like. (In Mac OS you may need to save, close, and reopen the file before Acrobat launches the email program.)

12 When you are finished, close any open files, and quit Acrobat.

Review questions

1 Where do you change the appearance of your digital signature?

2 Can you create multiple digital signatures?

3 Why would you want to apply password protection to a PDF file?

4 Why would you apply permissions protection?

Review answers

1 You change the appearance of your digital signature in the Configure Signature Appearance dialog box. You can access this dialog box from the Security Preferences dialog box. You can also change the appearance of your digital signature in the Sign Document dialog box during the signing process.

2 You can have numerous digital signatures. You can create different digital signatures for the different roles that you perform. You can have different signatures for use on corporate documents, personal documents, documents related to volunteer activities, and so on.

3 If you have a confidential document that you don't want others to read, you can apply password protection. Only users with whom you share your password will be able to open the document.

4 Permissions protection limits how a user can use or reuse the contents of your Adobe PDF file. For example, you can specify that users cannot print the contents of your file, or copy and paste the contents of your file. Permission protection allows you to share the content of your file without losing control over how it is used.

9 USING ACROBAT IN A REVIEW CYCLE

Lesson overview

In this lesson, you'll do the following:

- Discover multiple ways to use Acrobat in a document review process.

- Annotate a PDF file with the Acrobat commenting and markup tools.

- View, reply to, search, and summarize document comments.

- Initiate a shared review.

- Initiate live collaboration.

 This lesson will take approximately 60 minutes to complete. Copy the Lesson09 folder onto your hard drive if you haven't already done so.

Robust commenting tools and collaboration features in Acrobat keep review cycles efficient and make it easy for stakeholders to give feedback.

About the review process

There are several ways to use Acrobat in a document review process. No matter which method you use, the workflow contains some core elements: the review initiator invites participants and makes the document available to them, reviewers comment, and the initiator gathers and works with those comments.

You can share any PDF document by email, on a network server, or on a website, and ask individuals to comment on it using Adobe Reader, Acrobat Standard, or Acrobat Pro. If you post the document or email it manually, you'll need to keep track of returned comments and merge them on your own. If you're requesting feedback from only one or two other people, this might be the most efficient way for you to work. For most reviews, however, you can gather comments more efficiently using a managed review process. Additionally, in a shared review or live collaboration, reviewers can see and respond to each others' comments.

When you initiate an email-based review in Acrobat, a wizard helps you send the PDF file as an email attachment, track responses, and manage the comments you receive. Anyone with Acrobat 6 or later can add comments to the PDF file. You can also enable reviewers using Adobe Reader 7 and later to add comments.

When you initiate a shared review in Acrobat, a wizard helps you post the PDF file to a network folder, WebDAV folder, SharePoint workspace, or Acrobat.com, a free, secure web-based service. Through the wizard, you email invitations to reviewers, who then access the shared document, add comments, and read others' comments using Acrobat or Reader. You can set a deadline for the review, after which no reviewers can publish additional comments.

Using Acrobat, you can also initiate live collaboration, through which you hold a virtual meeting specifically connected to a single document. You or other participants can simultaneously move the document on all participants' screens at once, so that you are all literally on the same page.

Getting started

In this lesson, you'll add comments to a PDF document, view and manage comments, and initiate a shared review. By definition, collaboration requires you to work with other people. Therefore, many of the exercises in this lesson will be more meaningful if you work through them with one or more colleagues or friends. However, if you are working independently, you can complete the exercises using alternative email addresses, which are available free through websites such as Gmail.com and Yahoo.com. (See the legal agreements on email websites to determine how you may use their email addresses).

First, open the document you'll work with.

1 In Acrobat, choose File > Open.

2 Navigate to the Lesson09 folder, and double-click the Curetall_Protocol.pdf file.

Adding comments to a PDF document

You can add comments to any PDF file, unless security has been applied to the document to prohibit commenting. In most cases, you'll use the commenting features to provide feedback to a document's author, but you may also find them useful to write notes to yourself as you're reading documents. Acrobat includes several commenting tools, and you'll recognize some of them from the physical world. For example, the Sticky Note and Highlight Text tools are electronic versions of the physical tools you may have on your desk.

In this exercise, you'll use some of the commenting tools to provide feedback on a medical-trial protocol document.

About the commenting tools

Acrobat provides several commenting and markup tools, designed for different commenting tasks. Most comments include two parts: the markup or icon that appears on the page, and a text message that appears in a pop-up note when you select the comment.

The commenting and markup tools are in the Annotations and Drawing Markups panels in the Comment pane. For detailed information about using each tool, see Adobe Acrobat X Help.

- **Sticky Note tool** (⬭) – Create sticky notes, just as you would in the physical world. Click wherever you want the note to appear. Sticky notes are useful when you want to make overall comments about a document or a section of a document, rather than commenting on a particular phrase or sentence.

- **Highlight Text tool** (⬭) – Highlight the text you want to comment on, and then type your comment.

- **Attach File tool** (⬭) – Attach a file, in any format, to the PDF document.

- **Record Audio tool** (🔊) – Clarify your feedback in an audio recording. To record audio, you must have a built-in or removable microphone on your system.

- **Stamp tool** (👤) – Use a virtual rubber stamp to approve a document, mark it confidential, or perform several other common stamping tasks. You can also create custom stamps for your own purposes.

- **Insert Text tool** (T▲) – Add text at the insertion point. As with all the text commenting tools, your comments don't affect the text in the PDF document, but they make your intention clear.

- **Replace Text tool** (🔁▲) – Indicate which text should be removed, and type the text that should replace it.

- **Strikethrough tool** (🔀) – Indicate which text should be deleted.

- **Underline tool** (T̲) – Indicate which text should be underlined.

- **Add Note To Text tool** (T̲🔖) – Highlight text, and add a note regarding the highlighted content.

- **Text Box tool** (🔲) – Create a box that contains text, positioned anywhere on the page, and at any size. It remains visible on the page, rather than closing like a pop-up note.

▶ **Tip:** To create a custom stamp, click the Stamp tool and choose Custom Stamps > Create Custom Stamp. Then select the image file you want to use.

- **Callout tool** (🗨) – Specify the area you're commenting on without obscuring it. Callout markups have three parts: a text box, a knee line, and an end-point line. Drag handles to resize each part and position it exactly where you want it.

- **Line** (—), **Arrow** (⇨), **Oval** (◯), **Rectangle** (▢), **Cloud** (☁), **Polygon** (⬡), **Connected Lines** (⬠), **Pencil**(✏), and **Eraser** (🧽) **tools** – Use the drawing tools to emphasize areas on the page or communicate your thoughts artistically, especially when reviewing graphical documents.

Commenting in Adobe Reader

Adobe Reader X includes the Sticky Note and Highlight Text tools for use in all PDF documents. However, you can make all the commenting and markup tools available to Reader users for a particular document by saving it as an enabled document from Acrobat. To provide full commenting tools for Reader users, choose File > Save As > Reader Extended PDF > Enable Commenting & Measuring.

Adding sticky notes

You can attach a sticky note anywhere in a document. Because notes can easily be moved, they are best suited to comments about the overall content or layout of a document, rather than specific phrasing. You'll add a sticky note on the first page of this document.

1 Click Comment to open the Comment pane.

2 Click Annotations if the Annotations panel isn't already open, and then select the Sticky Note tool.

3 Click anywhere on the page.

A sticky note opens. The name in the Identity panel of the Acrobat Preferences dialog box automatically appears on the note, as well as the date and time.

4 Type **Looks good so far. I'll look again when it's finished.**

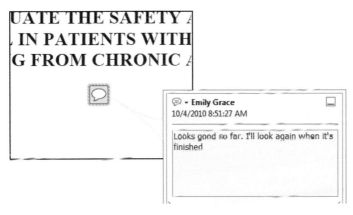

5 Click the arrow that appears before the name in the Sticky Note dialog box, and choose Properties from the pop-up menu.

6 Click the Appearance tab, and then click the Color swatch.

7 Select a blue swatch. The sticky note changes color automatically.

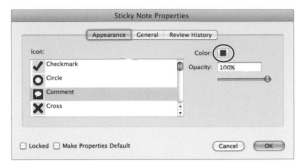

8 Click the General tab.

9 In the Author box, type **Reviewer A**.

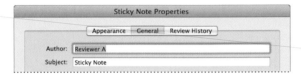

You can change the name attached to a comment. You may want to do that, for example, if you are using someone else's computer.

10 Click OK.

The blue sticky note is closed on the page. To reopen it, just double-click the sticky note icon.

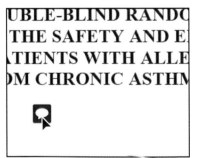

Emphasizing text

Use the Highlight Text tool to emphasize specific text in a document. After high-lighting the text, you can also add a message. You'll make a comment using the Highlight Text tool in this document.

1 Scroll to page 2 in the document.

2 Select the Highlight Text tool (📝) in the Quick Tools toolbar.

You can select the Sticky Note tool and the Highlight Text tool in the Annotations panel in the Comment pane or in the Quick Tools toolbar. You can add other commenting and markup tools to the Quick Tools toolbar by clicking the Customize Quick Tools button in the toolbar.

3 Drag the pointer over "Jocelyn M. Taget, RN" on the first line of the table. The text is highlighted in yellow.

4 Double-click the highlighted text. A comment message box opens.

5 Type **Double-check contact info.**

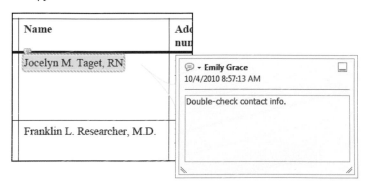

6 Click the close button (▢)in the upper-right corner of the comment box to close it. Alternatively, you can press the Escape key to close the comment box.

Marking text edits

You can clearly communicate which text should be deleted, inserted, or replaced using the text-editing tools. You'll suggest some text changes to the protocol document.

1 Scroll to page 3 of the protocol document.

2 Click the Replace Text tool (🔤) in the Annotations panel in the Comment pane.

3 Select the word "Patients" in the title of the study (in the fourth cell of the table).

4 Type **patients** to replace it.

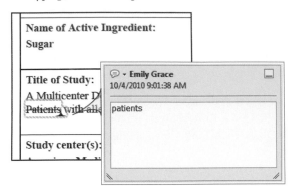

A comment box appears with the text "patients" in it, and the original text is crossed out. An insertion point appears in the original text.

5 Click the close button in the comment box.

6 Select the Insert Text tool in the Annotations panel. Then click an insertion point after "Evaluation of tolerability and evaluation of long-term" in the Objectives section of the table.

7 Type **efficacy** to insert text.

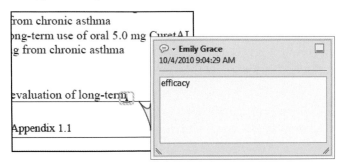

The comment box opens with the word "efficacy" in it. An insertion point icon appears in the original text.

8 Click the close button in the comment box.

9 Go to page 10 in the document.

10 Select the Strikethrough tool (⊕) in the Annotations panel.

11 Under "Potential Risks and Benefits" toward the bottom of the page, select the words "based on studies to date."

A red line appears through the text, indicating deletion.

12 Close the document. You can save changes or close without saving changes.

es (Appendices 2.1 through 2.12) in
or the indications stated.

umans ~~based on studies to date.~~ The
ic asthma who are also suffering fro
ge Regimen and Treatment Periods
remise that a 5mg tablet taken orally
study subjects.

▶ **Tip:** To check the spelling in your comments, choose Edit > Check Spelling > In Comments, Fields, & Editable Text.

Working with comments

You can view comments on the page, in a list, or in a summary. You can import, export, search, and print comments. You can also reply to comments if you're participating in a shared review or will be returning the PDF file to a reviewer in an email-based review. In this exercise, you'll import comments from reviewers, sort comments, show and hide comments, search for comments, and change their status.

Importing comments

If you use a managed shared review process, comments are imported automatically. However, if you're using an email-based review process or collecting comments informally, you can import comments manually. You'll import comments from three reviewers into a draft for an informed consent form.

1 In Acrobat, choose File > Open.

2 In the Lesson09 folder, double-click the Curetall_Informed_Consent.pdf file.

3 Open the Comment pane, and then click Comments List to expand it if it's not already open. There are no comments in the document yet.

4 From the options menu in the Comments List panel, choose Import Data File.

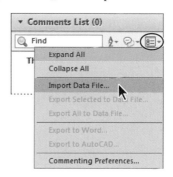

5 Navigate to the Lesson09/Comments folder.

6 Shift-click to select the following files:

- Curetall Informed Consent_ab.pdf
- Curetall Informed Consent_cd.pdf
- Curetall Informed Consent_ef.fdf

7 Click Open (Windows) or Select (Mac OS).

Two of the documents are PDF files with comments included; the FDF file is a data file that contains comments that a reviewer exported.

Acrobat imports the comments and displays them in the comments list.

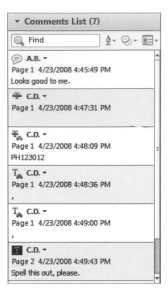

> **Tip:** As a reviewer, you can export comments to a data file (named with an .fdf extension) to reduce file size, especially if you're submitting comments by email. To export comments, choose Export All To Data File or Export Selected To Data File from the options menu in the Comments List panel.

Viewing comments

The comments list appears in the Comment pane when you import comments. The comments list includes every comment in the document, with the comment author's name, the type of comment, and the comment itself.

1 Scroll through the comments list. By default, comments are listed in the order they appear in the document.

2 In the Comments List toolbar, click the Sort Comments button (♣-), and then choose Type.

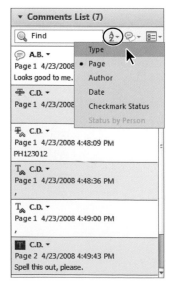 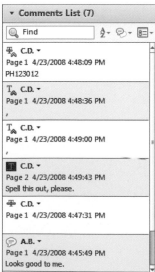

Acrobat rearranges the comments so that they are categorized by the type of comment, such as text insertions, highlights, or sticky notes, instead of page number.

3 Click the fourth comment, a highlight. When you click the comment, Acrobat moves the page to the comment location so that you can see it in context.

4 Click the check box next to the comment so that it has a check mark in it.

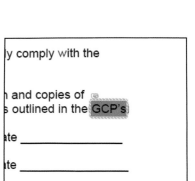

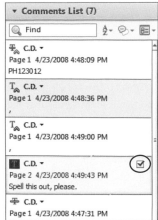

You can add check marks to indicate that you've read a comment, replied to it, discussed it with someone, or anything else that is meaningful to you.

5 Click the Filter Comments button (⊘ ·) in the Comments List toolbar, and choose Checked > Unchecked.

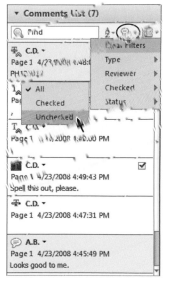

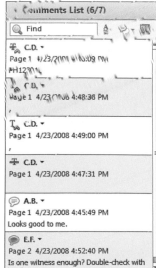

The comment you checked is no longer listed, but it remains in the document. You can use the filter options to declutter the comments list and focus on the comments you want to work with, whether you want to see only text edits, comments by a particular reviewer, or comments that meet other criteria.

6 Click the Filter Comments button again, and choose Show All Comments.

All the comments are listed again.

7 In the Comments List toolbar, type **witness** in the Find box.

One comment appears in the list, the only comment that includes the word "witness." You can use the Find box to search for any text in comments.

8 Select the comment, and then click the arrow in the comment, and choose Reply. A reply box opens in the comments list, with your name next to it.

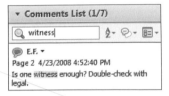
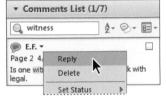

Note: The reviewer will see your reply only if you are using a shared review process or if you email a saved copy of the PDF file to the reviewer.

9 Type **Legal says one witness is fine, per Janet**.

10 With the last comment still selected, click the arrow in the comment again, and choose Set Status > Completed.

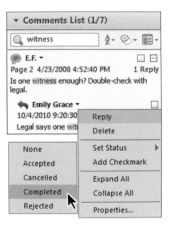
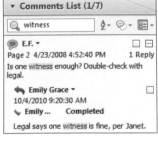

You can set the status of each comment for your own records and to show reviewers how their comments were handled.

11 Close the document without saving your changes.

224 LESSON 9   Using Acrobat in a Review Cycle

Summarizing comments

You can create a summary of comments, either as a list of only the comments, or as the document with comments referenced. From the Comments List panel menu, choose Create Comment Summary. In the Create Comment Summary dialog box, select the layout and other options for your summary. Then click Create Comment Summary. Acrobat creates and opens a separate PDF file with the comments summary layout you selected. You can view the summary onscreen or print it if you prefer to work with paper.

Initiating a shared review

In a shared review, all participants can view and respond to each others' comments. Using a shared review is an effective way to let reviewers resolve conflicting opinions, identify areas for research, and develop creative solutions during the review process. You can host a shared review on a network folder, WebDAV folder, SharePoint workspace, or Acrobat.com, a free web service. For this exercise, you'll use Acrobat.com to host a shared review. You'll need to invite at least one other person to participate. If you are working on your own, you may want to create an alternative email address using a free web service such as Gmail or Yahoo.

Inviting reviewers

You'll use the Send For Shared Review wizard to invite reviewers to participate in a shared review of a document.

1 Decide who you will invite to participate in a shared review and make sure you have their email addresses. If you are working on this lesson alone, create an alternative email address that you can send an invitation to.

2 Choose File > Open.

3 Navigate to the Lesson09 folder, and double-click the Aquo_Market_Summary.pdf file.

4 In the Comment pane, open the Review panel. Then select Send for Shared Review.

5 Select Automatically Download & Track Comments With Acrobat.com from the pop-up menu at the top of the Send For Shared Review dialog box.

6 Click Next.

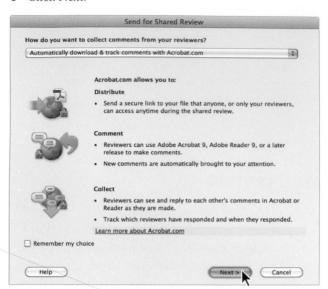

7 If you are prompted for your Adobe ID and password, enter them, click Sign In, and proceed to step 8. If you don't have an Adobe ID, do the following: Click Create Adobe ID, and then complete the form online. Read the services agreement, and then select I Have Read And Agreed To the Following. Then click Next. Click Agree if the Acrobat.com Services Agreement dialog box appears.

Acrobat.com authenticates your Adobe ID if you signed in or have previously signed in, or creates your Adobe ID if you required a new one.

8 Enter the email addresses for people you want to invite.

9 Customize the message that will be sent to participants, or accept the default message.

10 Select Open Access from the Access Level menu, so that anyone who has the URL can participate.

The Limit Access option restricts access to the participants you invite.

11 Click Send.

The Acrobat.com server sends invitation email messages with a link to the document on Acrobat.com. Acrobat saves your document to Acrobat.com and to your local hard drive. Depending on your email application and security settings, your email application may open.

12 Close the document.

About Acrobat.com

Acrobat.com is a secure, web-based service with many free features. Though it's called Acrobat.com, it's not actually part of the Acrobat application. In fact, you can share files of any format there, not just PDF files. To access Acrobat.com, go to www.acrobat.com in your web browser. To access the free features, you need only a free Adobe ID. For more information about Acrobat.com, visit www.acrobat.com.

Participating in a shared review

You or your colleague will participate in the shared review, adding comments for others to view.

1 If you're working alone, open the email invitation you sent to an alternative email address. If you're working with a colleague or friend, ask them to open the email invitation you sent and follow the steps below.

2 Click the link to the PDF file in the invitation to go to Acrobat.com.

3 If prompted, log into Acrobat.com with an Adobe ID.

4 Click Download. If prompted, click Pick A Location, and then select a location for the file on your computer.

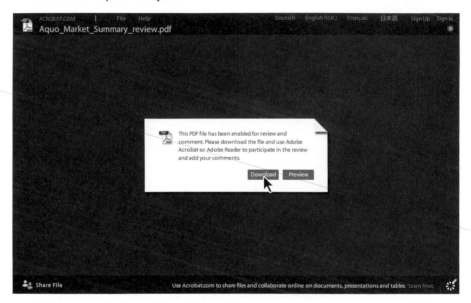

5 Open or double-click the downloaded file to open the PDF file in Acrobat.

6 If a Shared Review dialog box appears, click Connect, and then enter your Adobe ID if prompted.

7 In the Welcome To Shared Review dialog box, click OK.

8 Add several comments to the PDF file using the commenting tools.

9 Click Publish Comments in the document message bar to save comments to the server.

10 Close the document. You do not need to save your changes.

Tracking review comments

You can keep track of reviewers' comments and reply to comments yourself from within Acrobat. You'll open the review PDF file and check for new comments.

1 In Acrobat, choose File > Open.

2 Navigate to the Lesson09 folder, and double-click the Aquo_Market_Summary_ review.pdf file.

3 Click Connect in the Shared Review dialog box and OK in the Welcome Back To Shared Review window, if one appears.

Acrobat saves a review version of your document when you send it for shared review, and it automatically downloads any new comments that have been added.

4 In the document message bar, click Check For New Comments.

Acrobat reports and displays any additional new comments.

5 Select a comment, click the arrow in the comment, and choose Reply.

6 Type a reply to the reviewer.

7 Click Publish Comments in the document message bar.

Acrobat publishes your reply to the server.

8 In the Review panel, select Track Reviews.

Tracker opens.

9 Select the Aquo_market_summary_review.pdf file in the list. Tracker displays the list of reviewers you invited to participate and how many comments each reviewer has made. It also lists the deadline for the review, and lets you send email reminders to reviewers or add more participants. You can also change the deadline.

10 Close Tracker and then close the document.

> **Tip:** In Acrobat Pro, you can see what's changed between two versions of a PDF document. Choose View > Compare Documents, specify the document, and select the type of document. Acrobat highlights changes.

Starting an email-based review

In an email-based review, you send out a tracked copy of the PDF document, so that you can easily merge the comments you receive. To start an email-based review, select Send For Email Review in the Review panel in the Comment pane. Enter information in the Identity Setup dialog box, if the information isn't already available to Acrobat. Specify the PDF to include in the review, and then click Next. The PDF file you specify becomes the master file; you'll merge comments you receive from reviewers into this file. Type the email addresses of your reviewers or choose them from your email application's address book, and click Next. Customize the email invitation, and then click Send Invitation. Reviewers receive the PDF file as an attachment. When they open the attachment, Acrobat presents commenting tools and a PDF file with reviewing instructions.

After you receive comments from reviewers, open the attached files in email..

Exploring on your own: Initiating live collaboration

You can invite others to review a PDF with you live in an online session. In a Collaborate Live session, you can share pages, including magnification levels, so that everyone sees the same part of the document. You can use the live chat window to communicate your thoughts about the document. Though Acrobat is required to initiate a Collaborate Live session, participants can use either Acrobat X or Adobe Reader X.

In this exercise, you'll discuss the market summary document with a colleague. If you are working alone, use an alternative email address.

1 In Acrobat, choose File > Open. Open the Aquo_Market_Summary.pdf file again.

2 Select Collaborate Live in the Review panel of the Comment pane.

3 Click Next in the introductory screen.

4 If prompted, enter your Adobe ID and password, and click Sign In. If you don't have an Adobe ID, create one, and click Next to continue.

Acrobat.com authenticates your Adobe ID.

5 Enter the email addresses for the people you want to invite to participate in the live collaboration. Insert a semicolon or a return between each email address.

6 Customize the email subject and message if you want to.

7   Make sure Store File On Acrobat.com And Send A Link To Recipients is deselected for this exercise.

When this option is deselected, Acrobat sends the file as an attachment to the recipients.

8   Click Send.

Acrobat sends the email invitations. Depending on the security settings in your email application, you may need to send the messages from the email application. When Acrobat has sent the invitations, the Collaborate Live navigation panel opens in the document.

9   Ask your colleague to open the PDF attachment in the email invitation. If you're working alone, check your email and open the PDF attachment.

When a participant opens the PDF attachment, the Collaborate Live navigation panel opens.

10 Ask participants to sign in as guests. If you're working alone, sign in as a guest in the second copy of the document.

11 Click the Start Page Sharing button to start sharing pages with each other. Click OK in any message boxes that appear, alerting you that everyone will be viewing the same page, and that you can share a page view of the document.

12 Type chat messages in the box at the bottom of the pane. Click the color box if you want to use a different color for your chat text.

13 To share your screen in an Adobe ConnectNow meeting—which lets you share your screen, rather than simply a PDF document, choose Share My Screen from the options menu in the Collaborate Live pane.

14 When you have finished with your Collaborate Live session, choose Disable Chat & Page Sharing In My Copy or Disable Chat & Page Sharing In All Copies from the options menu in the Collaborate Live pane. Click OK if a warning message appears.

15 Close the document and quit Acrobat.

Review questions

1 How do you add comments to a PDF document?

2 How can you consolidate comments made by several reviewers?

3 What is the difference between an email-based review process and a shared review process?

Review answers

1 You can add comments to a PDF using any of the commenting and markup tools in Acrobat. Open the Comment pane to see all the tools available in the Annotations and Drawing Markups panels. To use a tool, select it, click on the page, and then select the text you want to edit, or draw your markup.

2 Open the original PDF file that you sent out for review, and then choose Import Data File from the Comments List panel menu. Select the PDF or FDF files that reviewers returned to you, and click Select. Acrobat imports all the comments into the original document.

3 In an email-based review process, each reviewer receives the PDF document through email, makes comments, and returns the PDF document through email; reviewers do not see each others' comments.

In a shared review process, you post the PDF document to a central server or folder, and then invite reviewers to make their comments. When reviewers publish comments, they can be seen by all other reviewers, so everyone can respond to each other. You can also enforce a deadline more easily with a shared review process, as commenting tools are no longer available to reviewers after the deadline.

10 WORKING WITH FORMS IN ACROBAT

Lesson overview

In this lesson, you'll do the following:

- Create an interactive PDF form.

- Add form fields, including text boxes, radio buttons, and action buttons.

- Distribute a form.

- Track a form to determine its status.

- Learn how to collect and compile form data.

- Validate and calculate form data.

 This lesson will take approximately 45 minutes to complete. Copy the Lesson10 folder onto your hard drive if you haven't already done so.

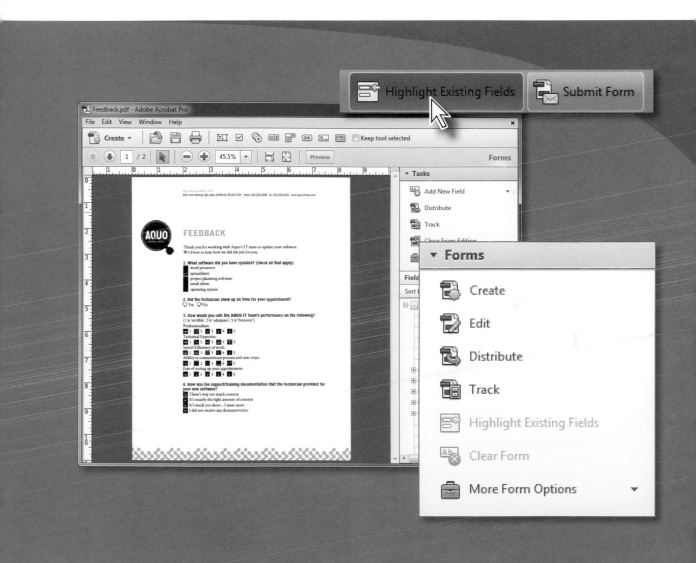

You can convert any Acrobat document, including a scanned paper file, into an interactive form for online distribution, tracking, and collection.

Getting started

In this lesson, you'll prepare a feedback form for the IT department of a fictitious beverage manufacturing company. You'll convert an existing PDF document into an interactive form, and use the form tools in Acrobat to add form fields that users can complete online. Then you'll distribute the form, track it, and collect and analyze the data, all using tools within Acrobat.

Converting PDF files to interactive PDF forms

With Acrobat, you can create interactive PDF forms from documents you've created in other applications, such as Microsoft Word or Adobe InDesign, or scanned in from existing paper forms. You will start by opening a flat form that has already been converted to PDF. You will then use the forms tools to convert it to an interactive form.

1 Start Acrobat.

2 Choose File > Open, and navigate to the Lesson10 folder. Open the Feedback.pdf file.

The PDF document contains the text for the form, but Acrobat doesn't recognize any form fields in the document yet.

3 Open the Forms panel in the Tools pane. Then click Create in the Forms panel.

4 In the Create Or Edit Form dialog box, select Use The Current Document Or Browse To A File, and then click Next.

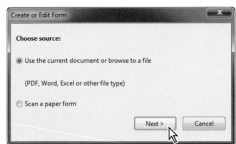

5 Select Use The Current Document, and then click Next.

Acrobat analyzes the document and adds interactive form fields. When it has finished, the Form Editing dialog box alerts you that you are in Form Editing mode. In Form Editing mode, you can inspect the document to ensure that Acrobat added form fields appropriately, and you can add fields manually where necessary.

6 Click OK to close the Form Editing dialog box.

Acrobat lists the form fields it added in the Fields panel on the right. The Tasks panel lists the tools available for working with forms in Form Editing mode.

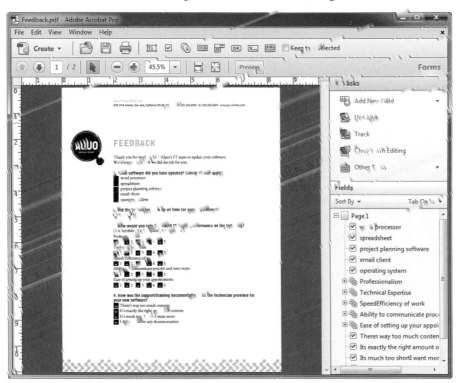

Adding form fields

● **Note:** If a document has been password-protected to prevent editing, you must know the password to add or edit fields. After a form has been enabled for Adobe Reader, so that Reader users can save the completed form, no one can edit it.

You can use the form tools in Acrobat to add form fields to any document. Because you've used the Create option to convert a document to an interactive PDF form, you're already in Form Editing mode. You can access this mode at any time by clicking Edit in the Forms panel.

Each form field has a name, which should be unique and descriptive; you'll use this name when you collect and analyze data, but it does not appear on the form the user sees. You can add tool tips and labels to help users understand how to complete form fields.

Adding a text field

Acrobat found most of the form fields in the document, but it missed a couple of fields on the second page. You'll add a text field for an email address. Text fields enable users to enter information, such as their name or telephone number, on a form.

1   If you are not in Form Editing mode, click Edit in the Forms panel.

2   Scroll to the second page of the PDF form.

3   In the Tasks panel, choose Text Field from the Add New Field menu. Your pointer becomes a cross-hair, attached to a text box.

4 Click to the right of "Email address (optional):" to place the text field.

5 Type **email address** in the Field Name box. Do not select Required Field, because, of course, this is an optional field.

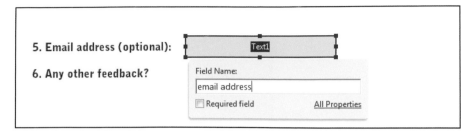

6 Drag the right edge of the text field to make it longer.

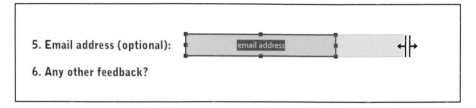

Adding a multiline text field

The next field is for additional feedback. Someone completing the form could type just a few words or a complete paragraph. You'll create a text field that supports multiple lines.

1 Choose Text Field from the Add New Field menu.

2 Click below "6. Any other feedback?" to add a text field.

3 Type **other feedback** in the Field Name box. This is another optional field, so do not select Required Field.

4 Drag the lower-right blue handle to increase the size of the box so that it could contain multiple lines of text.

5 Double-click the text field to edit its properties.

6 In the Text Field Properties dialog box, click the Options tab.

7 Select Multi-line and Scroll Long Text.

8 Select Limit Of _ Characters, and type **750** for the limit.

9 Click Close.

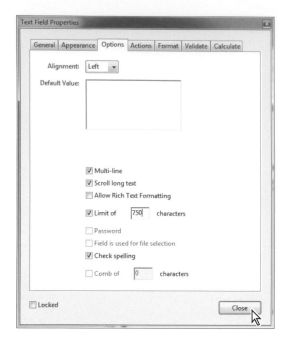

10 Click Preview in the Common Tools toolbar. If it isn't already selected, click Highlight Existing Fields to see how the fields will appear to users.

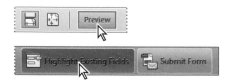

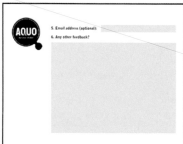

Specifying an answer format

You can use special formatting to restrict the type of data that is entered into a text field, or to automatically convert data into a specific format. For example, you can set a zip code field to accept only numbers, or a date field to accept only a specific date format. And you can restrict numerical entries to numbers within a certain range.

To restrict the format for a text field, open its properties. Click the Format tab, select the format category, and then select the appropriate option for your field.

Adding radio buttons

The second question on the feedback form requires a yes-or-no answer. You'll create radio buttons for that question. Radio buttons let the user select one—and only one—option from a set of options.

1   If you're in Preview mode, click Edit in the Common Tools toolbar to return to Form Editing mode.

2   Go to page 1 of the form.

3   Choose Radio Button from the Add New Field menu.

4   Click the circle next to the word "Yes" after question 2.

5   Select Required Field.

6   Type **Yes** in the Radio Button Choice box.

7   Type **on time** in the Group Name box.

8   Click Add Another Button at the bottom of the dialog box. Your pointer becomes a box again.

● **Note:** All radio buttons in a set need to have the same group name.

9   Click the circle next to "No."

10 Type **No** in the Radio Button Choice box, and confirm that the group name is "on time."

11 Click Preview in the Custom Tools toolbar. For the second question, click Yes, and then click No. Notice that you can select only one radio button at a time.

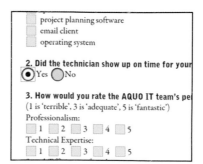

Adding an action button

Buttons let users perform an action, such as playing a movie file, going to a different page, or submitting a form. You'll create a reset button that will clear the form fields so the user can start over.

1 Click Edit in the Custom Tools toolbar to return to Form Editing mode.

2 Choose Button from the Add New Field menu.

3 Click in the upper-left corner of the form to create the button.

4 Type **Reset** in the Field Name box, and then click All Properties.

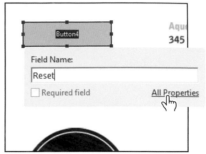

5 Click the Options tab.

6 Type **Start over** in the Label box.

The field name is used to collect and analyze data, but does not appear on the form itself. The label, however, appears in the field when the user is completing the form.

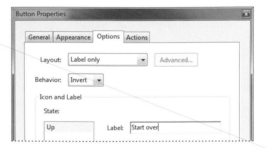

7 Click the Actions tab.

8 Choose Mouse Up from the Select Trigger menu, and then choose Reset A Form from the Select Action menu. Click Add.

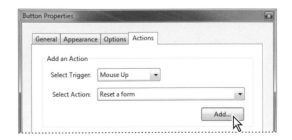

When the user clicks the button and releases the mouse (Mouse Up), the form will reset.

9 Click OK in the Reset A Form dialog box to reset the selected fields. By default, all form fields are selected.

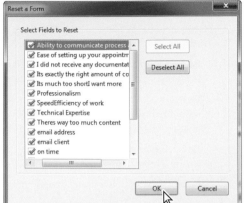

10 Click the Appearance tab.

11 Click the Border Color swatch, select a blue color, and then click the Fill Color swatch and select gray.

12 Choose Beveled from the Line Style menu.

The button will appear with a gray background and blue outline, and the beveled line will make it appear to be three-dimensional.

13 Click Close to close the Button Properties dialog box.

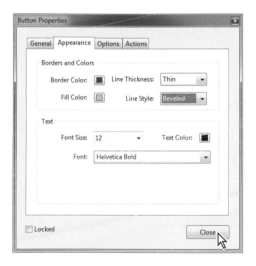

14 Click Preview. Select options for a few questions, and then click the Start Over button you created. The fields reset.

15 Choose File > Save. If the Save As dialog box appears, save the file with the same name.

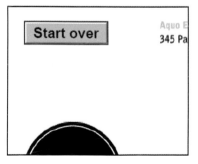

Types of form fields

You can include the following types of fields in a PDF form you create in Acrobat:

- **Barcodes** encode the input from selected fields and display it as a visual pattern that can be interpreted by decoding software or hardware (available separately).
- **Buttons** initiate an action on the user's computer, such as opening a file, playing a sound, or submitting data to a web server. You can customize buttons with images, text, and visual changes triggered by moving or clicking a mouse.
- **Check boxes** present yes-or-no choices for individual items. If the form contains multiple check boxes, users can typically select as many of these as they want.
- **Combo boxes** let the user either choose an item from a pop-up menu or type in a value.
- **Digital signatures** let the user electronically sign a PDF document with a digital signature.
- **List boxes** display a list of options the user can select. You can set a form field property that enables the user to Shift-click or Control-click to select multiple items on the list.
- **Radio buttons** present a group of choices from which the user can select only one item. All radio buttons with the same name work together as a group.
- **Text fields** let the user type in text, such as name, address, email address, or phone number.

▶ **Tip:** When you fill out a PDF form, you can press the Tab key to move to the next field. As the form author, you can set the tab order. To see the current tab order, make sure you're in Form Editing mode, and then choose Other Tasks > Edit Fields > Show Tab Numbers in the Tasks panel. Tab order numbers appear on the form. To change the tab order, drag fields into a different order in the Fields panel.

Distributing forms

After you have designed and created your form, you can distribute it in several different ways. If you have an email account, you'll send the feedback form to yourself, and then collect the response in email. You'll use the tools in Acrobat to distribute the form, but first you'll enable Adobe Reader users to save a completed form.

Note: You cannot edit a form or any other PDF document after you have enabled rights for Reader in it. Enable a form just before distributing it.

1 If you're in Form Editing mode, click Close Form Editing in the Tasks panel.

2 Choose File > Save As > Reader Extended PDF > Enable Additional Features.

3 Read the information in the dialog box, and then click Save Now.

4 Click Save to save the form with the same name.

5 Click Yes or Replace to replace the existing file.

Ordinarily, Adobe Reader users cannot save PDF forms that they have filled out. When you use the Enable Additional Features command, however, Acrobat saves the form as a Reader-enabled PDF file, so that people using Adobe Reader can save the completed form.

6 Click Distribute in the Forms panel.

7 Click Save if you are prompted to save, and click Yes if you are prompted to clear the form before distributing it.

8 In the Distribute Form dialog box, choose Manually Collect Responses In My Email Inbox, and then click Next.

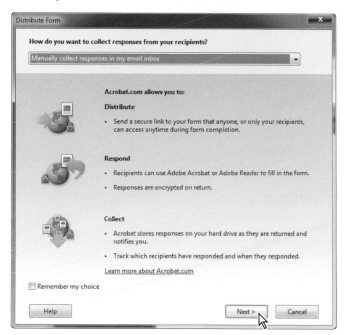

9 Select Send It Automatically Using Adobe Acrobat, and then click Next.

10 If prompted, enter or verify your email address, name, title, and organization name, and then click Next. If you've entered that information previously, Acrobat uses the information it has stored.

11 Type your email address in the To box. Make sure Collect Name & Email From Recipients To Provide Optimal Tracking is selected. Then click Send.

● **Note:** You can customize the subject line and email message that accompanies your form, and you can send the form to multiple people at once. For the purposes of this lesson, however, you are sending the form only to yourself with the default message and subject line.

Acrobat opens your default email application and sends the message with the attached form. Depending on the security settings in your email application, you may need to approve the message before it can be sent.

Acrobat moves the addresses you entered in the To box to the BCC field in your email application to preserve the privacy of the form recipients.

Acrobat opens Tracker to help you manage the form that you have distributed. Tracker lets you view and edit the location of the response file, track which recipients have responded, add more recipients, email all recipients, and view the responses for a form.

● **Note:** You can open Tracker at any time by selecting Track in the Forms panel.

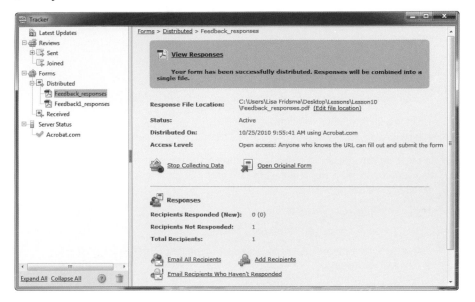

12 Check your email, and open the attached PDF file to complete the form.

The form opens in Acrobat, and a document message bar appears above it.

The document message bar displays information about the form. If the form does not contain a Submit Form button, one is included in the document message bar. Additionally, the document message bar informs Reader users about their usage rights for the form, and it specifies whether a form is certified or contains signature fields.

● **Note:** If form recipients are using earlier versions of Acrobat or Reader, the document message bar may not be visible or may contain different information.

Tracking forms

If you've used Acrobat to distribute your forms, you can manage the forms that you have distributed or received. Use Tracker to view and edit the location of the response file, track who has responded, add more recipients, email all recipients, and view the responses for a form.

To track forms in Tracker:

1 In the Forms panel, click Track.

Tracker displays reviews you've initiated and forms you've distributed.

2 In the left navigation panel, expand Forms.

3 Select the form you want to track.

In the main pane, Tracker displays the location of the response file, the method used to distribute the form, the date it was distributed, the list of recipients, and whether each recipient has responded.

4 Do one or more of the following:

- To view all responses for a form, click View Responses.
- To modify the location of the response file, in Response File Location, click Edit File Location.
- To view the original form, click Open Original Form.
- To send the form to more recipients, click Add Recipients.
- To email all recipients, click Email All Recipients.
- To remind recipients to complete the form, click Email Recipients Who Haven't Responded.

Options for distributing forms

There are several ways to get your forms to the people who need to fill them out. You can simply post a form on a website, for example, or send it directly from your email application. To take advantage of Acrobat form-management tools to track, collect, and analyze data, use one of these options:

- Host your form on Acrobat.com, and send recipients a secure link to it. From Acrobat, you can create your own user account on Acrobat.com, and then use Acrobat.com to upload and share most document types.

- Send the form as an email attachment, and manually collect responses in your email inbox.

- Send the form using a network folder or a Windows server running Microsoft SharePoint services. You can automatically collect responses on the internal server.

To distribute a form using any of these methods, click Distribute in the Forms panel, and then follow the online instructions. To learn more about distributing forms, see Adobe Acrobat X Help.

Collecting form data

Electronic forms aren't simply more convenient for users; they also make it easier for you to track, collect, and review form data. When you distribute a form, Acrobat automatically creates a PDF Portfolio for collecting the form data. By default, this file is saved in the same folder as the original form, and is named [filename]_responses.

You'll complete the form and submit it, and then collect the form data.

1 Complete the form you opened and select options for each question, as if you were the recipient. Type a few words in the multiline field for number 6. Then click Submit Form.

2 In the Send Form dialog box, verify the email address and name you're using to send the data, and then click Send.

● **Note:** Depending on the security settings in your email application, you may need to approve the message before it is sent.

3 In the Select Email Client dialog box, select Desktop Email Application if you use an application such as Microsoft Outlook, Eudora, or Mail. Select Internet Email if you use an Internet email service such as Yahoo or Hotmail. (You must send the file manually from an Internet email service.) Click OK.

If you receive a message about sending the email, click OK. Depending on settings in your email application, you may need to send the message manually.

4 Check your email. The completed form arrives in a message with the subject line "Submitting Completed Form." Double-click the attachment in that message.

5 Select Add to An Existing Responses File, and accept the default filename. Then click OK.

Acrobat compiles the data in the response file that was created when you distributed the form.

6 Click Get Started at the bottom of the PDF Portfolio welcome screen.

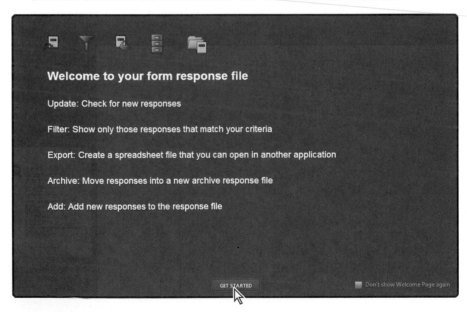

● **Note:** You can add multiple form responses to the responses file at once. Click Add, and then navigate to the responses you want to include.

Form data you've collected is listed in the PDF Portfolio. Each response is listed as a separate component. You can use the PDF Portfolio to filter, export, and archive data.

Working with form data

Once your data has been compiled, you can view each response, filter responses according to specific questions, export the data to a CSV or XML file for use in a spreadsheet or database, or archive the data for access later. You'll filter the data from the feedback form and then export it to a CSV file.

1 Click Filter on the left side of the PDF Portfolio.

2 Scroll down the Select Field Name menu, and choose Other Feedback.

3 Select Is Not Blank from the next menu.

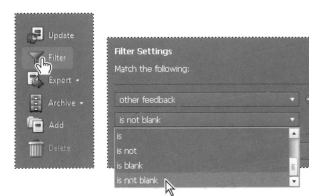

The form you completed is listed because it contains data in the Other Feedback field.

4 Select Is Blank from the second menu.

The form you completed disappears because it no longer matches the filter criteria. You can add filters to sort responses based on as many criteria as you like.

5 Select Is Not Blank again, so that your form reappears.

6 Click Done at the bottom of the Filter Settings pane.

7 Select the response.

8 Choose Export > Export Selected on the left side of the PDF Portfolio.

9 Select CSV as the file type, and click Save.

Acrobat creates a comma-separated data file that contains the data from the selected responses. You can open a CSV file in Microsoft Excel or another spreadsheet or database application.

10 Close any open PDF files and Tracker.

Exploring on your own: Calculating and validating numeric fields

Acrobat offers many ways to ensure that users fill out your forms correctly. You can experiment with creating fields that will allow the user to enter only information of a specific type. You can also create fields that automatically calculate values based on entries in other fields.

Validating numeric fields

To ensure that correct information is entered into form fields, use the Acrobat field validation feature. For example, if a response needs to be a number with a value between 10 and 20, restrict entries to numbers within this range. Here, you'll limit the price of instruments on an order form to no more than $1,000.

1 Choose File > Open, navigate to the Lesson10 folder, and open the Order_Start.pdf file.

2 Open the Forms panel in the Tools pane, and then click Edit to enter Form Editing mode.

3 Double-click the Price.0 field (the first cell in the "Price Each" column).

4 In the Text Field Properties dialog box, click the Format tab, and set the following values:

   • For Select Format Category, choose Number.

   • For Decimal Places, choose 2 to allow cents to be entered.

   • For Separator Style, choose 1,234.56 (the default).

   • For Currency Symbol, choose $ (the dollar sign).

Now you'll specify a validation check on the data entered in this field.

5 Click the Validate tab, and then select Field Value Is In Range. In the range fields, type **0** in the From box and **1000** in the To box. Click Close.

6 Click Preview. Then type **2000** in the field you just created, and press Enter or Return. A message warns you that the entry you have tried to make is unacceptable.

Calculating numeric fields

In addition to verifying and formatting form data, you can use Acrobat to calculate values used in form fields. For your PDF order form, you will calculate the cost for each line item, based on the quantity that has been ordered. You will then have Acrobat calculate the total cost of all items that have been ordered.

1   If you're in Preview mode, click Edit.

2   Double-click the Total.0 field (the first cell in the Item Total column).

3   In the Text Field Properties dialog box, click the Calculate tab, and do the following:

   • Select the Value Is The option.

   • For the value, choose Product (x). You'll be multiplying two fields.

   • To select the fields to multiply, click Pick. In the Field Selection dialog box, select the boxes next to Price.0 and Quantity.0.

4   Click OK to close the Field Selection dialog box, and click Close to exit the Text Field Properties dialog box.

5   Click Preview. Then enter **1.50** for the price and **2** for the quantity in the first row, and press Enter or Return. The Item Total column displays $3.00.

6   Close any open files, and quit Acrobat when you are finished.

Review questions

1 How can you convert an existing document into an interactive PDF form?

2 What is the difference between a radio button and a button?

3 How can you distribute a form to multiple recipients?

4 Where does Acrobat compile form responses?

Review answers

1 To convert an existing document into an interactive PDF Form, open the document in Acrobat. Then open the Forms panel in the Tools pane, and click Create. Select the current document, and follow the onscreen instructions.

2 Radio buttons permit the user to select just one of a set of two or more options. Buttons trigger actions, such as playing a movie file, going to another page, or clearing form data.

3 You can post a form on Acrobat.com and then send an invitation to recipients, email the form to recipients, or post the form on an internal server. Click Distribute in the Forms panel to select a distribution option.

4 When you use Acrobat to distribute a form, Acrobat automatically creates a PDF Portfolio file for your responses. By default, the file is in the same folder as the original form, and the word "_responses" is appended to the name of the original form.

11

USING ACTIONS

Lesson overview

In this lesson, you'll do the following:

- Run an action (Acrobat Pro).

- Create an action.

- Create an instruction step for an action.

- Set options in steps so the user doesn't need to provide input.

- Prompt the user for input on specific steps.

- Share an action.

 This lesson will take approximately 45 minutes to complete. Copy the Lesson11 folder onto your hard drive if you haven't already done so.

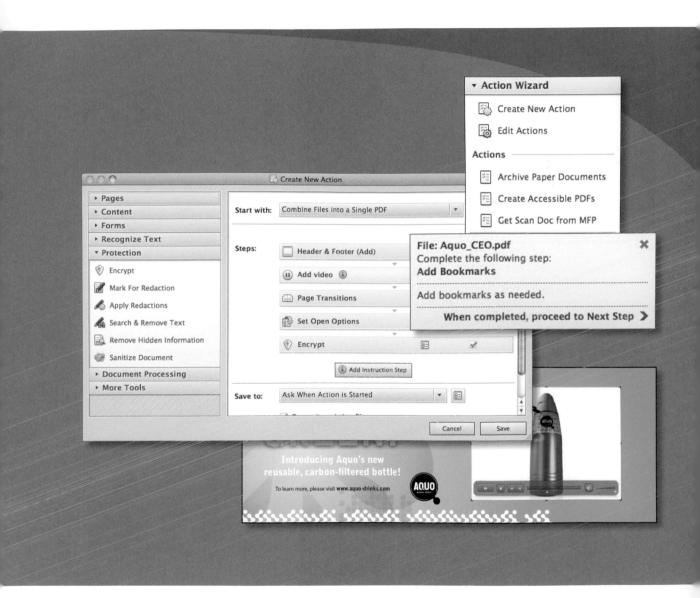

Actions in Adobe Acrobat X Pro automate tasks
and make processes more consistent. You can use
the actions that come with Acrobat or create your
own to use and share.

About actions

In Adobe Acrobat X Pro, you can use actions to automate multistep tasks and share processes with others. An action is a collection of steps: Some steps, such as adding tags to a document, can be performed automatically by Acrobat. Some steps, such as removing hidden information, require input as to which information to remove or add, or which settings to use. Other steps, such as adding bookmarks, cannot be done automatically because you need to use human discretion to create and name the bookmarks; in those cases, an action includes instructions for the user to perform the necessary step before the action continues.

Acrobat Pro includes several actions in the Action Wizard panel. You can use these actions to perform common tasks, such as preparing documents for distribution or creating accessible PDFs. You can also create your own actions, assembling steps in the order that works for your process, and including informational steps where appropriate for the people who will be using each action.

Actions that contain automated steps are particularly useful for tasks you perform frequently. Actions in general are handy for tasks you perform less frequently, but which require the same steps each time. Using actions, you can ensure that critical steps are included in the process.

Using predefined actions

To use an action, select it in the Action Wizard panel in the Tools pane. To gain practice using actions, you'll use the Prepare For Distribution action to prepare a document before posting it on an external website.

1   In Acrobat Pro, choose File > Open. Navigate to the Lesson11 folder, select Aquo_CEO.pdf, and click Open.

The Aquo_CEO.pdf document is a biography of the chief executive of a fictitious beverage company.

2   Click Tools to open the Tools pane, and then click Action Wizard to open its panel.

3   Select Prepare For Distribution in the Actions area of the panel.

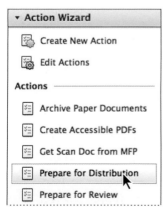

The opening window of the action appears. It describes the action, lists its steps, reports whether the action is started with an open document or not, and describes how the changed document is to be saved.

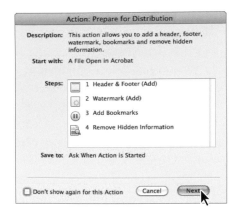

4 Review the description and steps for this action. When you've read the information, click Next to proceed to the first step.

The Add Header And Footer dialog box appears, because the first step of this action is to add a header and footer to the document.

5 In the Add Header And Footer dialog box, click an insertion point in the Center Header Text box, and then type **Aquo Corporate Information**. Click OK to add the header and close the dialog box.

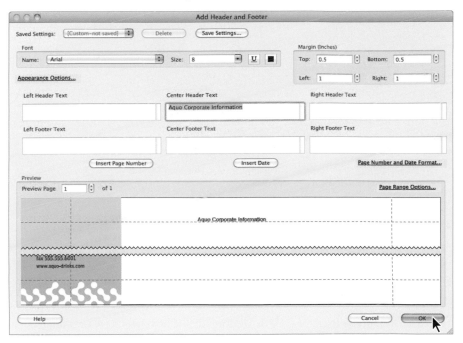

6 In the Add Watermark dialog box, click an insertion point in the Text box. Then type **Copyright Aquo 2011**. Select 20 for the font size, and set the Opacity to 25%. In the Position area of the dialog box, enter **1** point for the Vertical Distance, and choose Bottom from the From menu. Then choose Right from the From menu for Horizontal Distance. The watermark should appear in the lower-right corner of the document in the preview pane. Click OK to accept the watermark.

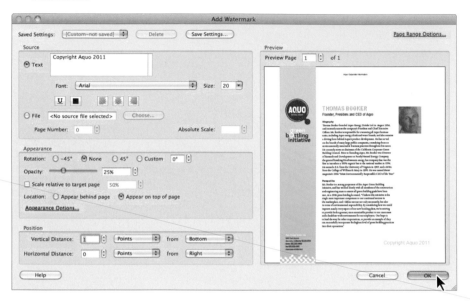

The third step of the action is to add bookmarks. However, this is a one-page document, so it doesn't require bookmarks.

7 Click Next Step in the instruction step window at the bottom of the application screen.

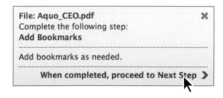

8 Click OK in the Remove Hidden Information dialog box to accept the default selections.

9 In the Save As dialog box, name the document **Aquo_CEO_dist.pdf**, and click Save.

10 Click Close in the Prepare For Distribution dialog box, which reports that the action has been completed and displays the name and location of the saved file.

11 Close the document.

Creating an action

You can create your own actions, assembling Acrobat steps and instructional steps to automate a process or to make it more consistent. Before you create an action, consider the steps involved and the logical order for those steps. For example, encrypting a document with password protection or saving it with Reader-extended features should be among the last steps in the action.

You'll create an action for assembling a multimedia presentation in Acrobat X Pro. The steps you'll use for creating a multimedia presentation are to combine files, add a header or footer to visually link the pages to each other, add video files, create page transitions, set the file to open in Full Screen mode, and then add a password to the document to prevent others from making changes.

1   In Acrobat, choose File > Action Wizard > Create New Action.

2   In the Create New Action dialog box, choose Combine Files Into A Single PDF from the Start With menu.

You can apply an action to an open file, prompt the user to select a file or folder, require the user to scan a document, ask the user how to apply the action, or start by combining multiple files. Presentations often include multiple document types, so you'll start this action by combining files.

3   Choose Ask When Action Is Started from the Save To menu. When the action runs, Acrobat will prompt the user to specify a location for the saved file.

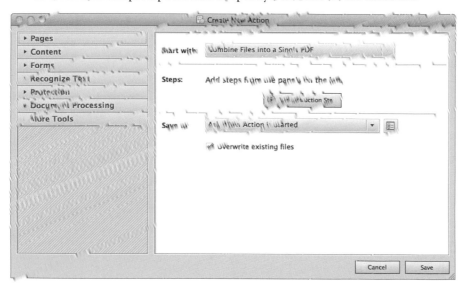

Adding steps to an action

▶ **Tip:** If you change your mind about a step, you can delete it. Move the pointer over the step, and then click the X that appears on the right side of the step. To change the order of steps, drag them into position in the Create New Action dialog box.

Now you're ready to add the steps.

1 Expand the Pages panel in the left pane of the dialog box, and select Header & Footer (Add).

The Header & Footer (Add) step is listed in the right pane.

2 Select Prompt User at the right side of the step. When the action runs, the user can customize the header or footer for the presentation.

The next step is to add video files. There is no Add Video step available in the Create New Action dialog box, so you'll add an instruction step for the user.

3 Click Add Instruction Step.

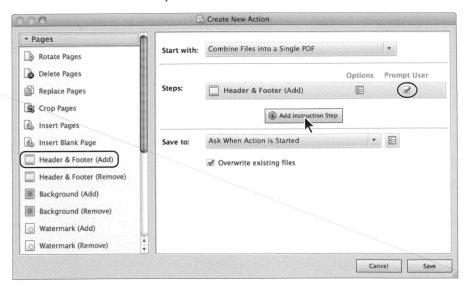

4 Type **Add video** in the Step Name text box in the Add/Edit Instructions dialog box.

5 In the Instructions text box, type **Add video files as appropriate. To add a video, choose Multimedia > Video in the Content panel, drag a box on the page, and select the video file and any settings.** Then click Save.

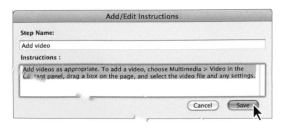

You can add as much or as little information as you want in an instruction step. If you're sharing your action with people who are less familiar with Acrobat, consider providing detailed steps. If you're creating an action for yourself, a reminder to perform the step, such as "Add video," may be enough.

6 Expand the Document Processing panel in the left pane, and click Page Transitions.

7 Click the options button in the Page Transitions step.

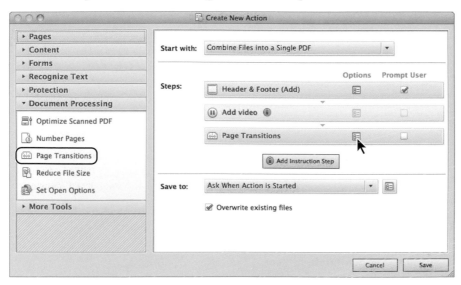

8 Choose Dissolve from the Transition menu, and then choose Medium from the Speed menu. Then click OK.

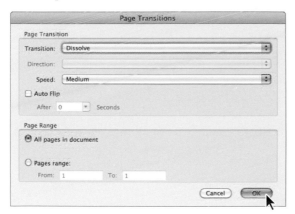

9 Make sure Prompt User is not selected in the Page Transitions step.

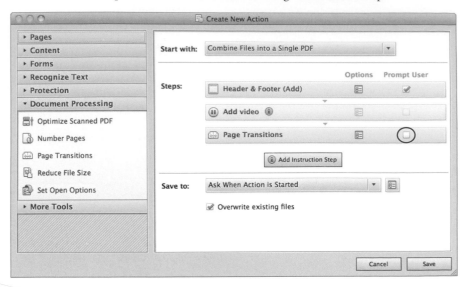

Acrobat will automatically apply the options you select for the Page Transitions step, without prompting the user.

10 Click Set Open Options in the Document Processing panel. Click the options button in the new step. In the Set Open Options dialog box, choose Yes from the Open In Full Screen Mode menu. Click OK.

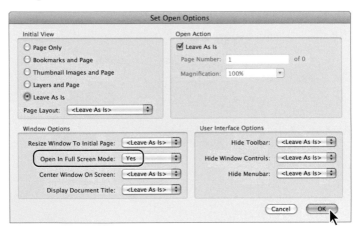

11 Expand the Protection panel, and then click Encrypt. Select Prompt User in the Encrypt step so that each user can set an individual password.

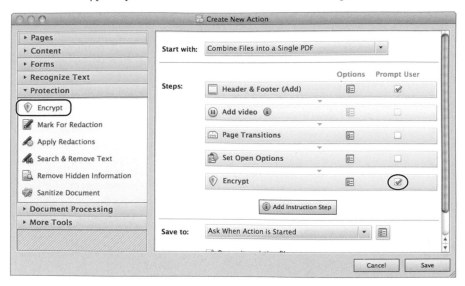

Saving an action

When you've added all the steps, confirmed that they're in the appropriate order, and specified the options you want, save and name the action.

1 Click Save.

2 Name the action **Prepare Multimedia Presentation**.

3 For the action description, type **Combine files for a presentation in full-screen mode with page transitions**. Then click Save.

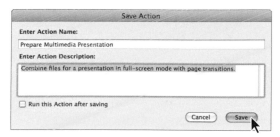

Give actions names that help you remember what the actions do. It's usually a good idea, especially if you'll be sharing the action, to describe the product of the action or when you should use it, such as when you're preparing documents for a particular client or purpose.

Testing an action

▶ **Tip:** You can also run actions from the File menu. Choose File > Action Wizard > [action name] to run an action.

You've created an action. Now you'll test-drive it to ensure it works the way you expect. You'll create a multimedia presentation for a fictitious beverage company.

1   In the Action Wizard panel, select Prepare Multimedia Presentation. (If you don't see it, click More Actions to see additional actions.) The action description and steps appear.

2   Click Next.

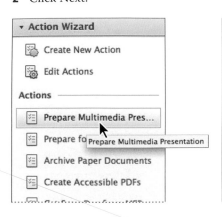 

3   In the Select Files dialog box, click Add Files, and then choose Add Files from the menu. Navigate to the Lesson11 folder, and then Ctrl-click (Windows) or Command-click (Mac OS) to select the Aquo_Bottle_Ad.pdf, Aquo_CEO.pdf, and Aquo_FAQ.pdf files. Click Add Files.

4   Arrange the files so that the Aquo_Bottle_Ad.pdf file is first, followed by the Aquo_FAQ.pdf file, and then the Aquo_CEO.pdf file. To move a file up in the file order, select it, and click Move Up. To move a file down, select it, and click Move Down.

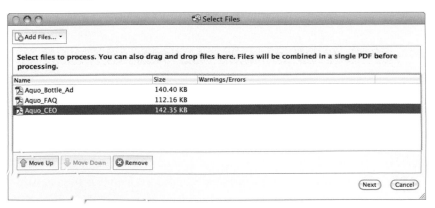

This is the order in which the files will appear in the final presentation.

5 Click Next to combine the files and move to the first step in the action.

6 In the Add Header And Footer dialog box, click an insertion point in the Left Header Text box, and then type **Aquo Shareholders Meeting 2012**. Click OK.

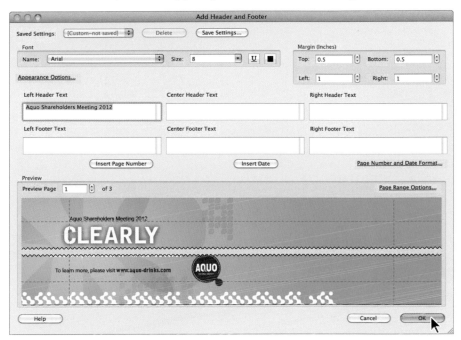

The instruction step you created appears on the screen. You'll add a video.

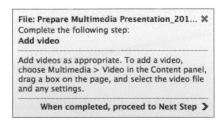

7 Open the Content panel in the Tools pane, and choose Multimedia > Video. Drag a box over the right half of the bottle ad page (the first page in the document). Click Choose or Browse, select the Aquo_T03_Loop.flv file from the Lesson11 folder, and click Open. Then click OK.

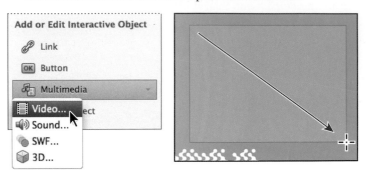

8 Click the Play button to preview the video file. When you're done, click the Pause button to stop it. Then click Next Step in the instruction step to proceed through the action.

Acrobat automatically performs the next two steps—adding page transitions and setting the presentation to open in Full Screen mode—because no input is required. The final step is adding a password, which does require input.

9 In the Document Security dialog box, choose Password Security from the Security Method menu. In the Permissions area of the Password Security – Settings dialog box, select Restrict Editing And Printing Of the Document. In the Change Permissions Password box, enter **Aquo1234** as the password. Then click OK.

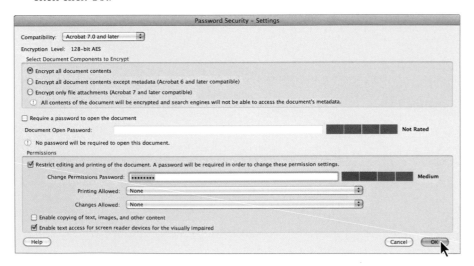

10 Click OK in the informational dialog box, enter the password again when prompted, and then click OK. Click Close to close the Document Security dialog box.

11 In the Save As dialog box, name the presentation file **Aquo_meeting.pdf**. Click Save.

Acrobat reports that the Prepare Multimedia Presentation action has been completed.

12 Click Close. Close the document file. If you want to see the presentation open in Full Screen mode with its header and page transitions, open the file in Acrobat. When you've viewed the presentation, press Escape to exit Full Screen mode, and then close the file.

Avoiding the Full Screen mode warning

By default, Acrobat warns you when a PDF file is set to be opened in Full Screen mode, because it is possible for malicious programmers to create PDF files that appear to be other applications. If you click Remember My Choice For This Document, Acrobat will not show the warning again when you open the presentation on this computer.If you are presenting material on your own computer, you can change the preference so that Acrobat will not display the warning at the beginning of your presentation. To change the preference, choose Edit > Preferences (Windows) or Acrobat > Preferences (Mac OS), and then click Full Screen on the left. Deselect the Alert When Document Requests Full Screen option.

Sharing actions

You can share actions you create or edit with other users.

1 Choose File > Action Wizard > Edit Actions.

2 Select the Prepare Multimedia Presentation action, and click Export.

3 Name the action **Prepare Multimedia Presentation** (the default name), save it in the Lesson11 folder, and click Save.

The action file is saved with an .sequ extension. You can copy .sequ files or email them to other users. To open a .sequ file that someone has sent you, click Import in the Edit Actions dialog box, and select the action file.

4 Click Close to close the Edit Actions dialog box. Then close any open documents, and quit Acrobat.

Review questions

1 What is an action in Acrobat X Pro?

2 How can you create a step in an action if the step isn't available in the left pane of the Create New Action dialog box?

3 How can you share an action with others?

Review answers

1 An action is a collection of steps: Some steps, such as adding tags to a document, can be performed automatically by Acrobat. Some steps, such as removing hidden information, require input as to what to remove or add, or which settings to use. Other steps, such as adding bookmarks, cannot be done automatically, because you need to use human discretion to create and name the bookmarks

2 To include a step that isn't predefined in Acrobat, click Add Instruction Step, and then type instructions to the user.

3 To share an action, choose File > Action Wizard > Edit Actions, select the action you want to share, and click Export. Then send the resulting .sequ file to the person you want to share the action with.

12 USING THE LEGAL FEATURES

Lesson overview

In this lesson, you'll do the following:

- Apply Bates numbering to a document.

- Apply redaction to eliminate privileged information.

- Search for text patterns to mark areas for redaction.

- Mark the same area across multiple pages for redaction.

- Combine multiple documents into one PDF.

 This lesson will take approximately 45 minutes to complete. Copy the Lesson12 folder onto your hard drive if you haven't already done so.

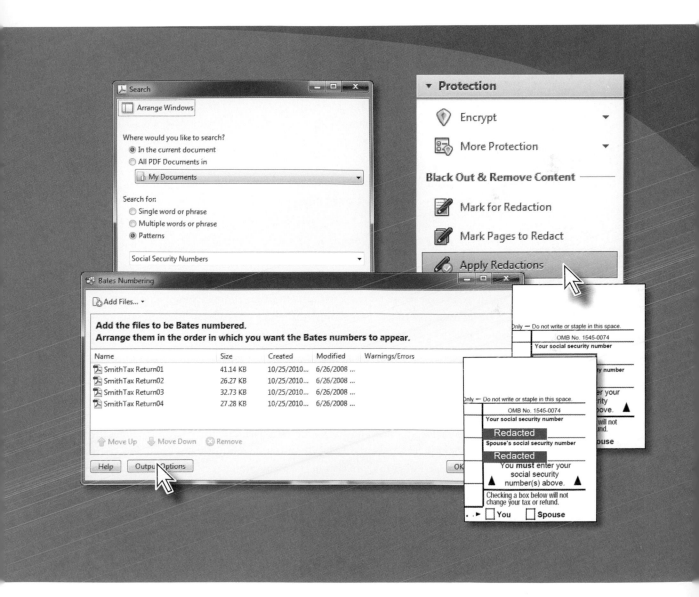

Adobe Acrobat X Pro includes features that are particularly useful for legal documents. You can apply Bates numbering to documents involved in a case, and apply redaction to ensure that confidential information stays private.

Legal features in Adobe Acrobat X

Increasingly in the court systems and in law offices across the United States, documents are processed electronically, usually as Adobe PDF. Acrobat X Pro offers several features designed specifically to enhance the workflow in this environment. In addition to Bates numbering and redaction, which are covered in this lesson, other features useful to the legal community include the following:

- PDF Portfolios make it easy for you to collect documents for e-Briefs and case management. For information on PDF Portfolios, see Lesson 7, "Combining Files in PDF Portfolios."

- The Forms tools help you manage data collection within your firm as well as from clients and outside counsel. See Lesson 10, "Working with Forms in Acrobat."

- Improved scanning and optical character recognition facilitate conversion of paper documents to smaller, more searchable PDF files. See Lesson 3, "Creating Adobe PDF Files."

- The Compare Documents command (in the View menu) lets you easily compare two versions of a document.

- Collaboration features make it easy to share documents online so all participants can view and work with the most current version of a document. You can even coordinate in real-time through web conferencing and screen-sharing. See Lesson 9, "Using Acrobat in a Review Cycle."

- The Split Document tool lets you split a large document easily and quickly into smaller documents based on file size to better meet court systems' upload requirements.

- The Find Hidden Information tool lets you inspect PDFs for metadata (such as the name of the document author), annotations, attachments, hidden data, form fields, hidden layers, or bookmarks. To find hidden information in a document, click Remove Hidden Information in the Protection panel. The Remove Hidden panel displays the information Acrobat finds; click Remove to delete any selected items.

About Bates numbering and redaction

In law offices, Bates numbering is routinely applied to each page of a document that is part of a legal case or process. Using Acrobat X Pro, you can automatically apply Bates numbering as a header or footer to any document or to documents in a PDF Portfolio. (If the PDF Portfolio contains non-PDF files, Acrobat converts the files to PDF and add Bates numbering.) You can add custom prefixes and suffixes, as well as a date stamp. And you can specify that the numbering is always applied outside the text or image area on the document page.

You can use the redaction tools to search a PDF document and automatically and permanently redact images, privileged or confidential words, phrases, or character strings (numbers and letters). You can search for patterns, such as patterns associated with phone numbers or social security numbers. You can even redact the same area on every page in a document.

Applying Bates numbering

You'll apply Bates numbering to several documents, adjusting the format of the numbering to avoid overlaying text in the body of the documents.

1 Open Acrobat. In the Welcome screen, click Open.

2 Navigate to the Lesson12 folder on your hard drive, select the SmithTax Return01.pdf file, and click Open.

3 Click Tools to open the Tools pane. Then click Pages.

4 Click Bates Numbering, and then choose Add Bates Numbering.

5 In the Bates Numbering dialog box, click Add Files, and then choose Add Files from the menu.

You can add Bates numbering to individual files or to the contents of folders, as well as to PDF Portfolios. If a folder contains files that Acrobat does not support for PDF conversion, those files are not added.

● **Note:** Bates numbering cannot be applied to protected or encrypted files, or to some forms.

6 Navigate to the Lesson12 folder, and select the SmithTax Return01.pdf file. Ctrl-click (Windows) or Command-click (Mac OS) to add the following files to your selection:

▶ **Tip:** If you need to add Bates numbering to paper documents, scan the paper document using the File > Create > PDF From Scanner command, and then apply Bates numbering to the resulting PDF file.

- SmithTax Return02.pdf

- SmithTax Return03.pdf

- SmithTax Return04.pdf

You can also add files in formats other than PDF, but the files must be in a format that can be converted to PDF.

7 Click Open (Windows) or Add Files (Mac OS).

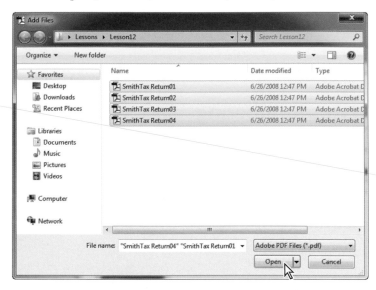

8 If necessary, use the Move Up and Move Down buttons to arrange the files in the following order:

- SmithTax Return01.pdf

- SmithTax Return02.pdf

- SmithTax Return03.pdf

- SmithTax Return04.pdf

You set the name of your Bates numbered file and the location for the saved file in the Output Options dialog box.

9 Click Output Options.

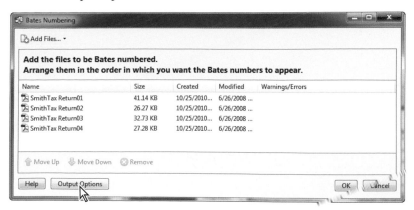

10 In the Output Options dialog box, select The Same Folder Selected At Start to specify where to save the files. The default is to save the files to the same folder as the unnumbered documents.

If you select A Folder On My Computer, you are prompted to browse to select a destination.

11 Under File Naming, select the Add To Original File Names option.

If you choose to keep the original filename, be sure to save the file in a different location from the original file; otherwise, you'll overwrite the original file.

12 Type **Bates** in the Insert After text box. You could enter anything you want to have appear before or after the page number in the Insert Before and Insert After text boxes.

13 Deselect the Overwrite Existing Files option, and leave the other options unchanged.

14 Click OK to apply your options and return to the Bates Numbering dialog box.

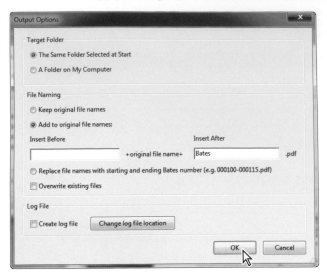

15 Click OK to close the Bates Numbering dialog box.

The Add Header And Footer dialog box opens. You'll use this dialog box in the next exercise to define the style of the Bates numbering to be applied.

Defining Bates numbering

You define the font, color, type size, and location of the Bates numbering in the Add Header And Footer dialog box. This is also where you opt to shrink the document contents to avoid overwriting content with the Bates numbering. Your Bates number can have 6 to 15 digits plus prefixes and suffixes.

First you'll specify the font, type size, and color.

1 In the Add Header And Footer dialog box, specify your type settings. Choose Arial for the font and 10 for the type size. Click the underline option to enable it, and then click the color swatch and select red for the page numbering.

2 Specify the size of the blank margin around the image or text area of the page in the Margin area of the dialog box. Accept the default values of 0.5 inches for the top and bottom margins and 1.0 inches for the left and right margins. This blank area is where the Bates numbering will be added in order to avoid overwriting text or images in the document.

3 Click Appearance Options.

4 Select the Shrink Document To Avoid Overwriting The Document's Text And Graphics option. Click OK.

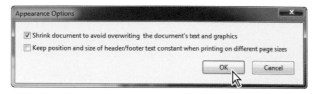

Now you'll choose where to place the Bates numbering—left, center, or right header (top of the page) or left, center, or right footer (bottom of the page).

5 Click in the Right Header Text box. Text you enter in this box will appear in the upper-right corner of the page.

You specify the format of your Bates numbering sequence in the Bates Numbering Options dialog box. You can specify a prefix, suffix, or both, as well as the number of digits in the numerical portion of the number.

6 Click Insert Bates Number.

7 Specify **6** digits (15 is the maximum), with a prefix of **Smith** (for the client's name) and a suffix of **Jones** (for the principal lawyer's name). Since this is the first document in the package, leave the Start Number at 1. Click OK.

The options you selected are reflected in the text box you chose in step 5. You can add the date as part of your Bates numbering, or you can add the date separately.

8 To add the date as part of the Bates numbering, click Page Number And Date Format.

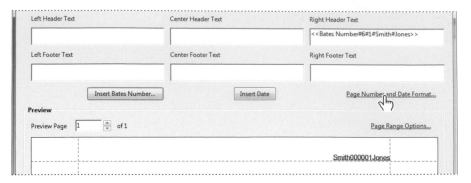

9 Choose mm/dd/yy from the Date Format menu. Choose Bates Number from the Page Number Format menu. Leave the Start Page Number as 1. Click OK to return to the Add Header And Footer dialog box.

10 Click Insert Date to add the date to the Bates numbering formula. You can preview your entry in the lower portion of the dialog box.

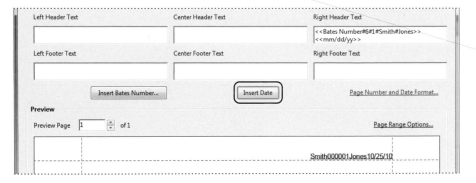

You can edit the Bates numbering options in this dialog box:

• To add space between the Bates number and the date, click an insertion point between the tags (here, in the Right Header Text box), and press the spacebar.

• To delete an entry, select it, right-click or Control-click, and choose Cut from the context menu.

- To move the date, drag over it to highlight it, and then drag it to precede or follow the Bates number.

- To change where the Bates numbering appears on the page, drag it to a different text box.

Now you'll save your settings.

11 Click Save Settings at the top of the dialog box, and name your settings **Smith_ Jones.** Click OK.

Saving the settings makes it easier to number additional documents later.

12 When you are satisfied with the Bates numbering style, click OK to apply the Bates numbering across your target documents. Click OK to clear the message box that reports that the documents were successfully numbered.

13 View the SmithTax Return01Bates. pdf file, which remains open. Bates numbering has been applied to the upper-right corner of this file as well as to SmithTax Return02Bates.pdf, SmithTax Return03Bates.pdf, and SmithTax Return04Bates.pdf.

14 Close any open documents.

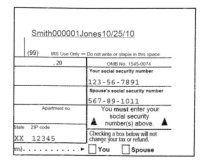

If you need to add documents to the collection at a later date, add Bates numbering to the documents following the steps above, but select your settings from the Saved Settings menu at the top of the Add Header And Footer dialog box. Then change the start page number to follow the last page of the existing collection. For example, if you added pages to this set, you would select 5 as the starting page number for additional documents.

To apply Bates numbering to the documents in a PDF Portfolio, select the PDF Portfolio in the Add Files dialog box, just as you would any individual PDF file.

Editing Bates numbering

You cannot edit Bates page numbering after you've added it to a document. You can, however, delete Bates numbering and apply a different Bates numbering formula.

Comparing different versions of a document

In Acrobat Pro, you can see the difference between two versions of a PDF document. When you use the Compare Documents command, the Compare panel lists the differences Acrobat identifies, and the new document is annotated to indicate the changes.

1 Choose View > Compare Documents.

2 Select the documents to compare.

3 If you want to compare only part of the documents, specify the page ranges. If you don't need to compare graphic elements, but just need to identify any changes in the text, select Compare Text Only in the Compare Documents dialog box.

4 Select the description most appropriate for the documents you are comparing, and click OK.

Acrobat analyzes the two documents, and then opens a results document with annotations indicating the changes. The first page of the new document summarizes the results of the comparison.

5 Review the differences reported in the Compare panel. You can customize the annotations by hiding them or changing the display options. Click a page thumbnail to go to that page.

6 To show each of the compared documents in its own window, choose Show Documents Tiled or Show Documents Side By Side from the options menu in the Compare panel. Choose Synchronize Pages if you want to synchronize the pages as they are displayed in their own windows.

▶ **Tip:** Because redaction cannot be undone, you should always work on a copy or archive an unedited copy of the file for future use. By default, Acrobat saves redacted files with the suffix _Redacted added to the filename. If you want to change this setting, choose Edit > Preferences (Windows) or Acrobat > Preferences (Mac OS), select Documents from the categories on the left, and then make your changes.

Applying redaction

Whenever the courts make documents public or law offices are required to produce documents that contain potentially confidential or privileged information, redaction may be applied to the documents to hide such information. Traditionally, redaction has been a time-consuming manual process. However, with Acrobat Pro, you can use the Redaction tool to automatically search for and permanently remove any privileged information. First, convert your electronic documents to Adobe PDF, or scan paper documents to PDF directly. You then use the Redaction tool to search for specific terms, such as names, telephone numbers, or account numbers, and permanently erase this information from a copy of your document.

You can also search for common patterns. You can search a page or a page range. You can redact privileged or confidential information using the simple equivalent of a black marker, or you can add overlay text to the redaction, identifying the privilege asserted, applicable statutory or code citation, or other basis for the redaction.

First you'll look at an example of redaction.

1   In Acrobat, choose File > Open, navigate to the Lesson12 folder, and double-click SmithTax Return03.pdf.

Notice, in both Part I and Part II, that the description of the property has been redacted.

2   With the Hand tool (✋) or Selection tool (➤),
    try to select the redaction. You can't. Once
    redaction has been applied, it can't be removed,
    nor can the material under the redaction mark
    be accessed in any way. For this reason, you
    should always save a file to which you've applied
    redaction under a new name. If you accidentally
    overwrite the original file, you cannot recover
    the redacted information.

3   Choose File > Close to close the tax return.

Changing the appearance of redactions

You can change redaction properties, including the color of the Redaction tool (the default is
black), whether to include overlay text, and how
overlay text is formatted. The properties affect
redactions you add after you modify them; existing redactions are not affected.

1   Open the SmithTax Return01.pdf file.

2   Open the Protection panel in the Tools pane,
    and then select Redaction Properties.

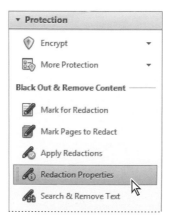

3 In the Redaction Tool Properties dialog box, click the color swatch next to the Redacted Area Fill Color label. Select a red color for the redaction mark.

4 Select the Use Overlay Text option.

5 In the Overlay Text area, choose a font for the redaction text. We used the default font.

6 Select the Auto-Size Text To Fit Redaction Region option. This option automatically sizes the text depending on the size of the redaction area. You can select a specific font size if you prefer.

7 For font color, choose white. Make sure the Repeat Overlay Text option is not selected, so that the redaction message is displayed only once per redaction. Select Center for the text alignment.

8 With the Custom Text option selected, type **Redacted** for the redaction text overlay.

If you want to indicate that information is redacted based on the U.S. Privacy Act or the U.S. Freedom of Information Act, select Redaction Code, and select the appropriate code set and code entry.

9 Click OK to apply your settings.

Searching text for redaction

You can use the search and redact feature to find a word, phrase, number, character string, or pattern, and mark it for redaction. You'll search for social security numbers and redact them before producing the documents in a post-judgment discovery of assets.

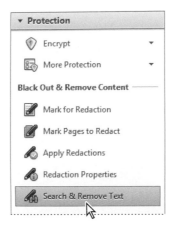

1 Select Search & Remove Text in the Protection panel. Click OK to clear the informational message.

2 In the Search panel, select In The Current Document to search the open document. You could also search all documents in a folder.

If you want to search and redact across only the current page or across a page range in a document, select Mark Pages To Redact in the Protection panel, and then specify a page range.

Use the Multiple Words Or Phrase search option if you want to search for and redact more than one word or phrase at the same time, rather than running separate searches for each word or phrase.

3 In the Search For area, select Patterns. Then choose Social Security Numbers from the menu. Click Search And Redact.

The Search panel shows the results. Each occurrence of the search string is listed.

4 Click on any entry in the Search panel to go to that occurrence in the document.

5 In the Search panel, click Check All to select all the occurrences of the social security number pattern listed.

6 To identify all the checked items as redaction candidates, click Mark Checked Results For Redaction in the Search panel. You can apply redaction after you have verified the marked redactions.

As you click each entry in the Search panel, the focus in the document pane moves to the entry marked for redaction. You can save and print this copy if you want to have colleagues check the redaction process before applying the redaction. Be sure to choose the Document And Markups option (under Comments And Forms) in the Print dialog box in order to print the redaction markups.

7 When you are sure the redactions are correct and complete, click Apply Redactions in the Protection panel. Click OK to clear the message box. Click No to close the next message box. (This PDF file of the tax return was created by scanning a simple paper form. There is unlikely to be any information on hidden layers or in metadata and therefore no need to scan for additional information.)

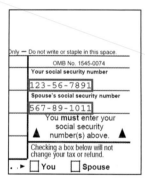  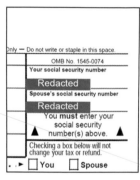

▶ **Tip:** If you cannot
select text or graphics
using the Mark For
Redaction tool, you can
still apply redaction
by pressing Ctrl or
Command as you drag
over the text or graphic,
and then clicking the
Apply Redactions tool.

8 Choose File > Save, and save your file. Because of the Documents preferences settings, the suffix _Redacted is automatically applied to the filename. You can page through the file to review the redaction.

9 Close the Search panel, and close the PDF file.

If you are working with a document that was created by scanning a paper version and converting the resulting file to PDF, some text or graphics may be converted as images. Such text and graphics are not searchable unless you apply optical character recognition (OCR). To learn about applying OCR, see Lesson 3, "Creating Adobe PDF Files."

Assembling PDF documents

You can assemble documents for e-Briefs and case management by combining multiple PDF files into a single document or, if you're using Acrobat Pro, by creating a PDF Portfolio. The advantage to using a PDF Portfolio is that documents remain separate so that you can easily reuse or share an individual document. Documents in a PDF Portfolio retain their individual security settings and default views. Each file can be read, edited, formatted, and printed independently of the other files in the PDF Portfolio. Any changes that you make to documents in a PDF Portfolio are not made to the original document. The original document remains unchanged. For information on working with PDF Portfolios, see Lesson 5, "Combining Files in PDF Portfolios."

If you don't expect to need to use individual documents again, you may find it simpler to merge PDF files into a single document for distribution or archival. You'll merge the four tax return files into a single PDF document.

1 Choose File > Create > Combine Files Into A Single PDF.

2 In the Combine Files dialog box, click Add Files, and then choose Add Files.

3 In the Add Files dialog box, navigate to the Lesson12 folder, and select SmithTax Return01_Redacted.pdf. Then press Ctrl or Command and select SmithTax Return02.pdf, SmithTax Return03.pdf, and SmithTax Return04.pdf.

4 Click Open or Add Files. The files you selected appear in the Combine Files dialog box. You can change a file's position by selecting it and clicking Move Up or Move Down. When the files are in the appropriate order, click Combine Files.

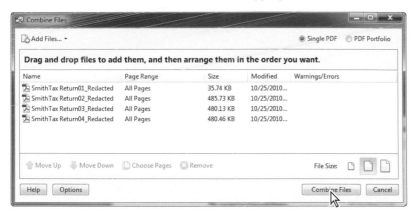

Acrobat merges the files into a new open document called Binder.pdf.

5 Choose File > Save As > PDF.

6 Name the file **SmithTaxReturn_set**, and click Save.

Splitting documents

If your files are consolidated into a single, merged PDF file rather than assembled into a PDF Portfolio, you can use the Split Document command to separate out the original documents. You can also use this command to split up a document that is too large for court upload requirements.

1   Open your combined PDF file, and click Split Document in the Pages panel in the Tools pane.

2   In the Split Document dialog box, specify whether to split the document based on a number of pages, a maximum file size for each document created by the split, or top-level bookmarks.

3   Click the Output Options button to specify a target folder for the split files and your file-naming preferences.

You cannot split documents to which you have applied security features.

You can split multiple documents using the same criteria with the Apply To Multiple button in the Split Document dialog box.

Marking redactions across multiple pages

You can use the Mark For Redaction tool to select text, an object, or an area of the page to redact, and you can redact that same area on multiple pages. You've assembled the tax return files into a single document, but the social security numbers were redacted only in the first original PDF file. You'll use the Mark For Redaction tool to redact the social security field on the last three pages of the combined document.

1   Type **4** in the page number box in the Common Tools toolbar, and press Enter or Return. Page 4 of the combined file is Schedule C. The social security number field is in the upper-right corner of the page.

2   Click Mark For Redaction in the Protection panel. Click OK to close the informational box.

3 Press Ctrl or Command so that the pointer changes to cross-hairs. Then drag it across the entire Social Security Number field. The selected area is shaded as you drag the pointer, and outlined for redaction when you release the mouse.

 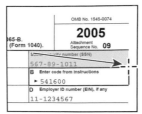 

The area is not actually redacted yet. You can undo the redaction until you select Apply Redactions.

4 Right-click (Windows) or Control-click (Mac OS) the selected area, and choose Repeat Mark Across Pages.

5 In the Repeat Redaction Mark Across dialog box, select Specify Range. Type **4-6** in the text box, and then click OK.

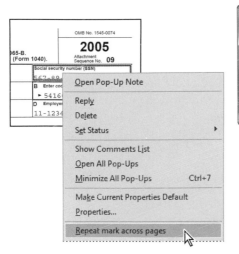 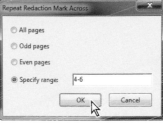

6 View pages 5 and 6. The area you selected is highlighted for redaction.

7 Click Apply Redactions in the Protection panel. Click OK to close the warning message. Click No when prompted to examine the document for additional information.

 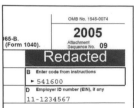

Acrobat saves the file with the _Redacted suffix, based on the settings in Documents preferences.

8 View the social security number field on the other pages in the document. The number has been redacted on each page.

9 Close the document.

Review questions

1 Can you remove redaction marks if you accidentally redact the wrong information?

2 How can you be sure that your Bates numbering doesn't overlap text or graphics in a document?

3 Can you edit Bates numbering after you have applied it to a document collection?

Review answers

1 No. Redaction is permanent. Always review the material marked for redaction carefully before applying redaction. Always save the redacted file under a different name to avoid overwriting the original file and losing it. Note, however, that if you haven't saved your document after applying redaction, you can select the redaction and remove it.

2 In the Add Header And Footer dialog box, click Appearance Options, and select Shrink Document To Avoid Overwriting The Document's Text And Graphics.

3 No. You can only delete the current Bates numbering and apply a different Bates numbering formula.

13 USING ACROBAT IN PROFESSIONAL PRINTING

Lesson overview

In this lesson, you'll do the following:

- Create Adobe PDF files suitable for high-resolution printing.

- Preflight an Adobe PDF file to check for quality and consistency (Acrobat Pro).

- View how transparent objects affect a page (Acrobat Pro).

- Configure color management.

- Use Acrobat to generate color separations.

 This lesson will take approximately 60 minutes to complete. Copy the Lesson13 folder onto your hard drive if you haven't already done so.

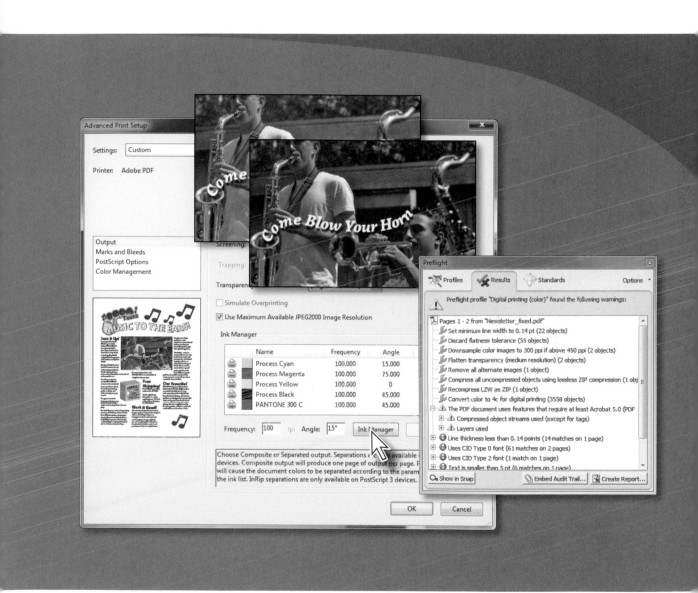

Acrobat Pro provides professional printing tools,
including preflighting and transparency previews,
to help you achieve high-quality output.

Guidelines for creating print-ready PDF files

By the time you submit a PDF file to a printer, the die has been cast. A printer can coax a quality print-out from some less-than-optimal PDF files, but for the most part, the printer is restricted by decisions made during the creative process. Following these guidelines, you can deliver the strongest, highest-quality PDF file to a printer:

- **Remember that the end product is only as good as its components.** For high-quality printing, a PDF file must contain the appropriate images, fonts, and other components.

- **Convert only when absolutely necessary.** Every time you convert text, objects, or color, you compromise the integrity of the file. The printed product will most closely resemble your original intent if you minimize conversions. Keep text in its original form, as fonts, rather than outlining or rasterizing it. Keep gradients live. Maintain live transparency as long as possible. And don't convert colors from device-independent or high-gamut color spaces, such as RGB, to device-specific or low-gamut color spaces, such as CMYK, unless advised to do so.

- **Use transparency efficiently.** Transparency comes into play any time you apply a blending mode or change the opacity of an object. For the best results, keep transparency live as long as possible; place objects you don't want the flattener to affect (such as text and line objects) above all nearby sources of transparency, preferably on a separate layer; and use the highest-quality flattener settings if and when you flatten transparency.

- **Proof and preflight before creating the PDF file.** Early in the workflow, you have more context for problems, and more options for fixing them. Carefully proof the content and formatting before creating a PDF file. Additionally, if the authoring application provides a preflight feature, use it to identify missing fonts, unlinked images, or other issues that could result in problems down the road. The earlier you can identify and fix a problem, the easier and less expensive it is to fix. Certainly, technical problems found while you're still working in the authoring program are easier to fix than problems found in Acrobat or on a printing press.

- **Embed fonts.** To minimize the chance of complications, embed fonts in the PDF file. Read the end user license agreement (EULA) before purchasing a font to ensure it permits embedding.

- **Use the appropriate PDF settings file.** When you create the PDF file, make sure you're using the appropriate settings. The PDF settings file determines how image data is saved, whether fonts are embedded, and whether colors are converted. By default, Acrobat PDFMaker in Microsoft Office creates PDF files using the Standard settings file, which does not meet the requirements for most high-end printing. No matter what application you're using to create a PDF file for professional printing, ensure that you're using the Press Quality PDF settings file or the settings file recommended by your printer.

- **Create a PDF/X file if appropriate.** PDF/X is a subset of the Adobe PDF specification, requiring that PDF files meet specific criteria, resulting in more reliable PDF files. Using PDF/X-compliant files eliminates the most common errors in file preparation: fonts that aren't embedded, incorrect color spaces, missing images, and overprinting and trapping issues. PDF/X-1a, PDF/X-3, and PDF/X-4 are the most popular formats; each is designed for a different purpose. Ask your printer whether you should save your file in a PDF/X format.

Creating PDF files for print and prepress

There are many ways to create a PDF file from your original document. No matter which method you choose, however, you need to use the appropriate PDF preset for your intended output. For high-resolution, professional printing, specify the Press Quality PDF preset or a custom PDF preset provided by your printer.

Adobe PDF presets

A PDF preset is a group of settings that affect the process of creating a PDF file. These settings are designed to balance file size with quality, depending on how the PDF file will be used. Most predefined presets are shared across Adobe Creative Suite applications, including Adobe InDesign, Adobe Illustrator, Adobe Photoshop, and Acrobat. You can also create and share custom presets to meet your own needs.

Some PDF presets are not available until you move them from the Extras folder to the Settings folder; the Extras folder is installed only with Acrobat Pro. For more detailed descriptions of each preset, see Adobe Acrobat X Help.

- **High Quality Print** creates PDFs for quality printing on desktop printers and proofing devices.
- **Oversized Pages** creates PDFs suitable for viewing and printing engineering drawings larger than 200 by 200 inches.
- **PDF/A-1b: 2005 (CMYK and RGB)** is used for the long-term preservation (archival) of electronic documents.
- **PDF/X-1a (2001 and 2003)** standards minimize the number of variables in a PDF document to improve reliability. PDF/X-1a files are commonly used for digital ads that will be reproduced on a press.
- **PDF/X-3 (2003)** files are similar to PDF/X-1a files, but they support color-managed workflows and allow some RGB images.
- **PDF/X-4 (2007)** has the same color-management ICC color specifications as PDF/X-3, but it includes support for live transparency.
- **Press Quality** creates PDF files for high-quality print production (for example, for digital printing or for separations to an imagesetter or platesetter).
- **Rich Content PDF** creates accessible PDF files that include tags, hyperlinks, bookmarks, interactive elements, and layers.
- **Smallest File Size** creates PDF files for displaying on the web or an intranet, or for distribution through an email system.
- **Standard** creates PDF files to be printed to desktop printers or digital copiers, published on a CD, or sent to a client as a publishing proof.

You can create a PDF file from any application using the Print command. Because we do not know which applications you use, we have not included a file for this exercise. You can use any existing document or create a new document.

1 Open any document in its original application.

2 Choose File > Print.

3 In Windows: Choose Adobe PDF from the list of available printers. Then click Properties, Preferences, or Setup, depending on the application. Choose Press Quality or a custom PDF settings file.

In Mac OS: Click PDF, and choose Save As Adobe PDF from the menu. Then, in the Save As Adobe PDF dialog box, select the Press Quality settings file or a custom settings file from the Adobe PDF Settings menu, and click Continue.

4 In Windows, select Prompt For Adobe PDF Filename from the Adobe PDF Output Folder menu, and then click OK. If you do not select this option, the Adobe PDF printer saves the file in the My Documents folder. (In Mac OS, you will be prompted for a filename and location automatically.)

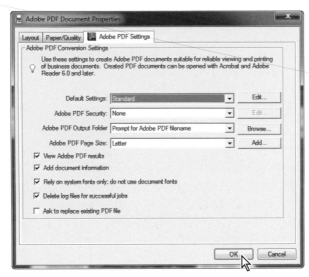

5 In Windows, click Print.

6 Specify a filename and folder for the PDF file when prompted, and click Save.

7 Close the PDF file and the original document.

For more information about selecting presets, see Adobe Acrobat X Help.

Creating PDFs with Distiller

You can also convert PostScript files to PDF using Distiller, which is automatically installed with Acrobat. How you print a document to PostScript depends on the authoring application. Some applications include specific options for printing a PostScript file; in others, you must set up a printer using a port configured to print to file. To create the PDF file, open Distiller, choose the settings you want to use, and then open the PostScript file in Distiller. Distiller converts the document using the settings you've selected.

To start Distiller within Acrobat, select Acrobat Distiller in the Print Production panel in the Tools pane.

Preflighting files (Acrobat Pro)

Before you hand off a PDF file to a print service provider, preflight it to verify that the document meets the criteria for print publishing. Preflighting analyzes a document against the criteria listed in the preflight profile you specify; in addition to identifying potential issues, many preflight profiles contain fixups that can correct problems for you.

Ask your print service provider which preflight profile to use to accurately preflight your document. Many print service providers provide custom preflight profiles to their customers.

You'll preflight a newsletter file to determine whether it's ready for digital printing.

1 In Acrobat Pro, choose File > Open, and navigate to the Lesson13 folder. Select the Newsletter.pdf file, and click Open.

2 In the Tools pane, open the Print Production panel. If the Print Production panel isn't available, choose View > Tools > Print Production to display it.

3 Select Preflight in the Print Production panel.

The Preflight dialog box lists the available preflight profiles, grouped into categories that describe the tests they perform.

4 Click the triangle next to Digital Printing And Online Publishing to expand the category.

5 Select the Digital Printing (Color) profile.

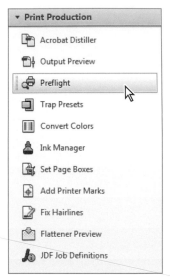

The full magnifying glass icon next to the profile indicates that it performs analysis; the full wrench icon indicates that it also performs fixups. When you select the profile, Acrobat displays its description. If a profile does not include analysis, or checks, the magnifying glass appears as an outline. If a profile does not include fixups, the wrench appears as an outline.

6 Click Analyze And Fix.

7 In the Save PDF File dialog box, name the fixed file **Newsletter_fixed.pdf,** and click Save.

Because the profile applies fixups, it makes changes to the file. Saving the file to a different name ensures that you can return to the original if you need to.

8 Review the results of the preflight.

Acrobat displays the results of the preflight in the Results pane. In this file, Acrobat performed several fixups, applying compression, color conversion, and transparency flattening, as well as other changes.

The Results pane also notes that the PDF document uses features that require PDF 1.4 or later, includes CID Type 0 and CID Type 2 fonts, and contains text smaller than 5 points. If you were professionally printing this document, you might want to contact your print service provider to ensure that these factors won't cause problems when your document is printed.

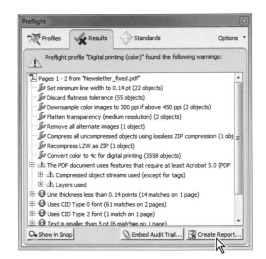

9 Click Create Report.

10 Click Save to save the report in the Lesson13 folder with the default name **Newsletter_fixed_report.pdf**.

Acrobat creates the preflight summary report as a PDF and opens it in Acrobat.

11 Close the Preflight dialog box and review the preflight summary report.

You can send the preflight summary report to your print service provider if you have any questions about preparing the file.

12 Close the preflight summary report and the Newsletter_fixed.pdf file.

▶ **Tip:** You can hide or show individual layers that were created in the authoring application, and determine which ones will print. To learn about showing, hiding, and printing layers, see Adobe Acrobat X Help.

Custom preflight profiles

You can customize the preflight profiles included with Acrobat, import profiles provided by your print service provider, or create your own custom profiles. To create a new profile, open the Preflight dialog box, and choose Options > Create New Preflight Profile. To modify an existing profile, click Edit next to its name, and then, if it's locked, choose Unlocked, and give the custom version a new name. Next, choose a group for the profile. Then click a category of criteria, and add or remove specific checks or fixups. Save the profile when you're done.

To import a preflight profile, open the Preflight dialog box, and choose Options > Import Preflight Profile. Navigate to the custom profile, which has a .kfp extension, and click Open.

To export a profile, select the profile you want to share, and then choose Options > Export Preflight Profile. Define the display name of the profile, and then specify the location where you want to save it.

PDF standards

PDF standards are internationally defined standards designed to simplify the exchange of graphic content (PDF/X), archived documents (PDF/A), or engineering workflows (PDF/E). The most widely used standards for a print publishing workflow are PDF/X-1a, PDF/X-3, and PDF/X-4.

You can validate PDF content against PDF/X, PDF/A, or PDF/E criteria in Acrobat Pro and save a copy of the document as PDF/X, PDF/A, or PDF/E, provided it complies with the specified requirements. You can also save a PDF file as a PDF/X or PDF/A file when you create the file using the Print command or the Export or Save command in an Adobe application.

When you open a PDF/X or PDF/A file in Acrobat X or Reader X, the Standards pane automatically opens to show you information about the file's conformance. If you are using Acrobat X Pro, you can also click Verify in the Standards pane to verify that the PDF file is a valid PDF/X or PDF/A file, using the preflight feature.

To save a copy of an existing PDF file as a PDF/X , PDF/A, or PDF/E file in Acrobat X Pro:

1 Select Preflight in the Print Production panel.

2 In the Preflight dialog box, click Standards.

3 Select Save As PDF/X, Save As PDF/A, or Save As PDF/E, and then click Continue.

4 Specify the version of the standard, and click Continue.

5 Select a conversion profile and one of the available viewing or printing conditions.

6 If you want to apply corrections during the conversion, select Apply Corrections.

7 To convert the PDF file based on the selected profile and settings, click Save As.

8 Name the converted file, and click Save.

9 Review the conversion results. If the conversion succeeds, a green check mark appears in the Preflight dialog box. If the conversion fails, a red X appears. The Results pane describes any reasons the conversion failed.

Working with transparency (Acrobat Pro)

Adobe applications let you modify objects in ways that can affect the underlying artwork, creating the appearance of transparency. You may create transparency by using an opacity slider in InDesign, Illustrator, or Photoshop, or by changing the blending mode for a layer or selected object. Transparency also comes into play whenever you create a drop shadow or apply feathering. Adobe applications can keep transparency "live," or editable, as you move documents from one application to another, but transparency must typically be flattened before printing. In Acrobat Pro, you can see which areas of your document are affected by transparency, and how those areas will print. ·

Previewing transparency

When you print to most printers, transparency is flattened. The flattening process separates overlapping areas of artwork into discrete sections that are converted either into separate vector shapes or rasterized pixels to retain the look of the transparency.

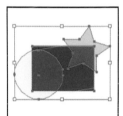

Objects before
flattening

Objects after
flattening

(Overlapping art is divided when flattened.)

● **Note:** If your print service provider is using a RIP that includes the Adobe PDF Print Engine, you may not need to flatten transparency.

Before flattening occurs, you can determine how much of the transparent area remains vector, and how much becomes rasterized. Some effects, such as drop shadows, must be rasterized in order to print correctly.

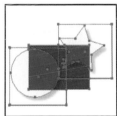

If you received a PDF file created by someone else, you may not know if or where transparency has been applied. The Acrobat transparency preview shows you where transparency is used in a document. This feature can also help you determine the best flattener settings to use when printing the document.

What is rasterization?

Rasterization is the process of changing vector objects, including fonts, into bitmap images to display or print them. The number of pixels per inch (ppi) is referred to as the *resolution*. The higher the resolution in a raster image, the better the quality. When flattening occurs, some objects may need to be rasterized, depending upon flattening settings.

Vector Object   Rasterized at 72 ppi   Rasterized at 300 ppi

You'll preview transparency in the Newsletter.pdf file.

1   Open the Newsletter.pdf file from the Lesson13 folder.

2   Navigate to page 2 of the newsletter. If the entire page is not visible, choose View > Zoom > Zoom To Page Level.

3   Select Flattener Preview in the Print Production panel.

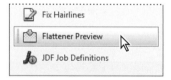

The Flattener Preview shows a preview of page 2 of the newsletter on the right side of the dialog box.

Specifying flattener preview settings

You can select different settings to preview different aspects of the way transparency interacts with objects in the document.

1   In the Flattener Preview dialog box, choose All Affected Objects from the Highlight menu. The photo and three musical notes are highlighted in red, indicating that they have transparent properties or interact with objects that have transparent properties.

2 Choose High Resolution from the Preset menu in the Transparency Flattener Preset Options area. The preset determines how much of the artwork remains vector and how much is rasterized. For professional printing, use the High Resolution preset unless your print service provider advises you differently.

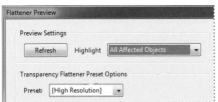

3 Click the left end of the Raster/Vector Balance slider or type **0** in the box. Then click Refresh, and choose All Affected Objects from the Highlight menu. Everything on the page is highlighted in red, indicating that everything would be rasterized at this setting.

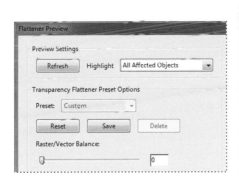

4 Make other selections to see how the settings affect the document. When you are finished, click the close button in the upper-right (Windows) or upper-left (Mac OS) corner of the window to close the Flattener Preview window without applying your settings.

▶ **Tip:** You can find more information on transparency output issues on the Adobe website at www.adobe.com.

If you want to use the selected transparency flattener settings when printing, click Apply in the Flattener Preview dialog box.

About flattening options in the Flattener Preview dialog box

- **Line Art And Text Resolution:** Because line art and text involve a sharper contrast around the edges, they need to be rasterized at a higher resolution to maintain a high-quality appearance. A resolution of 300 ppi is sufficient when proofing, but this should be increased to a higher resolution for final high-quality output. A resolution of 1200 ppi is typically sufficient for high-quality output.

- **Gradient And Mesh Resolution:** Gradients and meshes, which are sometimes called *blends*, will be rasterized, and should have a resolution appropriate for your specific printer. For proofing to a general-purpose laser printer or inkjet printer, the default setting of 150 ppi is appropriate. For printing to most high-quality output devices, such as a film or plate output device, a resolution of 300 ppi is usually sufficient.

- **Convert All Text To Outlines** ensures that the width of all text in the artwork stays consistent. However, converting small fonts to outlines can make them appear noticeably thicker and less readable (especially when printing on lower-end printing systems).

- **Convert All Strokes To Outlines** ensures that the width of all strokes in the artwork stays consistent. Selecting this option, however, causes thin strokes to appear slightly thicker (especially when printing on lower-end printing systems).

- **Clip Complex Regions** ensures that the boundaries between vector artwork and rasterized artwork fall along object paths. This option reduces stitching artifacts that result when part of an object is rasterized while another part remains in vector form (as determined by the Raster/Vector slider). Selecting this option may result in extremely complex clipping paths, which take significant time to compute, and can cause errors when printing.

- **Preserve Overprint** blends the color of transparent artwork with the background color to create an overprint effect. Overprinted colors are two or more inks printed on top of each other. For example, when a cyan ink prints over a yellow ink, the resulting overprint is a green color. Without overprinting, the underlying yellow would not be printed, resulting in a cyan color.

Setting up color management

Using color management can help you achieve consistent color throughout your workflow. Color profiles describe the characteristics of each device. Color management uses those profiles to map the colors possible for one device, such as a computer monitor, with the colors possible on another device, such as a printer.

1   Choose Edit > Preferences (Windows) or Acrobat > Preferences (Mac OS), and select Color Management from the list on the left.

2   From the Settings menu, choose North America Prepress 2. With this setting, Acrobat displays colors as they generally appear when printed using North American printing standards.

Note: You can synchronize color management settings for all the Adobe Creative Suite applications in Adobe Bridge. See Bridge Help for more information.

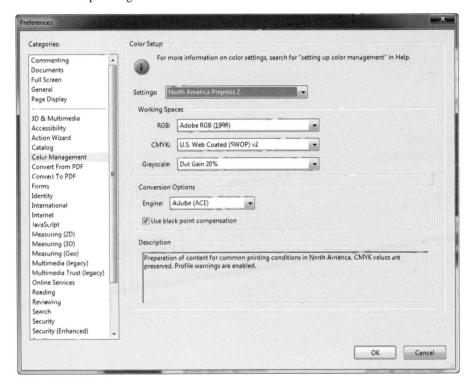

The setting you select determines which color working spaces are used by the application, what happens when you open and import files with embedded profiles, and how the color management system converts colors. To view a description of a setting, select the setting, and then position the pointer over the setting name. The description appears at the bottom of the dialog box.

ACE (Adobe Color Engine) is the same color management engine used by other Adobe graphics software, so you can be confident that color management settings applied in Acrobat will mirror those applied in your other Adobe applications.

3 Click OK to close the Preferences dialog box.

Previewing your print job (Acrobat Pro)

You've already previewed how transparency will print. Now you'll preview color separations and verify the resolution of individual objects. You'll also perform a *soft proof*—that is, you'll proof the document on the screen without having to print it.

Previewing color separations

To reproduce color and continuous-tone images, printers usually separate artwork into four plates, called *process colors*—one plate for each of the cyan, magenta, yellow, and black portions of the image. You can also include custom pre-mixed inks, called *spot colors*, which require their own plates. When inked with the appropriate color and printed in register with one another, these colors combine to reproduce the original artwork. The plates are called *color separations*.

You will preview color separations from this document using the Output Preview dialog box.

1 Choose View > Zoom > Zoom To Page Level.

2 Navigate to page 2 of the newsletter, if it's not already visible.

3 Select Output Preview in the Print Production panel.

4 Choose Separations from the Preview menu.

The Separations area of the dialog box lists all the inks that are included in this document for printing. There are four process inks (cyan, magenta, yellow, and black) and one spot color (PANTONE 300 C).

5 Drag the Output Preview dialog box to the side so that you can see the document. Then, in the Output Preview dialog box, deselect every ink except PANTONE 300 C. The items that remain on the page use the selected ink.

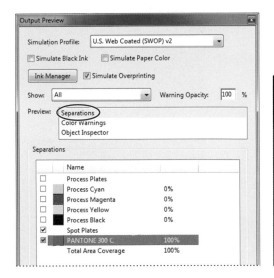

6 Deselect PANTONE 300 C, and select Process Magenta. Only those items that would print on the magenta plate appear.

7 Select all the inks again.

Soft-proofing your document

You can use the Output Preview dialog box to soft-proof a document, so that you can see onscreen how your document will look when printed. Use the simulation settings to approximate the color.

1 Choose U.S. Web Coated (SWOP) v2 from the Simulation Profile menu.

2 Go to page 1 of the newsletter.

▶ **Tip:** If you wanted to remap a spot color to a process color in order to limit the number of plates, and thus the expense, of a print job, you could use the Ink Manager, also available in the Output Preview dialog box.

3 Choose Apple RGB from the Simulation Profile menu.

4 Choose Adobe RGB from the Simulation Profile menu.

As you change the simulation profile, color shifts on the monitor. When you soft-proof a document, select the simulation profile that matches your output device. If you use accurately calibrated ICC profiles and have calibrated your monitor, the onscreen preview should match the final output. If you haven't calibrated your monitor or your profiles, the preview may not provide an exact match. For information about calibrating your monitor and profiles, see Adobe Acrobat X Help.

5 Choose U.S. Web Coated (SWOP) v2 from the Simulation Profile menu again.

Inspecting objects in a PDF file

You can take a closer look at individual graphics and text in a PDF file using the Object Inspector. The Object Inspector displays the image resolution, color mode, transparency, and other information about the selected object.

You'll check the resolution of the image on page 2.

1 Choose Object Inspector from the Preview menu in the Output Preview dialog box.

2 Scroll to page 2, and click the image of the waterside village.

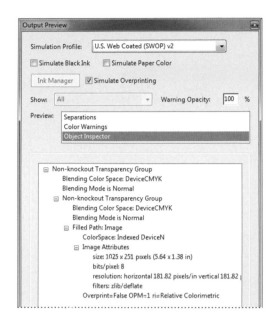

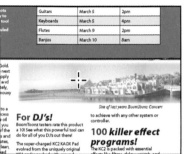

The Object Inspector lists attributes of the image you clicked, including the image resolution: 181.82 by 181.82 pixels.

3 Close the Output Preview dialog box.

▶ **Tip:** Overprinting is automatically displayed accurately in PDF/X files in all versions of Acrobat X and Adobe Reader X. You can change the settings to display overprinting accurately for all files in the Acrobat Preferences dialog box.

Advanced printing controls

You'll use the advanced printing features of Acrobat X Pro to produce color separations, add printing marks, and control how transparent and complex items are imaged.

1 Choose File > Print.

2 In the Print dialog box, choose a PostScript printer. In Windows, if you do not have a PostScript printer available, you can choose Adobe PDF.

Some advanced printing options, including color separations, are available only for PostScript printers. The Adobe PDF printer uses a PostScript printer driver, so it provides access to the options covered in this exercise.

3 In the Print Range area, select All.

4 In the Page Handling area, choose Fit To Printable Area from the Page Scaling menu.

The Fit To Printable Area option reduces or enlarges each page to fit the paper size.

5 Click Advanced.

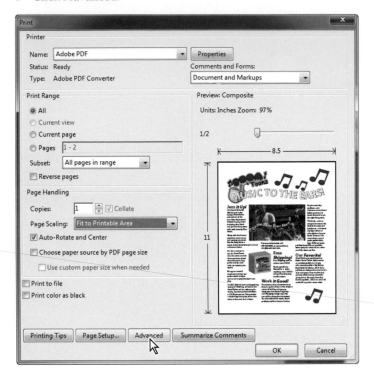

There are four options on the left side of the dialog box: Output, Marks And Bleeds, PostScript Options, and Color Management.

6 Select Output, and then choose Separations from the Color menu.

7 Click the Ink Manager button in the Ink Manager area.

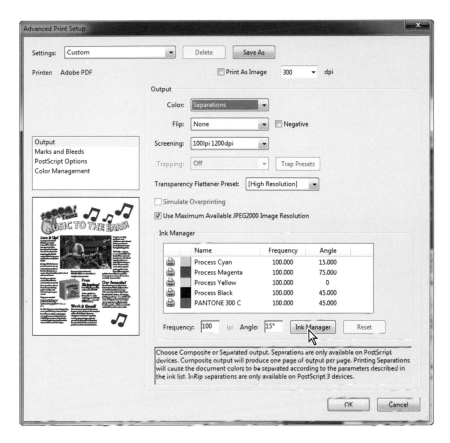

8   In the Ink Manager dialog box, select the icon to the left of the PANTONE 300 C name. The icon changes into a CMYK color swatch, indicating that this color will be printed as a process color, using the cyan, magenta, yellow, and black plates.

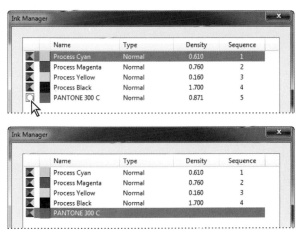

Acrobat will mix cyan and black to simulate the dedicated ink that is used to produce the PANTONE 300 C spot color. In many cases, it is more cost-effective to use a mixture of CMYK inks than to add an entirely new spot color ink.

To globally convert all spot colors to their CMYK equivalents, select Convert All Spots To Process.

9 Click OK to close the Ink Manager dialog box.

10 In the Advanced Print Setup dialog box, select Marks And Bleeds from the list on the left. Select All Marks to enable trim marks, bleed marks, registration marks, color bars, and page information to print on each plate, outside the edges of the document.

11 Select Color Management from the list on the left.

12 Choose Acrobat Color Management from the Color Handling menu.

13 Choose Working CMYK: U.S. Web Coated (SWOP) v2 from the Color Profile menu.

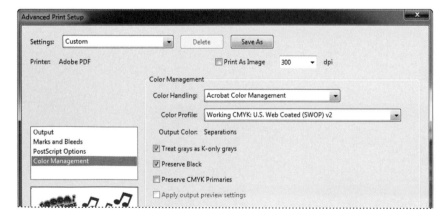

The color profile you select should match the device you will be printing to.

14 Click Save As at the top of the Advanced Print Setup dialog box, and save your settings using the name **Newsletter**. Then click OK.

Saved settings are added to the settings menu, so you can reuse them for future print jobs without having to re-enter the settings for certain jobs or specific output devices.

15 Click OK to exit the Advanced Print Setup dialog box. Then either click OK to print this document, or click Cancel if you prefer not to print at this time.

16 Close the document, and quit Acrobat.

Review questions

1   What is the Adobe PDF printer, and how do you use it?

2   How can you select a settings file when you create a PDF using the Print command in Mac OS?

3   What problems can Preflight detect within a PDF?

4   What is a spot color and how can you remap it to a process color?

Review answers

1   Adobe PDF printer is a printer installed by Acrobat for Windows. You can use it to print to a PDF file from any application in Windows. Simply choose it as the printer in the application's Print dialog box.

2   To change the settings file in Mac OS, first choose Save As Adobe PDF from the PDF menu in the Print dialog box. Then choose a preset from the Adobe PDF Settings menu.

3   Use the Preflight command to check for all areas of concern within a PDF. For example, if you are sending a PDF file to a professional printer, preflight the document to verify that fonts are embedded, graphics have the appropriate resolution, and colors are correct.

4   A spot color is a special premixed ink that is used instead of, or in addition to, CMYK process inks, and that requires its own printing plate on a printing press. If absolute color accuracy is not critical, and it is not practical to print a spot color plate as well as CMYK plates, you can remap the spot color to a process color using the Ink Manager. In the Advanced Print dialog box, select Separations, and then click Ink Manager. In the Ink Manager, click the icon to the left of the spot color to remap it to a process color for the print job.

INDEX

Production Notes

Adobe Acrobat X Classroom in a Book was created electronically using Adobe InDesign CS4. Art was produced using Adobe InDesign, Adobe Illustrator, and Adobe Photoshop. The Myriad Pro and Warnock Pro OpenType families of typefaces were used throughout this book.

References to company names in the lessons are for demonstration purposes only and are not intended to refer to any actual organization or person.

Images

Photographic images and illustrations are intended for use with the tutorials.

Typefaces used

Adobe Myriad Pro and Adobe Minion Pro are used throughout the lessons. For more information about OpenType and Adobe fonts, visit www.adobe.com/type/opentype/.

Team credits

The following individuals contributed to the development of this edition of *Adobe Acrobat X Classroom in a Book*:

Writer: Brie Gyncild

Project Manager: Lisa Fridsma

Lesson Development: Brie Gyncild

Illustrator and Compositor: Lisa Fridsma

Copyeditor and Proofreader: Wendy Katz

Technical Reviewer: Megan Tytler

Indexer: Brie Gyncild

Cover design: Eddie Yuen

Interior design: Mimi Heft

Adobe Press Executive Editor: Victor Gavenda

Adobe Press Production Editor: Hilal Sala

Adobe Press Project Editor: Connie Jeung-Mills

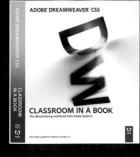
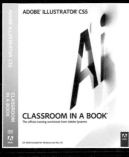